Five Lieutenants

Also by James Carl Nelson

The Remains of Company D:
A Story of the Great War

FIVE LIEUTENANTS

The Heartbreaking Story of Five Harvard Men Who Led America to Victory in World War I

JAMES CARL NELSON

St. Martin's Press New York

 For information, address St. Martin's Press, 175 Fifth Avenue, New York, N.Y. 10010.

www.stmartins.com

Library of Congress Cataloging-in-Publication Data

Nelson, James Carl.
Five lieutenants : the heartbreaking story of five Harvard men who led America to victory in World War I / James Carl Nelson.—First Edition.
p. cm
Includes bibliographical references.
ISBN 978-0-312-60423-3 (hardcover)
ISBN 978-1-250-01858-8 (e-book)
1. World War, 1914–1918—Biography. 2. Harvard University—Biography. 3. United States. Army—Officers—Biography. 4. Soldiers—United States—Biography. 5. World War, 1914–1918—Campaigns. I. Title.
D639.E4H364 2012
940.4'12730922—dc23

2012016322

First Edition: November 2012

10 9 8 7 6 5 4 3 2 1

For Daniel Newhall

Contents

Preface

Unlike the Civil War, World War I, at least from the American perspective, is not known as a literary war. Draconian censorship Over There limited the doughboys' abilities to describe their thoughts and experiences as they happened; diaries and journals were forbidden, lest they fall into the enemy's hands. In any case, so many of the young soldiers were immigrants from Europe and other places and thus limited in English, or simply from hardscrabble backgrounds in the United States and limited in education, that they would have been hard-pressed to relay any erudite description of what they were going through.

I encountered this problem while researching my previous book, *The Remains of Company D: A Story of the Great War.* The letters I located from the enlisted men who served in Company D of the 28th Regiment, 1st Division, were often terse and devoid of any descriptions of actions, emotions, hopes, and fears and any accounting of where the soldiers had been. However, I noted early on that this was not necessarily so with the company's officers, who censored their own letters home, and I began a concerted push to find letters and writings from other young officers from the 28th Regiment to add context and a sense of immediacy to *Remains*.

In the end, I found more than I had bargained for; the result is *Five Lieutenants*, based on the voluminous letters and diaries of five Harvard-educated young men who were selected for service with the 1st Division in 1917—and who encountered differing fates in the spring and summer of 1918 as America entered battle on the Western Front.

It's an account of their collective and individual journeys from Harvard Yard to Flanders Fields—and, I hope, as full and complex a narrative of World War I as experienced by the doughboys as has ever been produced.

I would like to extend my deep appreciation to Robert Gould Shaw, a great-nephew of George Guest Haydock, for providing me George's private diary. It was a key find and a key piece of the puzzle that became *Five Lieutenants*. Yes, he's a descendant as well of the famous and eponymous major featured in the film *Glory;* and yes, he has met its star Matthew Broderick.

I would like to thank Richard Newhall's son Daniel for his recollections and for his encouragement during the research and writing of this book. Thanks also to author Claire Douglas for her help and guidance in regard to William O. P. Morgan.

When I decided to pursue the story of Richard Newhall I was immediately presented with a problem: The material in the Williams College Archives and Special Collections had been packed away in anticipation of being relocated to a new library. Archivists Sylvia Kennick Brown and Linda Hall went out of their way to locate the dozen boxes I needed from the Richard A. Newhall Papers and have them ready for me when I arrived at the archives in August 2010. This book could not have been written without their kind help. Thank you, Ms. Brown and Ms. Hall.

Similarly, Eben Dennis, special collections librarian at the Maryland Historical Society, deserves a special shout-out for help in retrieving the papers and photos of George Buchanan Redwood.

Thanks also to Laurie Stein at the Lake Forest–Lake Bluff Historical Society for help with my research into the McKinlocks; Andrew E. Woods at the Robert R. McCormick Research Center; Phyllis Goodnow for her work at the U.S. National Archives in College Park, Maryland; Laurie Miller, Mireya Throop, and Barbara Koskie; and Michael Brophy for his help in the Harvard University Archives.

Of course, thanks to Marc Resnick, my editor at St. Martin's, for his interest and patience, and thanks once more to my agent, James D.

Hornfischer, for helping me whittle the possibilities for this, my second, book, and as well for his help in assembling the manuscript. Many thanks as ever to my wife, Janet J. Goodrich, and my boys, Ethan and Nathaniel; Dad's ready to come up from the basement now . . .

Eden Prairie, Minnesota
April 2012

Five Lieutenants

May 28, 1918
Somewhere in France

So this is a battle, he half-laughs to himself as he sits helpless and shattered in the bottom of a slit trench, his dead corporal oozing blood from half a dozen holes, shells landing about him, machine-gun fire peppering the ground, and men coming and going, rushing forward and falling back.

Thick chalky dust mingles with cordite; men yell, some screaming in pain, others with bloodlust, banshee cries welling from some unknown, dark place in their souls pushing them to action; individual duels, bayonet to bayonet, take place all across the field, macabre dances ending in a gush of blood and a battered, staved-in head. A few primitive French tanks—"animals," the men call them—wallow and emit thick black exhaust, some running over the prone forms of miserable and already dying doughboys, crushing legs and arms and torsos.

He thinks, fleetingly, of Haydock, and wonders if George has made it through the first German line; then the pain wells and takes over his mind. He sits helpless, shot through and through, nausea now coming in waves, his platoon moving on without him.

He wonders if anyone can see him. He wonders if anyone might come and help him. He wonders whether he will die, but he can't bring himself to pray.

Noise, confusion, dead bodies, and blood—his own.

So this is a battle.

I

A Rendezvous

*B*RING OUT THE LIVER! the instructor shouts. *Bring out the kidneys!*

Parry, thrust, turn—it doesn't matter that their enemy is made of cloth, the bayonets of wood.

Stick it in, turn it.

Kill.

Forty-six hundred young men work at the bayonet in the May sun, sweat darkening the unfamiliar khaki on their backs. Parry. Thrust. Turn. A cool breeze stirs occasionally from nearby Lake Champlain and then wafts away. A runty army regular screams commands and at times comes in close, so close they can smell the tobacco on his breath and feel his warm bark on the napes of their necks. *Give it to him,* he yells. *Kill.*

All morning they work at the bayonet, then turn to calisthenics, and after lunch there will be hours spent on signaling and the sighting of rifles, learning to balance the weapon in their arms and then slowly squeeze the trigger. After dinner they will work on skirmish drills and then hit the books to learn the army's many arcane rules and regulations.

Some will wash out today, some tomorrow, some in the coming weeks, and return to their civilian pursuits or stubbornly insist on enlisting as privates. The rest will carry on as best they can, intent on gaining a commission as a reserve officer, though many know not why exactly they have answered their country's call in this spring of 1917 by applying for officers' training camp at Plattsburg, New York.*

It's a contingent made up largely of college boys, with the Ivy League well represented. Among these Ivy Leaguers are 350 Harvard men, a smattering of undergraduates and graduates, mostly young, well educated, and the progeny of some of the leading families in American society; many have been here before, turning out in droves to attend the 1916 Plattsburg camp and learn the rudiments of war-making.

They have read the papers. They have watched from afar since 1914 as the world went mad after the assassination of an Austrian archduke of whom few had ever heard; watched as alliances and treaties clicked into place like a jigsaw puzzle picturing hell itself.

They have watched as an insecure and armed Germany invaded neutral Belgium and marched for Paris, to assert its long-wished-for hegemony on the Continent; watched as the British landed an expeditionary force to counter the move through northern France; watched as the Germans were checked at the Marne; watched as an ensuing race to the North Sea turned into stalemate, leaving the north of France split by a big ditch.

They have read of the reprisals in Belgium in which hundreds of civilians have been lined up and shot; read of the execution of the British nurse, Edith Cavell, her offense being to help prisoners of war escape to Holland.

They know of the burning of the library at Louvain, 230,000 books gone to ashes; know of the call of the German intellectuals, the heralds of German patriotism, who in the "Call to the World of Culture" defended the reprisals and praised the German soldier as the righteous keeper of the German flame, of its *Kultur*.

---

* The town's name is actually Plattsburgh. The spelling "Plattsburg" reflects contemporary practice, which apparently originated with the local post office in the 1890s as the result of misinterpreting new place-name guidelines. The missing *h* was discovered, investigated, and restored in 1951. See Greg Twerko, "'H' in Plattsburgh Always There," http://www.cardinalpointsonline.com/fuse/h-in-plattsburgh-always-there-despite-mix-up-1.2225705?pagereq=2#.TtgSJEobdUU (accessed December 3, 2011).

They have read of the further atrocities—some real, some invented by the clever British after the underwater cable from Germany to the United States was cut. They have also read of their own predecessors, more than five hundred Harvard graduates and students who, in August 1914 and thereafter, heard the call and left their civilian lives to enlist with the Canadians, the British, and the French.

By April 1917, thirty of these Harvard men will be dead, many of them scions of the British Empire who rushed to Canada and Britain in the empire's hour of need. A handful, however, are American, from the classes of '08, and '10, and '12.

"From scraps of information that are gradually being collected, it is now evident that a great number of Harvard men are playing a part in the European war," the *Harvard Crimson* would report on November 19, 1914.

"Some of these are actually on the firing line of the allies, but the majority are engaged in Red Cross work. Many graduates of the Medical School have volunteered as surgeons in the European hospitals, while other alumni are acting as ambulance drivers and attendants."

One of the American dead is Edward Mandell Stone, Class of '08, from Chicago, who had lived in France prior to the outbreak of the war and had become "deeply interested in this country and fond of its people," his biography would say. When Germany attacked France in August 1914, he enlisted as a private in the 2nd Regiment, of Battalion C of the Foreign Legion.

They wasted little time rushing Stone to the front. He was sent up with a machine-gun company in October and lasted a few months before being wounded by shrapnel on February 15, 1915.

"One day I got a call from his company to treat a wounded man," the regiment's surgeon would remember. "It was Stone, I found, with a hole in his side made by a shrapnel ball, which had probably penetrated his left lung.

"He was carried back by my squad of stretcher-bearers from the front line trench—the *'Blanc Sablon,'* our headquarters—where I applied the first dressing, and from there removed to a hospital about eight miles back. I did not see him again, and heard that he had died of his wound in the hospital."

The American Eddie Stone of Chicago lingered for twelve days, and died on February 27, 1915.

There are others, but perhaps the most famous of these Harvard volunteers is the New Yorker Alan Seeger, who, after graduating in 1910, left for Paris, where he refused to be "implicated in any kind of a job." As the Germans approached the city in late August 1914, he, too, volunteered for the French Foreign Legion—"out of love for France."

Seeger, Harvard '10, would write his mother: "Everybody should take part in this struggle which is to have so decisive an effect, not only on the nations engaged but on all humanity. There should be no neutrals but everyone should bear some of the burden."

Of his own prospects, he put the chances of surviving at "about ten to one." In the face of these odds, he wrote: "Death is nothing terrible at all. It may mean something more wonderful than life. It cannot possibly mean anything worse to the good soldier."

Seeger took his place in the trenches in the fall of 1914 and was wounded in Champagne in February 1915. Perhaps with a better understanding of his chances of surviving, he penned one of the most famous poems of the Great War:

I have a rendezvous with Death
At some disputed barricade,
When Spring comes back with rustling shade
And apple-blossoms fill the air—
I have a rendezvous with Death
When Spring brings back blue days and fair.

It wasn't in spring but in summer that Seeger had his rendezvous. On July 4, 1916—the fourth day of the massive offensive on the Somme—Seeger and his fellow Legionnaires attacked across a wide field already littered with corpses, their destination the village of Belloy-en-Santerre.

"I caught sight of Seeger and called to him, making a sign with my hand," a friend would remember. "He answered with a smile. How pale he was! His tall silhouette stood out on the green of the cornfield. He was the tallest man in his section. His head erect, and pride in his eye, I saw him running forward, with bayonet fixed. Soon he disappeared and that was the last time I saw my friend."

The village was taken, "though Seeger . . . fallen, among the first in the attack, could but cheer his comrades on as they dashed past the spot where he lay dying."

Seeger left behind another poem, "Memorial Day Ode," anticipating the United States' eventual entry into the war—"from which no people nobly stands aloof," he would write. "If in all moments we have given proof/ Of virtues that were thought American/ I know not if in all things done and said/ All has been well and good."

From the outbreak of the war, through the German invasion of Belgium, to the desperate stand on the Marne in September 1914, and through the bleeding of the French at Verdun and the catastrophic losses at the Somme, sympathy for the Allied cause at Harvard remained strong. The war itself held an enduring fascination for its undergraduates, raised as they were to appreciate the many glories of their forebears in the Civil War and the current and inspiring writings of Robert Bridges, Rudyard Kipling, Edmund Gosse, Thomas Hardy, and others. Of course, there was Alan Seeger's poetry, too, and his noble self-sacrifice on the Somme—a dose of glory that quickened the heartbeat of many a Harvard man.

Harvard men were also at the forefront of the "preparedness" campaign that proved a vibrant force in the mid-1910s. One of the school's most famous graduates, the former president Theodore Roosevelt, Harvard 1880, became one of preparedness's loudest and most forceful proponents, and in doing so proved himself a giant thorn in the side of the pacifist President Woodrow Wilson, who had campaigned in 1916 on a promise to keep the United States out of what was seen by some as an irrelevant struggle between lumbering and decrepit empires.

At Roosevelt's side stood his good friend and former commander in the Rough Riders, the former army chief of staff Leonard Wood, himself a graduate of the Harvard Medical School in 1884, now called the "prophet of preparedness." Roosevelt's sons Teddy Jr., Harvard '08, and Archie, Harvard '16, would also become acolytes and the faces of preparedness among their peers.

The movement urged the training of thousands in at least the rudiments of the military, and in fact had a specific origin in the meeting of several Harvard graduates at the Harvard Club on West Forty-fourth Street in Manhattan just days after the liner *Lusitania* had been sunk by a German submarine off the coast of Ireland on May 7, 1915, bringing to the bottom of the Atlantic with it 124 American citizens.

Among the attendees at that meeting was Theodore Roosevelt Jr., as well as the sons of other notable American statesmen—Elihu Root Jr., Hamilton Fish Jr., and Robert Bacon Jr., the son of the former U.S. ambassador to France. Afterward, they would publicly demand that Woodrow Wilson reply to the sinking of the *Lusitania* in some military manner, "however serious."

Wilson declined their request, demanding instead that Germany drop its program of unrestricted submarine predation. In turn, the young Roosevelt and his Harvard pals approached Wood and asked if he might help organize a summer camp for professionals and businessmen yearning to display their patriotism and untapped military prowess.

Despite objections, and worries that the proposed preparedness camps mirrored the military buildup in Germany that had led to war, the "Plattsburg movement" gained steam, and several training camps opened in the late summer of 1915. On the shores of Lake Champlain in New York, at Fort Sheridan above Chicago, and at other locales, more than 2,000 TBMs—or "tired businessmen," a cadre of out-of-shape mostly thirty- and forty-somethings—slept in tent cities, learned to drill, gathered around campfires at night, and took part in large-scale mock battles during the day.

Some 1,300 tired businessmen, each paying the thirty dollars necessary for a thin cotton uniform, attended the first and largest camp at Plattsburg beginning August 10, 1915. All happily put aside their civilian pursuits for several weeks with the understanding that they would be first in line for officers' commissions should America enter the war—as many of them were certain it eventually would.

Upon their arrival at Plattsburg, the novice soldiers were wound up by speakers. Among them was Col. Edward F. Glenn, who warned, the *New York Times* would report, that "in the present unprepared condition of the United States it would be possible for a first-class foreign power, once it gained control of the sea, to land an army of 450,000 men on the Eastern seaboard of the United States, gain control of the important territory that lies between Portland, Me., and the capes of Virginia, and then gradually, perhaps quickly, move westward."

The elder Roosevelt addressed the gathering toward the end of the camp. On August 25, 1915, he praised the camp's attendees for "fulfilling the prime duty of free men." He went on, as perhaps only he could, to denigrate the "professional pacifists, poltroons, and college sissies who organize peace-at-any-price societies."

In a pointed reference to Wilson's lack of military action following the *Lusitania* sinking, Roosevelt would add: "The man who believes in peace at any price or in substituting all inclusive arbitration treaties for an army and navy should instantly move to China. If he stays here, then more manly people will have to defend him, and he is not worth defend ing. Let him get out of the country as quickly as possible. To treat elocution as a substitute for action, to rely upon high-sounding words unbacked by deeds, is proof of a mind that dwells only in the realm of shadow and of sham."

His strong words would by association bring Leonard Wood an official reprimand from Secretary of War Lindley M. Garrison, but Roosevelt would remain a hero to the Plattsburg TBMs. On Labor Day—the last day of the course—"with yells and cheers the TBMs swarmed out of their tents to snake-dance" while the camp band played "Hail! Hail! The Gang's All Here!"

From the Plattsburg idea sprang the Harvard Regiment, one thousand members strong, who through the late winter and spring of 1916 could be seen marching around campus, clad in khaki uniforms from the Spanish-American War. For three hours a week, the regiment drilled and marched and dug trenches at Fresh Ponds, each of its members smug and secure with the conceit that Ivy Leaguers—and particularly the educated gentlemen from Harvard—were naturally better suited for instruction and leadership.

It was a given echoed by the regiment's commander, the regular army commander Capt. Constant Cordier. "In all this land there is no better material for officers than is found in the student body of Harvard," Cordier would say. "They are a splendid, manly set of fellows, and it is a pleasure to work with them.

"I am naturally more than pleased with what has already been accomplished, and I am sure that in another year, on top of the experience they will gain at the training camps this Summer, we will be in a position to supply a goodly number of prospective officers for our volunteer forces."

Harvard's president, Abbott Lawrence Lowell, also had no doubts about the leadership capabilities of Harvard's men. "I trust that none of you will ever have to take part in a war, and yet I know perfectly well that if you do you will do your part nobly and courageously," he would tell the regiment's men that spring.

"Every man here must prepare himself to be an officer, for officers are needed most by the Government now. The problems which confront officers today are far more perplexing, the duties that they have to perform are far more exacting, and the knowledge required much greater than the problems and duties officers had to face in the early wars in which the nation engaged."

When the summer of 1916 came, many of these same were among the 16,134 civilians that turned out for further instruction in the twelve Plattsburg-style camps organized across the country—just in case President Lowell's "trust" that they would never have to engage in war proved unfounded.

The Harvard contingent numbered 1,572—"representing all classes, from the late eighties down to the sub-freshmen," the *Harvard Alumni Bulletin* reported. "It was not only the athletes and sportsmen who turned out in force, there were teachers and parsons and bankers and doctors and lawyers and diplomats and scholars and literary men, and a little of everything else."

None of the attendees—not those from Cornell or Princeton or, perish the thought, Yale or Dartmouth—"worked harder than the Harvard men," the *Bulletin* added. Their showing, it went on, turned the head of at least one non–Ivy Leaguer, "a Westerner," who had held a "life-long prejudice against Harvard men.

"There were so many in his company who were so utterly unlike what he had been brought up to regard as the 'Harvard type' that he was forced to cut loose from his traditional opinion, and he boldly asserted that, whatever people might think out home, the Harvard men at Plattsburg were the best men in the camp."

After playing at war for some weeks the campers were allowed to return to their civilian pursuits, or to Harvard and its "contacts with truly great men, of a surprising diversity of interests, characters, and personalities," as one alumnus would recall. "We had liberty in the choosing of these influences, time to adjust and assimilate them, leisure to grow from our centres as well as absorb our points of contact. We were not regimented, standardized, herded, and labeled. We were not intimidated into imitativeness, browbeaten into conformity, or nagged into efficiency."

The declaration of war on Germany on April 6, 1917, put an end to such carefree intellectual pursuits. The army had a crying need for leaders, and these same Harvard men were considered to be the best available pool of men to be taught the army way, in the hope that some in turn would help convey that knowledge to the army of millions to be raised in that summer's draft—while others, their three months of training completed, would be sent straight to France, and eventually into the Allies' myriad and deadly trench system.

More than 11,000 Harvard men would see some kind of action in the Great War, the largest number from any American college or university; of those, 375 would be killed in action or die from wounds and accidents and disease, far more than from any other college or university. Harvard's Ivy League archrival, Yale, put 7,000 men into the service, of which 200 died; Princeton University sent 6,050 graduates and students into the fray, losing 147 of them, according to Charles Franklin Thwing's 1920 study of the war's effect on American higher education.

Even in the death count, Harvard stood alone.

This is the story of just five of those 11,319 men Harvard sent to war, five who traded their tweed for khaki and suborned their class, their privilege, their education, and their free will to be ordered about and harangued by their supposed social inferiors; five who traded the works of Rousseau and Aristotle and Keats for the army's *Infantry Drill Regulations;* five who surrendered the might-have-beens of their short-term futures for a chance to lead illiterate immigrants and the far less privileged youth of America's cities and towns in fearsome battle; five men loosely united by the stamp of a Harvard education whose lives were forever altered by world war.

It's the story of five men who were among the best the nation had to offer to the cause of defeating an enemy well experienced at and inured to the horrors of modern war, an enemy who had accepted that significant gains would be measured in feet and yards and the wastage of thousands of lives.

It's the story of five young men who exemplified the clash of cultures within an American army sent overseas to wallow in rat-infested trenches and wait for its chance to advance into the maelstrom upon the first shrill whistles of its overeducated platoon commanders.

It's the story of five lieutenants.

2

No Place for a Philosopher

Put him in khaki, put a weapon in his hands, put him among the herd, which he detests; work him fourteen hours a day in drill and calisthenics and digging trenches; strip him of his individuality, stifle his thoughts, and still the question remains: Can the army take Harvard out of Richard Ager Newhall?

More to the point: Can the army take Richard Newhall out of Richard Newhall?

He wonders the same, as he trains at Plattsburg with those thousands of others in mid-May 1917, who have arrived with their valises crammed with extra underwear and their heads stuffed with grand and noble ideas about war. They have leaped, followed the herd, succumbed to peer pressure and the notion that they were born to lead men in mortal combat—by right, by breeding, by virtue of their sterling educations.

Richard Newhall has thought this through more than most, worked through the what-ifs and pros and cons and decided that if—no, *when*—war comes he will offer himself to the United States Army, no matter that he is at once attracted to and repelled by all things military; no matter that he sees in it the same Prussianism that, he believes, caused this war; no matter that his eyes are bad and he has devoted his twenty-eight years not to the robust manly games of youth, as have so many, but instead has spent hours in dimly lit libraries, chasing a PhD in history, tracing the crests and swells of history in musty books.

He has thought this through and decided when the time comes he will take the leap from learning history to *making* it, in his own small way. He has decided he will apply for a place in the officers' training camps and throw in his lot with the army, repugnant as that seems, not out of blind patriotism but from a sense of personal responsibility to the world, to the idea that something has been rotten for too long, that democracy—true democracy—has been allowed to wither on the vine because of individual greed. The war has presented an opportunity to set things straight.

Richard Ager Newhall is a study in contrasts, something of an anomaly even among the educated, soon-to-be newly minted second lieutenants of the American Expeditionary Force. The son of a Minneapolis businessman who had himself attended Harvard only to quit when financial matters at home became too pressing for him to continue, he was raised comfortably in a solidly middle-class home on the city's south side, not far from the downtown and the massive Victorian homes lining Lake of the Isles but far, far from the ivy-coated East Coast bastions of higher education in Boston and Baltimore and New York.

Born June 12, 1888, the fifth of six children, Richard attended the public schools and spent "a normal enough childhood," a friend would write, though he seemed to have taken little joy in the usual schoolyard roughhousing or sports, instead finding solace in books. Blessed with a towering and independent intellect, he refused to suffer fools and was thus somewhat ostracized by classmates who found him standoffish and perhaps even a little imperious.

He also possessed a keen self-awareness and had the unusual ability to watch himself with "untroubled detachment," to "stand off and watch myself and laugh at myself," he would remember. "Even if I should ever get into battle I imagine that I will have the same feeling of naïve curiosity. 'So this is a battle! Well, I always did want to know what a battle was like . . .'"

He recalled with no bitterness that as a teenager, "I seem to have become aware of the fact that I wasn't popular (nor unpopular either), and to have accepted that fact with enough equanimity not to strive after popularity. Perhaps the fact that there was no social activity of any formal or organized sort to which I was exposed helped. So I became accustomed to diverting myself with books and public entertainments (theater, symphonies), none of which were sociable."

In 1906, he entered the University of Minnesota but continued to live at home. Where other undergraduates lived and died with the fortunes of the school's sports teams, Newhall, typically, had no interest. Instead he continued to indulge an interest in the theater and symphonies, to which he had been introduced in his teens by his mother. He took in productions of Ibsen and Thackeray—and even a performance by the dancer Isadora Duncan, whom he found "fascinating."

He wasn't "hurt" when he was not invited to join any of the university's fraternities but did recall "mild regret when I found that certain of my class-mates whom I liked seemed to become unavailable for me when they did join."

In contrast to his bookish persona, Newhall indulged a fascination with things military—perhaps spurred by his wide reading of history—by signing up for reserve training, and he drilled for part of the summer after his freshman year at nearby Fort Snelling. Newhall received his BA with honors in history in 1910 and was elected to Phi Beta Kappa.

He stayed on at Minnesota for a year to complete his master's degree in history, then in 1912 moved to Cambridge, Massachusetts, to become a teaching fellow while he worked on his PhD at Harvard—"some classy place, believe me," he would write of the fabled institution.

There, the midwesterner came in contact for the first time with the Easterner. At once he was both drawn to the "refined sociability" of the Harvard set and at the same time made painfully aware of his "provincialism." He attended teas every Sunday at the home of Harvard's President Lowell and was impressed by the gatherings. "There seems to be something . . . that these refined Easterners have which we lack. They enjoy culture and refinement for themselves and take real pleasure in them; they seem to be more leisurely, whereas we are so eternally hustling that we only enjoy things on the run."

In the fall of 1914, even as Europe quaked with the outbreak of war and piles of chalky soil marked the ever-lengthening trench lines across France, Newhall traveled to Europe to research his thesis on the Norman conquest of that country. Prevented by the maelstrom from beginning his work there, he instead landed in England, where he remained until spring, visiting castles and cathedrals and libraries.

In the spring of 1915, he ventured across the Channel and made it to Paris, Rouen, Lisieux, and Caen for a few months before returning to Cambridge. By then, the *Lusitania* had sunk off the coast of southern Ireland, and, perhaps more than most other youths of the age, the young historian followed closely the rapid turn of events, hoping the United States could stay out of the war.

He believed Germany posed a threat to American values, but at the same time he remained unconvinced that America had any real stake in the conflict. Still, Newhall was one of those Harvard men who drilled at Plattsburg in the summer of 1916, even though he viewed the "preparedness" campaign being pushed by Wood and Roosevelt to be repugnant and instead found himself supporting Woodrow Wilson, who was even then campaigning on a promise to keep America out of the overseas war.

He seems to have been drawn to Plattsburg more by the opportunity for camaraderie amid the outdoors setting than by any real concern about preparedness, believing that the arming of thousands of Americans might lead to the United States falling under the spell of the same undemocratic militarism he detested. "He worried about the psychological effects involvement in the war would have on Americans," a friend, Russell H. Bostert, would write. "He deplored 'crusading ardor' and extreme pro-American sentiment."

When Wilson won the presidency in late 1916, Newhall did an "intellectual war dance." Before long, however, Newhall saw the inevitability of American involvement and predicted, correctly, that Germany would resume its submarine campaign against American ships in a bid to isolate Britain and force an end to the stalemate. When the German move occurred on February 1, 1917, it meant war, Newhall was certain.

"My mind is so engrossed with the probability of war within the next few days that, so far, I have found it impossible to direct my attention to any of the jobs I have on my hands," he wrote his mother, Elizabeth, on February 4, 1917. "It looks to me as if we are about to witness the phenomenon of America entering the war with the greatest reluctance, after plenty of deliberation, after every possible attempt to settle the issues peacefully, and with no ulterior motive whatsoever. It is a phenomenon unique in history, I believe."

Despite his objections to the "semi-militaristic" mood of the United States, he was ready to join the army—if it would take him. "If there is a call for volunteers I will respond," he wrote, "although I must say I am a little skeptical as to my ability to be regarded as physically fit." He worried, as well, that "the mere fact of my wearing glasses may bar me."

Just two months later, on April 6, Congress voted for war—and Newhall found himself in a rush, hastening to finish his thesis while grading the papers and exams of his History I students. Harvard had moved up the end of the semester to accommodate the war, as hundreds of the nation's best and brightest made plans to enlist in the army, navy, or marines as soon as the term was over, everyone in a mad and glorious rush to get Over There and see the war.

It was almost a formality that Newhall was accepted for officers' training at the first camp for officers at Plattsburg. Because of his previous National Guard experience and his time at Plattsburg the previous summer, he was told he was to be commissioned as a second lieutenant right away.

He would enter Plattsburg not with blind patriotism but with high ideals and the hope that America's part in the war would help unite the different classes of American and European society, level the playing field, and bring social and economic justice to all.

He would also envision the eradication of nationalism and the beginning of an evolution toward a democratic world government—lofty ideals indeed. They were ideals shared by some, however, and were perhaps best expressed by the Englishwoman Frances Evelyn Warwick, the "Socialist Countess," who in 1917 wrote of the "disease" that lurked at the core of the war and, she claimed, had spread through Europe and even to America.

"With due apologies to every British apostle of the comfortable doctrine of self-righteousness," she would write, "I must decline to regard Germany as the villain of the piece. I can only see her as the sharp knife that lanced the festering ulcer of modern 'progress,' a progress that was traveling hard in the wrong direction." Germany, she would claim, was just the "unconscious agent, the dangerous remedy by which a desperate disease may yet be healed, and it seems to me that this disease was spreading fast all over Europe to say nothing of the New World."

The disease was "the pursuit of riches and power at any price," and in Germany and the Austro-Hungarian Empire it involved the building of military states. In England, "the pursuit of power and riches took another form. Of militarism we had little or none, but from ten thousand factories and workshops, from a thousand slums the cry of the worker uprose to God. 'The voice of thy brother's blood crieth unto me from the ground.' "

Newhall also noted the opportunity the war presented: "The bigness of the work in hand . . . is more than merely defeating Germany." Instead, he felt, the war was a "great step forward which the world is taking. It is the welding together of the liberty-loving peoples into a great co-operating society which is to be the triumph that will follow an allied victory."

The weakness of the world's democracies, he would write, "is that their liberty, of which they were so boastful, was a mere individualism which allowed every man to compete unscrupulously with all his neighbors.

"Now in the face of this German menace we are trying to learn how to curtail some of our individual 'liberties' in order to secure a national unity. Germany and Japan have secured the spirit of co-operation through the action of autocracies. It is for us to show that it can be achieved as well and in less dangerous form through democracy."

If it could not, "it is better to be killed before that impossibility has been demonstrated," he would add. "If it can be, then anyone who contributes towards the achievement of that end can be proud in proportion to his contribution."

Tall and blond and usually unsmiling, his face frozen in the stern and ever-serious mask of a fiery country preacher, the less-than-robust

Newhall continued to worry he might be rejected by the army. He had as his fallback plan an offer to teach history at Ohio State University in Columbus, which he had received on April 27. In the meantime, he traveled to Plattsburg to join the large number of college boys vying for commissions—nationwide, 40,000 officer candidates would vie for slightly more than 26,000 commissions as reserve officers in the army. On May 15, he found himself "enjoying the irresponsibilities of being a private" and soon lost himself in intense and long days of training at the camp with which he'd become so familiar the previous summer.

The need for officers was acute: On April 6, 1917, the army had just 5,791 regular officers in its ranks, who oversaw the activities of just 121,797 enlisted men. By the end of the war, 200,000 officers would be needed to lead a 4-million-man army—and almost half of these would come from the OTCs, or officers' training camps.

All sixteen camps were modeled on the original Plattsburg camps of 1915 and 1916. Their attendees were a mix of college upperclassmen and college graduates, reserve officers, national guardsmen, and some army veterans seeking commission—but college boys formed the overwhelming majority at Plattsburg, Fort Sheridan in Illinois, and other locales.

Their instructors were regulars who had spent years—and in some cases decades—paying their dues while climbing up the army's chain of command in peacetime. Now they found themselves in charge of a horde of educated and well-off college boys who after just three *months* would receive commissions as first and second lieutenants and, in some cases, captains.

The army in late 1916, the newly commissioned 2nd Lt. Charles T. Senay would write, was backward-looking, and many of its officers had stagnated in peacetime. "The big talk was still of the Spanish-American War—San Juan Hill and the Rough Riders; Gatling Gun Parker; General Shafter with his gouty leg . . . black powder and the Krag-Jorgenson rifle."

Cavalry dominated the army, in which the saber was still the decisive weapon. "The backbone of the Army was then . . . the long-suffering, ever-enduring infantry, trained to march in all kinds of weather at the rate of three miles an hour," Senay wrote. "There was a bit of artillery with its Civil War traditions of point blank fire. Long range concentrations were in their infancy, as were intricate breech lock mechanisms."

Company commanders, Senay would add, were about fifty years old. Peacetime routine flowed around the bottle: "There's an old Army saying, 'No liquor until the sun passes over the flagpole.' A high percentage of Army officers in 1916 were heavy drinkers. Some were rated as a bottle a day man. There were even two-bottle men."

One colonel, Senay wrote, "had been restricted to one drink a day. He asked me to join him in his drink at the club. I ordered a double Scotch on the rocks. Then he said, 'Waiter, bring mine.' The waiter brought a full bottle with a giant glass of crushed ice to match. That was the colonel's one drink a day."

With the advent of war, hundreds of regular army officers were detailed to train officer candidates such as Newhall. The immediate goal was not so much the production of line officers for the front but the making of instructors for the 1.5-million-man draft army that was to be raised over the summer, and for which 9 million men turned out to register on June 5.

The exigencies of "modern warfare" would require the imbuing of certain "moral qualities"—discipline being the most prized—both in junior officers and in the average infantryman, the handbook *America at War* would note: "To face destruction by the enemy's artillery when he is five or six miles from a point where he himself can inflict injury in return, suffer casualties in advancing over great stretches of ground without firing a shot, to face the thunderbolts of large calibre guns and howitzers, to endure the rain of death of shrapnel and high explosives, to meet the withering hail of the hell-spitting mitrailleuse, to face the steel-jacketed sheet of rifle fire, even to suffer death at the hands of one's own supporting artillery, cut the wire entanglement, mount the parapet, to give or receive the death thrust of the bayonet's cold steel. This is what modern warfare requires of the infantryman. To meet the test he must be faithfully and arduously trained. And to give him this training there must be developed the learned and successful officer who comprehends his task."

Richard Newhall quickly found himself to be just another face in the expectant horde gathered at Plattsburg—"an unimportant atom in a huge mass," he would write. He would also soon find his independent and egalitarian bent rubbing sharply against the military demands for blind obeisance and discipline.

Still, he tried his best to stifle his objections to being just one in the herd of almost 5,000 men accepted to the camp, where the days began with reveille at 5:30 A.M. and ended with taps at 9:45 P.M.

The pace was quick, "in tabloid form, administered in lightning doses with staggering rapidity," Maj. Merch B. Stewart, the senior instructor at Plattsburg, would say.

"The difficulties of teaching men fresh from civil life the duties of Lieutenants, Captains, and Majors in three months in war time may be appreciated," the *New York Times* would note that July.

Then again, no one was expecting the successful candidates to be ready for the trenches at the camp's conclusion. "The men now in the officers' training camps will not be soldiers, in the strictest sense, when they complete their work this summer," the *Times* added. "It is hoped, of course, that they will have absorbed enough from their army instructors to appreciate the necessity for discipline."

That "necessity for discipline" would at times rankle the independent and freethinking Newhall. "Truly the army is no place for a philosopher who values kindliness above efficiency," he would lament in one letter home that summer.

He would note immediately upon his arrival at the camp that its makeup had changed from the previous summer. "There is a marked difference in the general character of the crowd here now and the one last July," he wrote. "There are none of the elderly, paunchy men who were rather common last summer." The officer candidates instead were "young, without being youthful—middle and late twenties or early thirties for the most part. Most of them have had previous military work so I do not believe we will have to spend much time on the rudiments of close order drill, but can get on to new things more directly connected with actual warfare."

He noted, too, that his own state of mind differed. What had been a boyish lark had suddenly turned to deadly serious business—a fact he appreciated. "That was a vacation, and I sought to avoid all necessity for thinking which I could," he would write. "This is business and I will welcome all new responsibility which they will put on me. The little practical experience I had last summer comes in very handy when it comes to showing how to put together a pack or to take apart and clean a rifle."

He would admit to being envious of the men in his unit "who seem to have more enthusiasm for military matters than I have, but I have not found any way of stimulating it in myself."

Overall, he would write, "I am glad to get back to camp life again. It agrees with me. If I can find some pleasant companion I should be quite happy. The men here now seem a pleasant sort and I may be able to make some new acquaintances."

Newhall also found himself pleased to be under a regular army officer who knew his stuff—and how to impart it to his subordinates. The teacher became the eager student, as the neophyte officer Newhall sought instruction in leadership more than anything else.

Capt. Thompson Lawrence was "a peach," Newhall would write. "Everyday we have 'conference' of a couple of hours in which he tells us a lot of practical things in connection with the various assignments set us to study.

"He can illustrate his remarks with his own experiences in the Philippines, Asia, Europe, and on the Mexican border. He knows how to handle men and that is something which I would like very much to learn. I am impressed with the fact that these regular officers are good teachers, very good teachers, and I am trying to find out just what it is that makes them so."

One lesson, he noted, was "the need of holding aloof from the men, and he practices it consistently in his relations with us. That is quite counter to all my theories of academic teaching, but I can see how different military teaching is from academic.

"The latter aims to cultivate individualism, the former to suppress it.

The former is trying to make a machine that will respond quickly and surely to the touch of its master, and it must recognize the mastery absolutely in order to do so. Too much kindliness or camaraderie can be most pernicious in its effects on a company."

He was impressed as well "with the fact that one does not learn to be a good officer out of the book," he added. "Most of our captain's excellence comes from personality and experience rather than from an encyclopedic knowledge of the different manuals."

At the end of May, Newhall's commission arrived, and, pending a physical examination, he was placed on active duty—a status, he confessed, that made him "a little uneasy, but there is nothing to do but to take it and abide the decision."

Even with his commission, there was no guarantee Newhall would be one of those chosen to be assigned as a reserve officer in the regular army and possibly be sent overseas. In any event, he continued to vacillate between wanting and not wanting to be in the army.

"Sometimes when I contemplate the possibility of living this sort of life for a year I am simply appalled," he wrote in early June, "but I guess I will get used to it." Then, too, he noted, "there is always the possibility that I won't be continued on active duty after August, though I have the feeling that, eventually at least, they will need all the officers they can get. It won't be so bad during the summer months but I don't like the idea of a winter in barracks."

He had already experienced enough of army life to have developed a strong distaste for its "tendency to emphasize details which seem petty," he wrote after five weeks of training, in a refrain that would become quite familiar over the next year.

"Things that I can see a reason for I do with enthusiasm but things that are to be done merely because it is so ordered by an arbitrary and not too intelligent (and not at all sympathetic) authority, for these I have small stomach.

"The whole idea of determining the worth of individuals by certain strictly regulated formulas is one against which I baulk, both at Harvard and here. It is worse than at Harvard, perhaps because they are attempting to handle such a large crowd with so few instructors."

By then he saw very clearly that his inability to simply do instead of questioning why was putting him on perhaps unsteady ground. "I am becoming more and more conscious of my limitations as a military man and won't be at all surprised if I am not utilized after this camp is over," he wrote.

"I may be able to acquire more of the military spirit. I am no worse than large numbers of the men here, which, however, is small comfort. We are all very civilian. The chief difference, I guess, is that most men are willing and eager to cultivate the military state of mind and I am not, or at least only half-heartedly."

At times, he would lament, "I get depressed, thinking that I am punk as an officer, but I am hardly worse than the general run, and I am improving and learning where my deficiencies are and trying to think out corrections."

Either way, he would allow things to take their course.

"I accept with resignation, often without conscious consideration, the complete disorganization of my future," he wrote. "Perhaps the military work helps that. It certainly makes you learn to accept what is assigned to you as inevitable and act accordingly. I am trying not to philosophize. It is unmilitary, fills me with doubts, and generally impairs military efficiency.

"This is no life for thinking."

Instead, he would "learn to act, to do something practical, to know without thinking what the most intelligent and practical thing to do is, to act without asking questions, to guess correctly what is wanted of you when you are not told what to do, to assume a position of domination even when you are not quite sure of yourself and then pull yourself together without being seen.

"All these are things I am slowly learning to try to do, which is educating and valuable. If they give me time I think I can pull myself out of my academic rut and make an efficient officer."

Beyond the "pettiness" that he found so distasteful, Plattsburg training offered exercises the practical Newhall found interesting.

At Plattsburg, as at other American camps that summer and fall, the requisite instruction in digging and holding trenches was imparted—

but from American Expeditionary Force commander Gen. John J. Pershing on down, the dominant emphasis was on teaching "open warfare," as the Americans were insistent that they would not become bogged down in the trench warfare that had stalled the ambitions of the Germans and Allies since the autumn of 1914.

In the 1904–5 Russo-Japanese War, machine guns had proved their murderous effectiveness on infantry, and barbed wire its usefulness in slowing attacks. Nevertheless, Japan's aggressiveness in attacking fixed machine-gun positions successfully had left the most lasting impression among American observers. The army's 1914 *Field Service Regulations* pointed specifically to the value of attack, stating unequivocally: "Decisive results are obtained only by the offensive."

Even the press praised offensive spirit and called for training that focused on the attack. The *New York Times,* referencing the experience of the British on the Somme, would note: "Frequently British attacking parties have had open country in front of them, but they were trained in trench warfare and they did not know how to follow up their advantage. They retired, or dug themselves in, and trench routine began again . . . The British mistake will not be repeated by the American General Staff. Emphasis is laid at the beginning on the elements of open field fighting, on deployment, on patrol work, on advance guards, and on outposts. Later will come the specialties of trench warfare, with veteran British and French officers to assist."

Newhall was enthusiastic about one such practical exercise in open warfare, which, at least for a day, forced him to use his brains instead of his brawn: "The battalion is marched out onto the road, a situation stated (where the enemy is supposed to be, how large our force is supposed to be, what we have been sent out to accomplish). Then we are told to write out the necessary orders for the various commanders.

"Then the situation is carried farther. The battalion undertakes to carry out the orders issued. After a couple of hours the instructors, who are regulars, assemble the whole crowd, and the whole morning's work is discussed and criticized.

"It soon becomes evident that there may easily be several good ways of solving an out-post problem, for instance, and that none of them are flawless. It is a change from working out of a book, and a very welcome one."

As well, there were trench-building lessons, long marches, bomb-throwing displays, and "Battle Fire" training, in which squads fired and advanced at targets on the rifle range—all hands-on, practical experiences around which he could wrap his mind.

"The men took to the work with an enthusiasm which they have not shown recently," he wrote of digging trenches. "Evidently they felt that here, at last, was something which had some direct bearing upon the war in which they would participate."

All the while doubting he had shown enough interest and military spirit, near the end of the camp Newhall took a large step toward active-duty status as a result of his performance during a battalion-strength night exercise in which he led his company through the night against "enemy" trenches.

Working stealthily, he brought his men to within one hundred yards of the position before they were discovered. He then ordered an attack with bayonets fixed. "That rush was, for me, a very exciting half minute," he wrote, "and I am surprised that in the excitement no one was hurt. The whole maneuver was pronounced a great success—and a probable victory for our battalion because we had got so close to the enemy before being discovered."

He would remember that his performance in command that night may have been better than his captain expected. For the first time, "I thought well of myself, and I had shown no hesitation in doing what was called for, did some of the small things correctly on my own initiative and gave the right answers when questioned."

On August 11, the training ended—and the wait to discover one's fate began. "There was one long crescendo of worry until Friday morning when the appointments were announced," Newhall wrote. "Since then the camp state of mind is epitomized in the following remark in a tone of bewildered surprise. 'John Smith a captain! Gee whiz!' "

About thirty from Newhall's group didn't make the grade and were let go, but Newhall, despite his worrying, kept his commission as a reserve second lieutenant in the infantry. Only 500 of those 4,600 candidates accepted for the first Plattsburg camp failed the test.

The camp's commanding officer, Lt. Col. Paul A. Wolf, was pleased. "I would rather command a regiment officered by these new, young officers, than an organization with officers from the regular army as it is constituted at present," he would say. "Nor am I crying down West Point, which, after all, is the greatest military school in the world."

He extolled the virtues of the newly commissioned officers at Plattsburg, who came in with little or no military experience, or attendant preconceptions, and who were "practically all college men. They are at the pliable age when they are willing to learn from the more experienced regulars. They have received proper instruction as to how to instruct other men, and they have nothing to unlearn."

The twenty-nine-year-old Newhall, though pleased to have made the grade as a reserve officer in the regular army, bristled at the parting words of Captain Lawrence. (Not for the last time, Newhall had changed his initially enthusiastic opinion of a commanding officer). Lawrence, Newhall would relate, told the new officers "how they must enforce the outward recognition of their superiority at all times and in every detail of our relations with the men under us."

Newhall complained: "The element of hypocrisy in assuming to be the best men in the platoon and demanding outward recognition of this very questionable fact disgusts me. For my own part, I know that I have given willing obedience to the captain's orders during the last two months without ever admitting that he had anything but technical superiority to me.

"Indeed in respects I consider myself the better man. Again we come upon two absolutely diverse standards of values. So far I have refused to alter mine."

Richard Newhall vs. the United States Army would continue in France, to which he would soon enough sail with dozens of other newly minted junior officers to fill the ranks of the 1st Division, in which many officers had gained automatic promotion with the expansion of the regular army and which had a desperate need of junior officers.

Newhall years later would continue to wonder why he—still decidedly *in* the army but not *of* it—had been chosen to be among the first shipment of officers to France.

"I don't think the captain thought I was very promising military material," he wrote, "and, according to his West Point outlook, he was correct."

3

His Death Warrant

He thinks that perhaps he shouldn't be here, even as he drills and digs and tries to figure the army way of doing things. He doesn't have a militaristic or unkind bone in his body; he has never ordered anyone around; he has only an inkling of interest in all of this furious activity of getting America's might up to speed. Perhaps, he thinks, he shouldn't be here. Perhaps he should have stayed home in Milton, Massachusetts, and continued on at the textile mill where he had worked his way from menial labor to a desk job in short order following graduation from Harvard.

Instead, he's into it up to his neck, even as he wonders what he's doing here.

George Guest Haydock is twenty-two years old. He is quiet and reserved, serious, but unsure of himself. His is a kind face, with a ready smile, no shadow or hint of anger. Born of Quaker heritage, he has been raised in the Friends' stronghold of Germantown, Pennsylvania, attending the Friends school there and learning the peaceful ways of the sect.

He is a natural athlete, a legendary pole vaulter at Harvard, and were it not that he had been born in 1894 he might well have become an above-average businessman and led a quiet, reserved life in Milton, to which his parents removed upon his father's retirement.

Instead he has come of age in the midst of a world war, and despite the concerns of his parents, Robert Roger and Annie Louise, he is one of those Harvard men vying for a commission at Plattsburg. He tells his parents that he is off to seek a commission as a reserve officer not from bloodlust or a bent toward militarism, but so he can in his own small way help end this war, and all wars.

Still, there's more than a sense that George Haydock simply couldn't stand by and watch as his Harvard mates rushed to the camps. So now he is parrying and thrusting and in games and drills showing off his athletic abilities and crawling through freshly dug trenches that, so the instructors all say, exactly mirror the conditions in France, right down to the tumbleweeds of barbed wire and the collecting mud and water.

He learns to shoot a rifle and studies the drill manual. Despite his uncertainties and insecurities, he performs well and is well liked by the other men and instructors.

George, Guest Haydock, it seems, is doomed to earn his commission and stay in the army.

In the spring of 1916 George Haydock had been one of those young men running around Harvard Yard in the decrepit threads of an old war, one of those who drilled and dug at the Fresh Ponds, the sweat pouring from his brow. Not enough sweat to wash away that grin, though, and that laugh, that famous self-deprecating laugh, the laugh of one not yet certain of his abilities or potential, the laugh of one who doesn't quite yet know who he is but knows who he *isn't*, knows he isn't army, though he may be a soldier, and one who hopes to find out more about himself in the great forge of war.

As have his peers, for the past three years George Haydock has read of the war raging overseas, read of the German atrocities and the numbing losses on all sides: the 20,000 British soldiers killed on July 1, 1916, the opening day of the Somme offensive; the hundreds of thousands killed at Verdun and at Loos and at Ypres and Champagne and the Marne.

And yet . . .

Yet with all that, "one would think that . . . it would have been all but impossible to get anyone to serve without duress," the former doughboy William L. Langer would write. "But it was not so. We and many thousands of others volunteered . . . I can hardly remember a single instance of serious discussion of American policy or of larger war issues. We men, most of us young, were simply fascinated by the prospect of adventure and heroism. Most of us, I think, had the feeling that life, if we survived, would run in the familiar, routine channel. Here was our one great chance for excitement and risk. We could not afford to pass it up."

This is so even though their junior-officer counterparts in Europe were famously turning into the Lost Generation, a cadre of noble and brave and doomed lads who were the first out of the trenches, shrill whistles in their mouths, cajoling and urging their supposed lessers on toward the fortified German trenches in the spirit of glorious suffering and self-sacrifice. The U.S. War Department, meanwhile, had taken note of the losses of junior officers Over There and calculated a "wastage" of 2,000 officers a month once America was in the thick of the fighting.

George Guest Haydock would say or write little of the larger issues of the war. He expressed no higher ideals, little interest in international issues, and, though his blood ran deep into England, no sentiments that he was off to war to settle a score for his English cousins.

Nor would he comment much on the quickly moving events of the late winter and early spring of 1917—how the war had finally willed itself across the Atlantic Ocean as steadily as a ponderous tsunami and swept aside the peaceable intents of President Woodrow Wilson and his ilk, arriving on the eastern seaboard on February 1 in the form of the announcement by Germany that it would resume unrestricted submarine prowling on American ships headed to Europe.

Wilson, restrained in his reaction to the sinking of the *Lusitania* almost two years before, this time cut diplomatic relations with Germany. Though still hopeful of the peace he had promised, he had watched, frustrated, as America's merchant fleet stuck to its harbors through the month, afraid to venture out into the suddenly perilous waters.

Wilson had sought a way around war, finally landing on the option of "armed neutrality," under which the merchant fleet bottled up in its ports would be provided guns and naval gunners. The measure, the Armed Ship Bill, stalled in the U.S. Senate, where the Wisconsin senator Robert La Follette and a few sympathizers stymied it with a filibuster.

In response, Wilson played a different hand, releasing the so-called Zimmermann Telegram, in which the German foreign minister, Arthur Zimmermann, offered Mexico the return of its former possessions of New Mexico, Texas, and Arizona if it would kindly stir up further trouble on the border in the event America entered the war—and in the event Germany was victorious.

The public furor over the delayed revelation of the bumbling German treachery blared across the country's front pages on March 1, and subsequent events—which began with the sinking of three American merchant ships by German torpedoes on March 18—led inexorably to Wilson's *finally* asking Congress for war. On April 6, just one day later, he got his wish.

What George Haydock thought of these great national and world events, which would soon involve him body and soul, isn't known; his writings—in his diary, in his letters home—mention nothing of a need for resolution of the situation in the Balkans, or patriotism, or any serious issue with Kaiser Wilhelm II—Kaiser Bill—who as the face of detested Prussianism would become the object of much doughboy invective.

What is known is that George Guest Haydock saw the war as an opportunity to settle a score with himself, to see if he had the stuff to fight, to lead men, to suffer, and to endure; and to find, as John Dos Passos had written in *One Man's Initiation,* the answer to the one question many young men asked themselves that spring:

"We had spent our boyhood in the afterglow of the peaceful nineteenth century . . . What was war like? We wanted to see with our own eyes."

George Haydock also wanted to see—even if it meant cutting across the grain of his peaceable upbringing.

The blood of the Friends ran deep in George Guest Haydock, handed down from a grandfather four times removed, Roger Haydock. Roger and his brother John had spread the good word at meetings throughout England and Ireland and the Netherlands in the late 1660s, and been persecuted for their faithfulness.

Their offense? They would preach the Truth, as they understood it: Seek the "inner light" of God within yourselves, instead of Scripture; do away with bricks-and-mortar church and trained clergy and seek God yourselves; believe each man and woman has goodness within; renounce all wars and violence no matter the ends. To the Puritans, it amounted to blasphemy.

George Guest Haydock was the youngest of the four children of Robert Roger—named after his rabble-rousing Quaker forebear—and the former Annie Louise Heywood. Edith, ten years older than George, was born in 1884; his brother, Robert, was born in 1888, and Louisa Lowe—her name a nod to the family's original Quaker's bride—made her appearance in 1890.

George, named after an uncle, came into the Haydocks' comfortable home in Germantown, Pennsylvania—established by the German Quaker Daniel Pastorius—on September 15, 1894.

True to their origins, the Haydocks sent young George to the Friends' School in Germantown and, in 1909, on to prep at the Middlesex School. "There, besides playing on the football and baseball teams, he entered heartily into the various interests of the place, and greatly endeared himself both to masters and boys," a biography says.

Following his older brother, Robert, to Harvard, George enrolled in the Class of '16 and "devoted himself with special interest to studies in English." Eschewing baseball and football, George moved on to track; he put his energy into working on his vaulting the summer prior to moving to Cambridge.

"I can't think of your house without George practising pole vaults in front of the stable for hours at a time, very patiently and very determinedly, all by himself," one friend of the Haydocks would remember.

At Harvard, his athleticism would bring acclaim. At the end-of-season awards in 1916 George "was the greatest individual winner and took three cups back to his room in Holworthy Hall," the *Boston Advertiser* would note on March 17.

Outwardly cheerful and self-deprecating, inwardly George Haydock tended toward self-doubt and insecurity. Though he embraced new experiences and adventures, he approached them with some trepidation. He was not one to rush in but one to ease himself in, peering around corners for what might hit him next, always falling back on a certain sense of the absurd and a comic view of himself. Others would find it endearing, but in fact it only expressed the conflicts between thought and action that at times paralyzed his soul.

Given those conflicts, it may have been a simple matter of caving to peer pressure that brought the Quaker-raised George Haydock into the Harvard Regiment when it was formed in his senior year on January 10, 1916, and thence to the Plattsburg camp that summer. While his soldiering caused some worry in the Haydock home, George countered the pacifist inclinations of the Friends by pointing to the larger picture.

George, his father would write, "abhorred" war "but entered from a strong sense of personal duty, and when once embarked carried through with the best that was in him."

Still, there seemed to be some worry within the family that George Haydock might find himself loving war too much.

"I am afraid thee may think . . . that I am trying to pretend that I am a fire-eater," George would write Annie Haydock on one occasion, "but as a matter of fact I am just as peace-loving as ever and will be more than thankful to get home at the first opportunity."

The camp over, he headed home to the Boston area and landed a job at Sutton's Mills in North Andover. He began his business career inauspiciously at the ground level, working as a "picker," and he went on to work in various departments of the mills until there was need of a Harvard man in the office.

"Throughout the Mill," a company newsletter would say, "he was well-known, and much liked by the employees with whom he came in contact, and in the office, where his training and ability were especially appreciated, he was looked upon as a hard worker and a student of the business, and was loved as a true friend."

The declaration of war found George Guest Haydock still at Sutton's Mills, working his way up the company ladder. He resigned his position there on April 28 and applied for officers' training, and on May 11 he headed to Plattsburg to throw in with the several thousand other college men vying for commissions.

Assigned to Company 6 of the 1st Provisional Training Regiment, for three months Haydock relearned the rudiments of war making. He drilled, dug, and led his company in open war exercises, and in mid-August, with the trials completed, Haydock was one of those milling about the post nervously, waiting for the names of those chosen for commissions to be announced.

Toward the end of training, the camp's officers called the names of twenty-five men, and these were sent on to a lecture in the camp stadium "by a man who had been an observer in France, and was very thrilling, but I still had that awful feeling that something was wrong and thought I had no chance for getting into the quota," Haydock wrote.

His fears proved unfounded. "I was called up right after the lecture and the first thing I knew I was being sworn in as a first lieutenant. I talked and tried to sign my name but remember being very much surprised at hearing how calm my voice sounded because I was perfectly scared queer."

That night, as the reality of his situation sank in, Haydock tossed and turned in bed, but he "doped the whole thing out and the next morning felt a good deal older and perfectly determined to get away with my job if I possibly could."

As always insecure, he worried that his abilities had been overestimated by his superior, a Captain Lang, "but he said he had made his recommendations not on what we knew and were now, but on what he thought we would turn into, which was a very neat way of putting it up to us perfectly straight that we would have to make good."

Several days later, the captain called together those who had been commissioned and asked for volunteers for "field service abroad" in France. Eight second and two first lieutenants were needed—but George balked.

"My first thought was nothing doing, the U.S.A. is good enough for me," he would write. "Then I thought there would be no chance of my getting it as he only wanted two firsts, so I said here is where I might as well get credit for being a sport, even if I am not one, and up went my hand.

"While he was writing the names down I thought of mother and down came my hand again. Then it occurred to me that it might mean the men were to go to school over there and it would be a good chance.

"The Capt. however had implied that we would be put into the line, but I figured that we would get more training first and the gambling instinct rose, so up went my hand again just in time to be the last one on the list."

That night, he tossed and turned again. "I stayed awake thinking about a mile a minute until after 3, but a big change came over me during that night. I made up my mind to take whatever came my way as though I had expected it, and then to get away with it if I possibly could."

The next morning, Haydock was called to see Captain Lang, who looked him in the eye for a long moment with a "funny little smile." Haydock nervously stared back, until Lang finally pushed some papers toward him and said:

"Well, Mr. Heydick, here's your death warrant!"

Taking the macabre joke in stride, Haydock picked up his orders for France. "I asked him a few questions and he told me that I was getting a chance that nearly every regular in the army was dying to get.

"He then said he had chosen men he was sure would make good, which seemed to me ironical because it looked more as though he had chosen us to get us out of the way, however, he said it in a way to make me believe it, and that with the hand shake he gave me when I said goodbye to him in the afternoon made me think he meant it and I resolved for my part to prove to him that he had made no mistake in judgment."

He would add: "Lang has the power to make a man feel like a prince or a skunk as he chooses, but I think he is a good deal of an actor. I hope he was sincere when he was talking to me, but even if he wasn't he gave me a good deal of self-confidence which I think after all is what he was aiming at.

"I guess he saw that I was the kind of person that has to have some one patting me on the back all the time if I am going to have good results and do my best work."

Just eighteen days shy of his twenty-third birthday, 1st Lt. George Haydock found himself aboard a train on August 28, 1917, on his way to the docks at Hoboken, on his way to war, trying to tamp down the uncertainties that lurked deep within him and to put a bright face on all of the unknowns that lurked on and across the sea.

"Well I am off for Hoboken and God only knows where I will end up," he would write once he had settled aboard. "This business I am in for now is so big that I hardly know what to think and find that I seem to have adopted the policy of not thinking at all, which I believe may be the best one after all. At any rate I am a fatalist now and do not worry about what is going to happen to me.

"The only thing that really bothers me is the family. Mother I know takes it very hard, but she has been perfectly splendid and tried not to show it. She has been as cheerful as she could be whenever I was around but I am afraid she did not sleep much at night."

As the train clacked south from Plattsburg, George Haydock confessed that his own worries went beyond family. "I get pretty scared now and then and wish the whole darn business was over even before I start, but I guess it will make a man of me if anything can.

"This last month has been a big one in my life. The last two weeks at camp were really hectic. We all got tired out, and the nervous strain of waiting for my commission was fierce. I have never been quite so far up in the air in my existence. I had no idea how I stood with the powers that be, and although I felt pretty sure I would get something there was a lurking fear of being left out which made it very uncomfortable waiting."

If there was any consolation, George's sister Louisa was already in France with the Red Cross, and knowing she was there took some of the sting and worry from the predicament in which he found himself.

Still, as his train moved ever south down the Hudson Valley, George Guest Haydock sensed that he was in over his head. With all of his worrying over gaining a commission a thing of the past, he, for the first time, came face-to-face with his own mortality, the potential direness of his situation, and the fact that he was in the army now—and there could be no turning back.

On September 7, George and scores of other Plattsburg men boarded the *Orduna,* and at 2:15 P.M. the gangplanks were pulled and she set sail. Fearful of spies, the military tried to keep a lid on the contents of the ship—although anyone watching from the docks could have easily known the ship was filled to the gills with American fighting men.

"Things were kept pretty quiet and there were only a few tearful women to wave us off," he wrote. "We were ordered to keep below and out of sight until out of N.Y. The tugs pushed us around and we got our last glimpse of the city from the doors and windows. Not long after we had left the Statue of Liberty we were allowed on deck."

On September 11, the *Orduna* steamed into the busy port of Halifax, Nova Scotia, where the *Manchuria* and the *Adriatic*, both also filled with newly commissioned American officers, plus the Massachusetts National Guard, were already in port, waiting to form a convoy for the trip to England.

At 5:00 P.M. the next day, the *Adriatic* began to nose its way from the harbor. "She started out with the band playing 'Over There,' 'Columbia the Gem,' 'Rally Round the Flag,' and 'Auld Lang Syne,'" Haydock would write.

Soon enough, the *Manchuria* followed, and then the *Orduna*. People lining the shore cheered the ships as they floated out of the harbor. "As we came through the narrows into the outer harbor by thc city we passed two British cruisers with the men all lined up along the bow, and the bands on the upper deck," Haydock wrote. "They played 'The Star Spangled Banner' and gave us three cheers which we returned for all we were worth. It was our first contact with the Allied fighting force."

As the convoy slipped farther toward the open sea, Haydock noticed several cottages onshore flying the American flag "and lots of enthusiastic people yelling at us."

There was also one ominous note to the send-off: "As we went by someone there played 'Taps,' which we thought was rushing things a little."

On September 15, Haydock turned twenty-three—"which seems rather odd," he would note. With nothing much else to do, Haydock sought to learn French, attending a class run by a man named Gordon. As the days aboard ship passed, he found some of his shipmates less than pleasant company—among them an English major who "seems to want it pretty generally known that he started as a second lieutenant and worked up, and that he has been in the war since the start without being hit," Haydock noted.

The major also offered up some horror stories for the American boys.

"He says that his battalion has not taken prisoners since the Spring of '15, because at that time the Germans put the wounded from his battalion on their barbed wire and then sprayed them with liquid fire.

"Pleasant thought," Haydock would add wryly.

As the *Orduna* sailed into its second week on the ocean, Haydock pored through the popular book *Carry On: Letters in War Time* by the novelist and soldier Coningsby Dawson, a transplanted Englishman who, after the war broke out in August 1914, left his home in Massachusetts to enlist in the Canadian Army.

After training at the Royal Military College in Kingston, Ontario, Dawson was offered a commission in the Canadian Field Artillery, and July 1916 found him in the cataclysmic Battle of the Somme. The novelist in him couldn't help but notice the glories of war, even as set against its dehumanization.

"I hope I come back again," Dawson wrote his family as he prepared to sail for France. "There are so many finer things that I could do with the rest of my days—bigger things.

"But if by any chance I should cross the seas to stay, you'll know that that also will be right and as big as anything that I could do with life, and something that you'll be able to be just as proud about as if I had lived to fulfill all your other dear hopes for me."

Dawson would write later of the front: "There's a marvelous grandeur about all this carnage and desolation—men's souls rise above the distress—they have to, in order to survive," and, in another letter, "Every man I have met out here has the amazing guts to wear his crown of thorns as though it were a cap-and-bells."

Dawson's prose would stir the hearts of many a young American going off to war that fall—among them George Haydock, who after reading the book was in a reflective mood.

"He seemed to be, in the first part, in just such a position as we are," he noted of Dawson, "and his thoughts seemed to be a good deal the same, only well expressed. It is funny the state of mind that one gets in, and the way each step seems to follow the one before it perfectly naturally. Last winter, I never could have dreamed that this fall I would be in the army.

"I have kidded myself along a good deal into thinking I might go to war, but down deep I felt that I never would. But when I do go it all seems perfectly natural and I am not surprised. When I went to camp I never thought that I would go across, and now that I am going across I feel that I will never really do any fighting, yet I am talking and acting just as if I confidently expected it, so that when the time comes I hope I will be ready to do my job."

As the *Orduna* headed ever east toward war, Haydock—perhaps steeled by Dawson's words—found himself hoping he would be in the thick of it one day.

"Somehow or other it has come across to me really hard recently, and I am beginning to feel now that I will be disappointed if I don't get into action," he wrote. "It is a funny thing to say and I guess perhaps I will think differently when I see a little more, but now I feel as though I wanted to see if I could stand the test.

"I suppose when the time comes I will go to the front just as I went to camp, getting a new experience and wondering if I could make good, and then if I get plugged that will be the next step."

In the end, he would convince himself that he was in the right place: "This is a wonderful big thing, and it makes me feel a little proud to feel that I am really taking a part in it, and I feel that it is the only worth while thing that I have ever done.

"I guess that is the reason I want to see it through. If I 'go West' as they say it will certainly be a good a route as any one could ask to go over, and if I come through it I think I will be worth something, because this sort of stuff certainly does deepen you."

Nearing England, talk aboard ship turned more urgently toward war and, perhaps naturally, America's participation.

"The English Major talking last night said that the allies would be very critical of us, and that we must show them that we were there for business and they would greet us with open arms," Haydock wrote. "He said that we would get in very wrong if we did a lot of waving of the Stars & Stripes. To put it baldly and disgustingly, the American stands very low in Europe.

"He said that it is natural that men who have been living through hell at the front can see no excuse for our not coming in, and now that we are in we have a pretty high standard to come up to before they will grant us anything."

On September 22, Haydock got his first glimpse of land as the *Orduna* neared the coast of Ireland and that afternoon crossed the Irish Sea. At 9:00 P.M. the *Orduna* reached Liverpool. Allowed off the ship just after noon the next day, the contingent of Americans headed for the train station and, after a mad rush, found places on the train that would take them to Southampton.

The Americans found themselves celebrities as they crossed England. "All along the tracks there were thousands of the funniest looking little kids I ever saw," Haydock wrote. "They were all yelling their heads off. We had quite a reception all along the line because it turned out there were signs in the stations that American Troop trains were to pass through, and there had been several before us."

Arriving at Southampton at 1:30 A.M., the Americans were put aboard a small transport. The ship began its trip across the Channel at 9:00 P.M. and at 7:00 A.M. reached the French port of Le Havre. As the transport eased into harbor, Haydock watched as a boat filled with Tommies coming back from leave approached. "They looked as though they had been through it all right," he wrote, "and were pretty blue at going back."

Soon enough, Haydock and the others took their first steps on French soil. Marching through town, they passed "French, English, Portugese, and German prisoners working under guard."

When they reached a rest camp, the first of many sortings and transferrings began, as the eager young Americans were parceled out to different British schools for further training. Haydock bid farewell to the familiar faces of those with whom he'd crossed the ocean.

"I had to leave the clan," Haydock wrote, "but picked up with WOP Morgan."

4

The Fiancé

He can hardly wait to get into the trenches, that violent and mysterious netherworld in which French, British, and German have been crouching and shooting at each other for three long and deadly years, and of which he has read of in newspapers, books, and magazines. *The trenches.* He finds the words alluring, signifying danger and drama and the chance for glory, the chance to test himself in a battle of good versus evil, the chance to find out what it is he is made of, all for the greater glory of the Cause.

He's sure that in the trenches he will find what he is looking for, grow within their muddy, grimy walls to be a man, a real man, and come home transformed, not the winsome, kind, and drifting lad he was when he went in but a *man,* one who will lean on his experience in war to take life by its horns and fashion it to his liking. Unlike his friend George Haydock, he is certain the war is the best thing that could have happened to him—and to the world.

He is sure he will enjoy war.

"I sometimes feel so impatient to be where I can really see these Huns and possibly take a shot at them," William Otho Potwin Morgan writes in October 1917. "You could scarcely believe me when I should tell you how much I should like to stick one of the Boches with my bayonet."

Yes, the majestically named W. O. P. Morgan is pretty sure he's ready—ready for what the world, and the war, will throw at him in the coming months. With still a year to go at Harvard, he has left school, as have so many others, to join the cavalcade heading into training camps and overseas, where "the Boches" wait with heavy artillery and counter-barrages of machine-gun fire, where slick and slimy mud oozes through the chalky earth, where the bleaching bones of hundreds of thousands killed on the Somme, at Loos, and now at Passchendaele mark the pathway to death like stepping-stones.

Just months before, he was gliding across the ice as a member of the Harvard "seven," his life a routine of classes and ice hockey and clubs. Like Richard Newhall, he hails from the Midwest, growing up in the upper-crust suburb of Highland Park, north of Chicago. Unlike Newhall, he has had little real-life experience, growing up coddled and isolated as he did.

He is one of the new scions of science and industry. His grandfather, Otho Herron Morgan, a Civil War veteran who lived through Chickamauga and other battles in which the 7th Indiana Battery fought, returned from war to begin the Chicago Varnish Company with his father-in-law, Anson Potwin. By 1918 their company had a capital of a million and a half dollars and had grown into one of the larger factories in the city.

The captain's marriage to Julia Potwin produced six children, the first of whom, William Potwin, was born on December 7, 1865. Willie, as he was called, attended the Chicago public schools, Lafayette College, and the University of Michigan before finishing school abroad, "chiefly at Coblentz and Vienna," his obituary says.

He returned to Chicago to work for the family varnish business in the chemistry department and in October 1893 married Clara Marks, whose family was involved in merchandizing and real estate. William Otho Potwin Morgan entered the world on May 14, 1895, and soon after tragedy entered his young life.

His mother fell ill not long after Bill was born, and soon afterward his father came down with pneumonia and was told by doctors to move to a warmer climate. He died within a year, leaving Clara Morgan—

whose own father had died at the age of thirty-one—to obsess over her toddler son. He would grow up under the despairing eye of an overprotective mother, who for some reason insisted on treating her young son as if he were a girl, putting him in dresses and leaving his hair in long tresses until he was six years old.*

Clara finally released Bill Morgan from her hypochondriacal clutches as he was about to enter ninth grade, sending him to St. Paul's School in New Hampshire, one of those eastern boarding schools to which Chicago's elites sent their sons to unlearn the rough habits of the Middle West. There young Bill Morgan flourished in social and athletic activities.

Moving on to Harvard in 1914, he was accepted into the prestigious AD Club, but his off-hours were spent mainly in athletics. After growing up dominated by an overbearing and worrisome female, he naturally gravitated toward the locker-room comraderie of his own sex.

However, blond and well built as he was, and with an easy smile that conveyed all of the idealism and innocence of his native country at the turn of the twentieth century, in the spring of 1917 he came under the spell of the pretty and more experienced Christiana Councilman, the nineteen-year-old daughter of William Councilman, the Shattuck Professor of Pathological Anatomy at Harvard Medical School.

A tomboy when a girl, she had by age fifteen become a sought-after partner at society dances, and by the time she met Bill Morgan she had already had several intense, if innocent, affairs. On the cusp of America's entry into world war, they became an item, he entranced by her girlish charms, she enthralled by his good looks and his noble plans to offer his young life on the battlefields of France.

"He has never been around with girls at all and so doesn't seem very polished, but he isn't at all awkward," Christiana would write of Morgan. "He is very much of a man's man and has perfectly splendid ideals and is really thoroughly fine through and through . . . He appreciates books

---

* Account of Bill Morgan's boyhood, his romance with Christiana Councilman, and their prewar letters and diary entries from Claire Douglas's *Translate This Darkness: The Life of Christiana Morgan, the Veiled Woman in Jung's Circle.* Princeton, N.J.: Princeton University Press, 1993.

a lot & gets a lot out of them, although he isn't at all brilliant. He has a delightful sense of humor and can be awfully funny."

Still, she would write, "Somehow I don't think of him as a masterful man, but a perfectly dear boy."

Morgan, meanwhile, told Christiana that he had found in her his "ideal"—and would spend the next two years trying to prove his manhood to her, describing every experience and feeling he had to her in long, impassioned letters.

Within weeks of their meeting, Bill Morgan's application for officers' training at Fort Sheridan, near his home on Chicago's North Shore, was accepted. Taking a walk on the eve of his departure from Cambridge, "we sat there under the pine trees and saw the sun come out and it really was so pathetic because over it all hung the cloud of war, & I felt as tho' he were going out on that great unknown & all the suffering of it, so little knowing what was coming," Christiana recalled.

Pathetic, perhaps; but Bill and Christiana both reveled in the drama of their parting, and of the image of the soldier boy grimly marching off to war while she fulfilled her female role of waiting and hoping he might somehow survive. The added uncertainty of his potential shipping overseas, while curtailing their ability to get to know each other, had the equally mitigating effect of adding romantic luster to their relationship.

"I remember your saying that it would be wonderful to feel you were giving to the war some man who meant everything to you," he would write Christiana, "and it is wonderful for a man to feel he can sacrifice himself for a girl."

It was more than a simple case of romantic sacrifice that sent Bill Morgan toward the trenches, though. "It was impossible to volunteer without knowing why," he would write after the war. "What actuated me most was to end all wars."

The quest to end all wars began with a crash course at Fort Sheridan in all things military, the ultimate aim modeled after the opening lines in the army's *Infantry Drill Regulations:* "Success in battle is the ultimate object of all military training; success may be looked for only when the training is intelligent and thorough."

"A man must know his drill regulations precisely," the camp's history would note. "Generalities, however true, meant nothing . . . Work in the drill regulations the first month covered the School of the Soldier up through the School of the Battalion. Also definitions, orders, commands and signals. The men became skilled in the manual of arms, in sighting, sub-caliber practice, and in the use of the rifle in physical drill.

"The men learned how to roll their packs and to carry them full for hikes of several miles. They learned how to keep their quarters in an orderly manner, to care for their rifle, and to conduct Saturday inspection. More than learning to command, their first month, they learned the really first essential—to obey."

The summer months brought nights in the trenches they had dug themselves and mock battles between the "Reds" and the "Blues." In early August, just prior to being handed their commissions as second lieutenants, they gathered and listened to the camp's commander impart a few tips on leadership.

"Many of you men have never been leaders," William J. Nicholson told them. "You have always been told what to do. Now you are going to tell other men what to do and teach them. So remember this—all men appreciate justice and a square deal. You must be square and just in all your dealings. Be honest and direct.

"Don't be afraid to go up to a man and take hold of him if necessary. The law permits you to use necessary force. Keep yourselves above reproach and never do anything that will enable a man to say, 'Oh, well, if that man does anything to me, I'll inform on him.' Keep your consciences clean, live like men, and nothing will ever make you ashamed or afraid."

By mid-August, Morgan had his commission as a second lieutenant and was one of those selected for immediate duty in France. He looked forward to his small part in the making of a brave new world—and was one of those who, as the historian Henry F. May would write, did not see the war as "the doom of their culture" but instead "believed it would bring about its revival: the war was a severe but necessary lesson in moral idealism."

"It seems as if a great door had suddenly opened—revealing beyond another world—the one I have thought of so often—the one in which men come to their own and at last are really valued as men should be valued, for what is at the bottom of them," Morgan would tell Christiana, "a world where men have seen things with new visions and feel things in a way only future generations will realize."

Visiting Christiana at the Councilmans' summer home in Maine before he shipped out for France, Morgan proposed marriage to her—and she accepted. She would claim that with their engagement she knew "what love really is"; but it seems probable that she as well could not resist the romantic swell of seeing her now-betrothed off to war.

"God alone knows what the future may hold," she would write, "but if need be I pray that I can make my sacrifice as nobly as others have made theirs, and if he comes back, I pray that we can make a life together worth living."

Her parents did not approve of the engagement, noting not only the couple's youthfulness and naïveté but the speed with which events had led to betrothal. They eventually relented, at least partly because there was, in fact, something of a chance that Bill Morgan would certainly *not* return.

Not having the heart to tell his impassioned daughter no, William Councilman turned on Christiana with "bitter mockery." Raising his glass to Christiana and Bill, he very loudly presented a toast.

"To the babes in the woods," he said.

In early September, Morgan headed south for Hoboken, and on September 12, 1917, he boarded the *St. Paul* for passage to France. While the scores of newly minted American officers aboard rubbed elbows with English and Irish passengers returning to home and, in some cases, the war, Morgan took the chance to reflect on his coming grand adventure:

"It is strange what a weird feeling I get at times about going into this war. I think I am actually afraid of the trenches, and yet I don't know because I believe it is just the uncertainty of what my job will be there that makes me feel this way . . .

"As long as you can fight and struggle for your life I seem to have confidence and no fear, and I hope that is the way it will be in the trenches. I sort of feel it will be, yet I can't get over an inevitable dread of being ordered into them until the war ends."

Entering the "danger zone" in which the threat of submarines lurked, all lights on the ship went dark at night, leaving Morgan feeling uneasy.

"It was queer to me," he wrote. "There was a faint afterglow illuminating cold, black clouds. There was something very grim about it all, and you realized that men were trying to take your life.

"I have never been anywhere where life was hunted after, yet the gray funnels and masts, slipping through the inky sky and water, reminded me that from now on, war would be a reality to us; our lives will really be taken if the opportunity comes."

He would find it hard to believe "that all my education, all my bringing up, has been for this, the cold killing of men who are fundamentally the same as I. Out here we don't get into the spirit of it, and for that reason it is the more appalling.

"I will say this right now that after this war, I am going to be the most rabid of pacifists, and I will be able to say it, for I can face war as well as anyone else, and I realize that now we must go into this war, as being the only means to secure a lasting peace."

Out on the rolling seas, the motion of the *St. Paul* inspired some grand imagery in young Morgan's mind:

"I believe that civilization has gone too fast for the evolution of man He has not yet learned to command his animal instinct, which, after all, is to fight; and like a great wave gathering in volume, civilization rears its crest higher and higher until finally it breaks and falls, a seething mass of foam.

"It is because its base is held back by the shallow beach that its head overruns and topples. It all collapses and lies for a moment on the beach, powerless, and then it rushes back to add to the strength of the next wave. Only gradually are we able to discern its mark upon the altered shore line."

He hoped that it was "necessary that this great war should be, in order that thus tremendous changes may be brought about."

With great prescience, he would add: "Some of us must go over here, and for us life can never be the same—there will be a shadow in the background."

Despite his anxieties, he claimed to look forward to his biggest test. "I shall be glad to get to France and to come in contact with men who have been in the war," he wrote. "I realize that this great effort which lies ahead of me—this test which is taking every bit of my will to face—will be a great thing for me.

"For after I have been thru it I shall have the confidence to undertake anything. Obstacles which come in my way will be small indeed, and I shall be able, as I should never be otherwise, to meet and to conquer them. It would be worth risking anything to acquire strength to make my life worth having lived, for to make a failure of my life would be something far worse than falling in battle on the soil of France."

On September 23, the *St. Paul* heaved to at Liverpool, followed closely by the *Manchuria* and George Haydock's *Orduna*. Within hours, Morgan and scores of other young Americans were put aboard a train for Southampton, their ultimate destination a British training camp near Le Havre, France.

Morgan piled on to the *Antrim* and made the trip across the Channel with Haydock and the others. "Aeroplanes overhead in the daytime and searchlights sweeping skys though no raids on Southampton," he would note on September 24. "However street lights are dimmed and no lights from windows.

"All conductors on double deck trams are girls . . . There seem to be no young men left. Everyone seems cheerful and the papers are full of peace talk. I saw one large sign, 'To all you who pass by to fight for us in foreign parts, good luck to you, and we thank you with all our hearts.' They are especially enthusiastic about the Americans."

After landing at Le Havre, the Americans marched five miles to Rest Camp I, "on a high hill overlooking the Channel," Morgan wrote.

The march was illuminating.

"Poor France," Morgan would write. "She is suffering terribly. Women and old men are all you see and EVERYONE is in mourning. It was pitiful to see two old women come out of early mass as we marched by. They did not wave—only stood and watched us silently.

"If only America could see France, could see her grief, it would not be so hard to leave, for this is such a big thing; it seems as if every human being were going to the front and it seems as natural a thing to do, as natural as our drift toward death in the States.

"I don't know why," he would add, "but I feel so far away from America and my wonderful happiness with Chris. I am glad that it seems so for I live from day to day now, looking forward to the trenches."

5

Why Don't We Attack?

They were so close now they felt as if they could reach out and touch them, and through a cold, sputtering rain and heavy mist they squinted intently past the detritus of no-man's-land, past the craters and curling and rusting bands of barbed wire to where the dark forms seemed to loll without a care in the world, hanging wash and cooking their bread and sausages under thin plumes of white smoke. It seemed so silly not to just go over and take them in a rush. Wasn't that what they were there for?

"Lieutenant," one of them said, "are those the German lines over there?"

"Yes."

"Well, why don't we attack?"

A long way from Cambridge, Massachusetts, Richard Newhall in mid-November 1917 found himself in charge of sixty men who stood knee-deep in mud and peered with malicious intent across a ruined swale of ground toward the German lines. He expected one day to lead them in battle, but for now he patiently spent his energies on making sure his green but eager charges did not do something stupid that couldn't be undone.

Their time would come, he told them, but not now; not today.

He had been here before, not long before, performing his medieval studies in musty and ill-lit libraries in Paris and Rouen and Lisieux and Caen, even as the war's nascent years had seen line after line of attacking German and French and English soldiers lie down and go still as if a straight-line wind had bowled them over.

Richard Newhall's studies had shifted now, moving from an ancient sword- and lance-bearing Crusade to a new one, an American onslaught bent on liberating half of France from the Germans, some of whose officers descended from some of those same Teutonic knights that had once protected pilgrimages to the Holy Land.

Perhaps more cognizant than many of what he had gotten himself into, Richard Ager Newhall had left Plattsburg, commission in hand, to return home to Minneapolis to say his good-byes in mid-August 1917.

Returning east by train to New York, where he was to report to the Army Transport Service for the "first available transportation to France," he noted that while he was not of the army, and never would be, his freshly pressed uniform set him apart from the civilians on board and made it easy to make friends with the other former college men also heading for New York and, in most cases, France.

"There must have been more than a dozen other officers on the train," he would write on September 2, "most of whom had orders similar to mine. The uniform was sufficient introduction, and as we came from many different camps it was very easy and pleasant to compare conditions and swap experiences.

"It is very easy for me to see how a class consciousness among military men can develop. None of us had been more than three months out of civilian life, but already we were beginning to feel a certain camaraderie among ourselves and a 'differentness' from the other travelers. The war will help it still more."

Even among the easy and natural camaraderie of his fellow officers, he was wary of the mass mobilization of which they were part—and worried about its implication for the country.

"I am indeed uneasy of the thought of the political probabilities which the growth of the big armies now needed contains," he wrote. "The more I see of the military organization, its character and spirit, the more I come to regard it as an evil, even though it be so essentially necessary just now."

Just a small part of that necessary "evil," Newhall soon found himself on his way to France. Within a day of leaving the Statue of Liberty behind, Newhall was seasick—a condition made worse by the anxiety caused when his transport suffered engine trouble and fell behind the convoy.

The ship slowly made it across, with no sign of submarines—although some commotion ensued one day when "a man on watch on the bridge mistook a porpoise for a torpedo but the commander of the bridge knew the difference. Twice we sighted whales but no subs.

"There are rumors of various sorts, such as are inevitable in a crowd of men who are all thinking about the same thing. I have no doubt that we are in a certain danger, but I know I can't do anything and that the naval men seem to know their business, so there seems no reason for worrying."

On September 20, the ship entered the estuary of the Loire River, which led it to the port of St. Nazaire. There Newhall and his shipmates "received a most thrilling welcome, of a sort to stir my emotions very deeply. The shores were dotted for two or three miles with people, women for the most part and children, waving handkerchiefs and American flags. At the harbor entrance was a large crowd which cheered itself hoarse.

"The band in our boat played the Star Spangled Banner and the Marseilles as we came in, and our arrival certainly seemed to arouse a real patriotic enthusiasm on both sides such as I have never seen before. Here was something truly thrilling for you couldn't but feel that the people welcomed us with real jubilation. I only hope that our men will deport themselves so that we have a good reputation."

By September 27, Newhall found himself at the British 4th Army School for Scouting, Sniping, and Observation, one of a number of British and French schools established to teach "the details of modern minor tactics" to the young and green officers being quickly sent over to replenish the junior-officer ranks of the 1st and other divisions, Shipley Thomas, of the 26th Regiment, would recall.

That fall, it was hoped, each of the subalterns would become "expert" in one of many different specialties that included school in the bayonet, trench mortars, grenades, wiring, sniping, "or the thousand and one technical requirements which three years of trench warfare had developed," Thomas added.

Newhall was one of twenty Americans, plus a smattering of Brits, at the school. On the first day he took a walk around the local village, Bouchon, and "became aware that heads were popping out of peasant houses, and women were coming to the door, and the phrase 'C'est un Americain' was running down the street. I was a novelty. I tried to look friendly."

The weather was lousy—cold and rainy. As the days of training passed, Newhall's comrades, cooped in their huts, stimulated his "naturally irritable" mind with their blather about military matters.

"Behind me there is a group of amateur American officers arguing strategy and tactics," he wrote on October 7. "It always irritates me to hear the law laid down by men who don't know much what they are talking about. The less a man knows on a technical subject the more disposed to talk about it he seems to be."

The British instructors viewed Newhall and his quarrelsome mates as novelties as much as had the local peasants—and taught Newhall a lesson about his own parochialism.

"When the British officers asked questions about America I was astonished at some of the answers given until it dawned on me that my own knowledge of America was confined to the area north of Mason & Dixon's line and the Ohio River and east of the Mississippi," he wrote. "For the first time the size and diversity of America became more apparent, plus the unpleasant fact that I wasn't particularly attracted to my fellow citizens from other parts."

The sniper's work, however, fascinated him, and he found his instructors to be a welcome relief from his insufferable, theorizing comrades. As well, the work was hands-on and practical.

"We are learning to crawl scientifically, how to watch enemy trenches, how to read maps and use the configuration of the ground for purposes of concealment, how to build loop-holes which can't be seen," he wrote.

"I wish you could get some pictures of us at work. Our 'crawling suits' are awfully funny. In order to simulate night conditions we have dark goggles through which it is often very difficult to see anything at all. Consequently it looks ridiculous to see a crowd groping their way about like blind men. On the whole I think it is better to do our practice at night. This we sometimes do and we have learned a lot of things not to do and a very definite idea of the difficulties of work in the dark."

The Americans took the course much more seriously than the British officers who had just come off the line, and had in any case already endured months or years in the trenches. The Brits regarded the school as "a sort of relaxation," Newhall wrote, "but for us it was more realistic and practiced than anything we had known."

The Americans, true to their frontier heritage, put on a show of marksmanship. "One result was that the shooting scores for the whole group were better than anything in the school's record," Newhall wrote. "I suspected the British instructors of, perhaps, relating this to traditions of Daniel Boone and the frontier. If so this was funny since our group was thoroughly urban and civilian, no more given to 'natural' sharpshooting than I."

Newhall was impressed with the British officers' ability to teach, and the unexpected chummy relationship he noted between the officers and their underlings—a relationship that one British platoon leader would ascribe to the nightmarish conditions at the front, which erased distinctions of class that existed between the enlisted men and officers during peacetime.

"In England, officers hardly know their men," Donald Hankey, the doomed author of the popular 1916 book *A Student in Arms*, would write. "They live apart, only meet on parade, and their intercourse is carried on through the prescribed channels . . .

"But at the front you have your own platoon; and week after week, month after month, you are living in the closest proximity; you see them all day, you get to know the character of each individual man and boy, and the result in nearly every case is this extraordinary affection . . .

"I have heard a Major, a Regular with, as I thought, a good deal of regimental stiffness, talk about his men with a voice almost choked with emotion. 'When you see what they have to put up with, and how amazingly cheery they are through it all, you feel that you can't do enough for them. They make you feel that you're not fit to black their boots.'"

Newhall would soon enough gain the same appreciation for the rank and file, and have it returned in kind, but for the moment he could only be intrigued by the genuine affection that seemed to exist between private and captain, corporal and major, within the British Army, and that seemed to run against the harsh advice his Plattsburg commanders had given on how to treat the men under him.

"The British officers are very pleasant instructors, better teachers than our own I think," he wrote. "They are essentially gentlemen and treat us as such. Before I get away from here I want to get some idea how they undertake to discipline their men because there seems to be a pleasant relationship which I like and which I did not encounter in America."

At the end of the training, the students culminated the sniping course with some "snap-shooting," Newhall would write. "This was a series of shots at moving targets, a man poking his head over a trench parapet, a man's head appearing at any one of four different windows, the head of a man walking along a trench.

"Each rifleman had an observer with a telescope to announce the appearance of the target and watch the shot. I was pleasantly surprised to make the second highest score of the twenty."

However, he would write years later, "nothing which I learned at the school ever had to be used, nor taught to any of my men. Presumably our assignment here had some of the quality of 'busy work' in school, something to keep us occupied until the mechanics of assigning us to regular outfits could be worked out effectively."

By mid-October, Newhall was on his way to just such a "regular outfit." On October 20, he reached Trévary, where he was assigned to Company L of the 28th Infantry Regiment, part of the U.S. 1st Division, which had been cobbled together from the 16th, 18th, 26th, and 28th Regiments and which had been strung out in sleepy border posts on the Rio Grande when war was declared. In mid-June 1917 the new division was sent to France in four transports carrying about 10,000 officers and men—65 officers and 2,414 enlisted men in the 28th Regiment alone.

AEF commander in chief John Pershing had decreed that the size of the American divisions would be enlarged to twice the size of those of the British and French, his theory being that larger divisions of about 30,000 men would be able to break through the German line with more ease.

Formed as a "square," each infantry division would consist of two brigades of two regiments each; each regiment consisted of three battalions containing four 250-man companies. Each company was in need of a minimum of five officers—a captain and four lieutenants, firsts or seconds, each one in charge of a platoon of about sixty men.

That June, the 1st's four regiments were severely understaffed, both in men and officers, even as it sailed to war. The four transports carrying the division contained a mix of 20 percent regulars and 80 percent recent recruits, many of the experienced fighting men being left in the United States to train draftees.

While all of the senior officers were regular army, many of the junior officers had only recently been commissioned. George Marshall, the division's assistant chief of staff in 1917, would write that he had "never seen more splendid looking men" than those junior officers with whom he sailed to France; after the war he would write that he could not recall a single one who had survived.

After landing at St. Nazaire, Company K of the 28th Regiment became on June 26 the first American unit to step onto French soil, followed by Company I, which stayed behind to police the city of 100,000 while the rest of the division marched east to a camp a mile inland. In mid-July, the entire division moved to Gondrecourt, 120 miles east-southeast of Paris, where the surrounding terrain was fit for performing large-scale maneuvers and practicing trench warfare.

There, the regiments were dispersed to surrounding villages, and a daily training regimen began under the eye of the Alpine Chasseurs, also known as the Blue Devils, some of the best fighting men France had to offer.

"They were stocky, tough old timers," Charles Senay, in command of Company I of the 28th Regiment, wrote. "They taught us the fine points of trench warfare: digging trenches, extending verticals (saps) from them to later be interconnected into new front lines, tunneling, mining, reinforcing with revetments, digging dugouts and knowing how to use the earth for protection.

"Added to this was the erection of barbed wire, use of bangelore torpedoes to destroy enemy wire and proper use of wire cutters. We spent hours on bayonet practice, fencing in the French manner. It was *piquet haut, piquet a bas, piquet droit* and *piquet gauche* for hours. There was much grenade practice with both offensive and defensive grenades. Often we lit and hurled sticks of dynamite. There were long marches and maneuvers."

There was also a large learning curve for the men. Newhall would note after the war that while the division was referred to as being composed of "regulars," the term by the fall of 1917 was hardly accurate. "To most, no doubt, this term will conjure up a picture of hardened soldiers, veterans of Philippine campaigns and border patrol duty, led by West Point graduates who had devoted their lives to the army," he wrote.

In fact, that image by October 1917 "was a thing of the dim past. At that time probably ninety percent of the enlisted men were in their first enlistment period, the majority in their first year of army life. In other words, they were recruits who had joined the army because war was in prospect, and after some service on the Mexican border had been shipped to France to learn modern warfare."

That training would be left mostly to the noncoms who had been promoted and to the graduates of the OTC courses—who themselves had no experience at war and very limited experience in leading men. The higher-ranking officers likewise ascended in the new army, being bumped up by the masses of new lieutenants and noncommissioned officers below.

Still, Newhall would write that the men of the 1st Division, though recent recruits themselves in many situations, were of a different ilk than those of the National Guard divisions, which were "hastily recruited, partially trained organizations officered by amateurs."

Whether greenhorn or battle-hardened veteran, the 1st's men "had a conscious pride in being part of the regular army," Newhall would reflect after the war, "a pride greatly enhanced by the fact that their particular part had been selected as the first to come to France. They thought of themselves as professional soldiers. They had behind them the tradition of the old, rigorously disciplined army, however much the 'old-timers' might bemoan the lowering of the standards under which they themselves had been trained.

"However smartly he might click his heels and salute, a second lieutenant of the line from the First Division regarded himself as superior to a lieutenant-colonel from any other division, was inwardly hostile toward all staff officers, and openly contemptuous of anyone from the S.O.S. (Service of Supply)."

Yet many of the enlisted men and junior officers shared Newhall's mission of getting there, getting the job done, and going home, with no plans for making the army a career—and no patience for the drill and other boring routine upon which the military mind, out of necessity or mere sadism, insisted.

"They did not like the army," he would write generally of the men with whom he served (it was an attitude with which he certainly sympathized). "They were not professional soldiers in that respect, they were merely fighting men. Such close order drill as they had became very irksome. They grumblingly wondered how the war was to be won by doing 'squads east and west,' and often the junior officers wondered the same.

"They had no military ambition, no love of glory, no particular hatred of the enemy. It was a dirty job which must be done, and the quicker the better. Divisional headquarters tried to instill hatred of the enemy by sending memoranda on atrocities or Pan-Germanism. These were read to the troops according to orders, but the men remained indifferent."

Their irks with the enemy were more personal, he noted. "Let them be reminded, however, that the Germans were to blame for their being in France, where they were exceedingly uncomfortable and homesick, and the desired fighting spirit would be aroused. 'Let's finish this damned war and go home,' was the prevailing attitude of mind."

He soon found that most of his peers in the 28th Regiment were, like him, just civilians in uniform, men who had been sent to France at the end of the first series of officers' camps. Among them was 2nd Lt. Jim Quinn, a twenty-six-year-old native of Memphis, Tennessee, with whom Newhall quartered in the small village of St. Amand-sur-Ornain.

Garrulous and energetic, Quinn had been working as a cotton buyer when war was declared. Despite not having had any education past high school, he had been accepted for officer's training at Fort Oglethorpe near Chattanooga. His motives for enlisting stemmed less from patriotism than pageantry and no doubt failed to impress the cerebral Newhall, whose own motives were a tad loftier.

"Both of my granddads back in Memphis were soldiers," Quinn would say. "One fought for the Union and the other for the Confederacy during the Civil War, and every time there was any kind of celebration in town they'd put on their uniforms and parade. I joined up so I could march in parades the rest of my life like them."

If nothing else, the Southern good-old-boy chatterbox seems to have amused the serious Northern intellectual. Newhall would remember Quinn as "someone who did a lot of talking without saying anything significant, but who was very amiable."

(Quinn, later assigned to the 28th Regiment's Company G, would win the Distinguished Service Cross for his almost single-handed taking of a German strongpoint on July 18 at Soissons, despite being severely wounded. He would march at the head of many a hometown parade before his March 30, 1934, death in a car accident, returning home as Memphis's greatest World War I hero.)

Their host, Mme. Paul Thierry, lived in a simple cottage "somewhat detached from the rest of the village, perhaps a thousand yards from the main street, separated from the village by a rivulet," Newhall recalled. "It was at the foot of a bluff on top of which were the 'remains' of a Roman camp, locally labeled 'Caesar's camp.'"

Madame Thierry was "quite a person, energetic and practiced," he added. "She had never, she said, been outside the department, nor seen a town bigger than Ligny-en-Barrois, the nearest place large enough to be called a town. She worked hard and was most friendly and accommodating.

"There were two little girls, Yvonne and Marie. My disposition to be reasonably friendly and courteous evoked a pleasant response, and I think the children came to regard me as someone who could and did produce small gifts."

Such friendly arrangements were common that winter and fall, as the division's young lieutenants were taken in by French locals happy to have America in the war—and happy as well to have a man around the house once again.

Company M's twenty-three-year-old 2nd Lt. Paul Dillard Carter, of Knoxville, Tennessee, would note that fifty-five men in St. Amand "have been killed during the war." His host, an elderly woman, regarded her boarders as family. "The old French lady calls herself our French mamma because our American mamma is so far away that we need a French mamma to take her place temporarily. She is great to us."

When his billet mate, 2nd Lt. Jerome Brown, fell ill with a cold, the woman every night brought him hot milk and medicine and rubbed his chest with iodine. "She has three daughters and they help us keep the room in good shape, make up our bed, and tend to us just like we were their brothers," Carter wrote. "They think a great deal of us and treat us royally."

Newhall and Quinn enjoyed the amenities of the American base and took in the sights around St. Amand. "It is nice to get back to American meals—real coffee, meats in quantity and variety, pan cakes, drinking water," Newhall wrote. The countryside reminded him of New England, "especially now when the trees are turning. We took a walk yesterday over the hills and through woods such as I might have taken in the vicinity of Cambridge.

"It is hard to realize that in Cambridge the college work is just getting underway, that there is a new Freshman class just being introduced to the Goths and Vandals, that things are going on there just as formerly only with different faces. Yet I wouldn't be happy if I were back there."

Soon enough, Newhall found himself in command of about sixty men in the 2nd Platoon of Company L, whose commander was Francis Marion Van Natter, a twenty-six-year-old native of Muncie, Indiana, and, like Charles Senay, a 1916 graduate of the University of Illinois.

He enlisted in the Indiana National Guard upon graduation and soon found himself heading for the Mexican border to join the growing contingent responding to the raids of Pancho Villa, even as Newhall played at war at Plattsburg.

"It was war!" Van Natter would write of the sudden excitement that caused the Guard's members to leave their jobs for a trip down south. "We were going to catch that Mexican bandit, Villa. We were going to do our bit on the border. We would be gone only a short while. Just a before-breakfast bell affair."

Arriving at Camp Llano Grande on July 15, 1916, Van Natter and his cohorts found not Villa but a hellish existence under the subtropical sun of the Rio Grande Valley: "The sky was cloudless, the thermometer at 120 and the water not fit to drink. Everything seemed ready to stick or sting us. The trees had thorns, the toads had horns and the ground was full of sandburrs.

"We grubbed mesquite under a tropical sun. We shivered in freezing northers. We always went for a hike when it rained or it always rained when we went for a hike, and the adobe mud stuck to us like creditors."

The initial excitement ebbed as the weeks wore into long, weary months. "The drill never ceased; the monotony never decreased. There were alarms. Random shots were exchanged across the river. Troops were double-timed to the muddy, placid Rio Grande. But we never got a glimpse of Villa."

As the months dragged by, "paydays seemed to grow farther apart and the monotony increased. To the coyotes' plaintive howl was added the memorable cry: 'I want to go home!' "

An actual war interrupted the misery, as the men in the spring of 1917 were quickly shipped back to Indiana for training at Fort Benjamin Harrison, near Indianapolis. To Newhall's eventual disgust, Van Natter would consider his camping trip on the border as being superior to the training at Plattsburg and the other OTC camps.

"To have served on the Mexican border in 1916," Van Natter would write, "was frequently the only recommendation needed for promotion in the World War."

While Newhall settled into Company L, Jim Quinn soon departed for Company G, where he found more of a like mind in its twenty-nine-year-old commander, Clarence Ralph Huebner.

Huebner, from tiny Bushton, Kansas, had worked his way up to captain the hard way. After attending grade school in a one-room schoolhouse, he graduated from Nebraska's Grand Island Business College and went on to work as a court reporter for the Chicago, Burlington, and Quincy Railroad.

Finding the work boring, he joined the army in 1910 at the age of twenty-one and was assigned to the 18th Infantry Regiment at Wyoming's Fort McKenzie. Like Senay, Huebner showed promise, and he was commissioned as a second lieutenant in the summer of 1916. Sent to France with the 28th Regiment in June 1917 he soon found himself running a company—the first step of command that would result in his leading the 28th Regiment by the end of the war. (He would move on to command the 1st Division on D-day, and later an entire corps.)

Huebner immediately appreciated having the energetic Quinn in his unit, writing later that he was "so young and so full of enthusiasm for anything that might come up . . . He never seemed to tire, and his platoon was one of the best trained in the division."

Though ever the loner, Newhall paradoxically craved companionship and seemed always to be on the lookout for a confidante—a real friend—with whom to share his experiences, especially amid the busily impersonal construction of the AEF that winter.

Though they had not exactly been soul mates, he lamented the transfer of Quinn. "Changes have been so continuous for the last few months that I have come to accept this state of flux as normal and am indisposed to attempt to settle down or to form any attachments," he wrote. "The whole business seems to be a series of meetings and partings. You make many pleasant, temporary acquaintances, but no friends. Choice of your associates is denied you. It becomes a mere matter of policy to like the men with whom you work."

His training at the sniping school also went by the boards. "It looks as if the things which I learned at the British school were not going to be utilized very soon for I have been put in command of a platoon to perform the duties of an ordinary line officer and not of a 'specialized' sort," he would write. "Still it is all one to me. There is an element of novelty about the work and yet it is the sort of a job which I know how to perform so that I have a feeling of perfect confidence."

Newhall's first impression of his captain, Van Natter, was that he was a "perfectly likeable young man who has been as nice as he could be."

He had worried that he would come under the sway of an officious martinet—"some officer who would be disposed to be rather contemptuous of a reservist, who would be disposed to over-emphasize the minutiae (which I am disposed to under-emphasize), and who would feel called upon to exercise his authority upon his subordinates in order to teach them their place.

"I have seen such officers and I am very thankful to have escaped being placed under them. Responsibility inspires self-confidence—in me at least. Indeed it irritates me very generally to encounter at nearly every turn an assumption by the military man over all the rest of creation. More and more I am proud . . . to know that I am hopelessly civilian."

In the same "unmilitary" vein, Newhall couldn't help but have a natural empathy for his own men. Given the task of censoring their letters, he noted that "at first it seemed rather ungentlemanly to be reading other men's letters, especially those addressed to young ladies and filled with endearing phrases. (Imagine finding your love letters counter-signed by some army officer.)

"With a little effort, however, I succeeded in developing an impersonal point of view, especially as most of the men merely wrote that they were well and had not had any mail for a long time."

He would find "a pathetic simplicity about most of these letters. For the most part they merely say that the writer is in good health and hopes that the recipient is the same. Then there are comments on the weather and inquiries about various relatives and friends.

"Not infrequently one comes on expressions of great tenderness, bluntly put, which I presume are the result of a fit of homesickness. Occasionally you get a glimpse of something which looks tragic. Now and then you get a new point of view on a man which enables you to estimate his worth better, usually to his advantage."

The same empathy extended to his occasional duty as commander of the guard, making his rounds "at various hours, P.M. and A.M., interrogating sentinels, seeing that men go in before taps even if they were a little wobbly on their legs," he wrote.

"There is something pathetic, sometimes, in the figures of these young Americans all alone, out in the rain, in the small hours of the morning, thousands of miles from home. I would like to have chatted with them to find out what they were thinking about and how they liked the soldiering game, but it would not have been 'military' to do so."

In a driving, cold rain, the 1st Division on October 21 entered the trenches in the quiet sector of Sommerviller in Lorraine. The 1st Battalion of each of the four regiments took its assigned place under its watchful French overseers, then spent ten uneventful days slipping and sliding and wading in the knee-deep, rat-infested mud, well within sight of their mysterious enemy, who peered back across a few hundred yards of no-man's-land and wondered whether the Americans had finally arrived.

"The trenches were very old and deep, with woven brush revetments, gabions, and fascines," Charles Senay remembered. "There was a sea of rusted barbed wire between the lines. My dugout was deep and shored and lined with wood.

"Myriads of brown rats swarmed behind the woodwork. At night, they would fight for any food scraps on the floor. They would run along the woodwork and sometimes bounce from one's body when they descended to the floor."

Outposts consisting of one or two men were set up in shell holes in no-man's-land. "These had to be inspected," Senay wrote. "One night an inspecting sergeant was shot and killed by a jittery outguard."

Returning to the lines had its own dangers. "The French used the sign and countersign for recognition," Senay remembered. "One night, the sign was CASTELNAU and the countersign was CASTIGLIONE.

Rather awkward for some of our farm boys. Stammering men were at a perilous disadvantage."

On the night of November 2, the 1st battalions were relieved by the division's 2nd. If the men thought they were in for as placid a time as their predecessors, thcy were quickly disabused of the notion.

At 3:00 A.M. on November 3, a raiding force of fifty handpicked German commandos stole across no-man's-land and swarmed the line held by Company F of the 16th Regiment. In the dark and confusion the intruders were mistaken for friends—and when one figure leveled a pistol at Cpl. James Gresham, he yelled, "Don't shoot—I am an American!"

"I am shooting all Americans," the grim form replied and dropped Gresham with two shots.

Two more Americans—Pvts. Thomas Enright and Merle Hay—were killed in the vicious melee, and then the Germans left almost as quickly as they had come, dragging eleven prisoners with them.

Thus in the early morning of November 3, 1917, did America—and the 1st Division—suffer its first combat deaths.

"Pershing, on being told of the attack, wept," the historian Martin Gilbert would write. An investigation would decide that the American troops were not yet trained well enough to man the front lines and should be removed. Gen. Paul Bordeaux, commander of the French overseers, said he was in doubt of "the courage and ability with which the Americans had defended themselves."

He would later be pressured to reverse that statement and came to see the useful symbolism of the deaths of Enright, Hay, and Gresham. "We will inscribe on their tombs, 'Here lie the first soldiers of the famous United States Republic to fall on the soil of France, for justice and liberty,'" he said.

"The passer-by will stop and uncover his head. The travelers of France, of the Allied countries of America, who come here to visit our battlefield of Lorraine, will go out of their way to come here, to bring to their graves the tribute of their respect and of their gratefulness."

Within days, Newhall's Company L and the rest of the 28th Regiment's 3rd Battalion joined the other regiments' 3rds in the trenches. The 28th was posted in front of the village of Luneville, in a stretch of the same supposedly quiet trenches in which Hay, Gresham, and Enright were slaughtered.

Their deaths put everyone on edge.

"Had the enemy learned that these troops were entering the lines?" Newhall would write postwar. "Was he 'laying for us?' It seemed very possible. The state of mind was not improved when it became known that the French artillery had failed to respond to the signal calling for a barrage, and that consequently the German raiding party had escaped, probably with little or no loss.

"It was later discovered that the French artillery officers had deliberately held their fire on the presumption that the Americans were merely nervous and that there was really no need for a barrage. At least such was the story current in the division."

The raid made a serious impression on the young officers now leading their men into the trenches, even if the sector continued to be considered quiet.

"The confidential pamphlets on trench warfare were studied minutely by company officers who felt themselves about to face the realities of war concerning which they had been reading for three years," Newhall wrote. "Sectors were occupied and relieved to all the prescribed details.

"The 'plan of defense' was issued in mimeographs to every officer and carefully studied. Each lieutenant made a sketch of the entire position, and familiarized himself with it before making his first relief. It was the quietest sector the division ever knew, but the most elaborate precautions were taken preliminary to occupying it, and a degree of alertness was maintained during the occupation, which was worthy of the Ypres salient."

Though no raids occurred while the 3rd Battalion performed its first tour of the trenches, there were enough other dangers to occupy the men's minds. "Our company did not lose any men, although the Germans shelled our positions and turned machine gun fire loose on us," Paul Carter would write.

"The roads over which we brought provisions were shelled continuously but we pulled through without any casualties. The Germans used their heavy guns in shelling the road and large craters were made by each shell. I was in charge of the wagon train and we had to bring up wood, food, and water each day, but we were not hit in going or coming.

"They did not send over any gas shells which was fortunate for us, because we are not used to distinguishing the gas shells from the ordinary shells and we might have had casualties. This was our first real taste of war and it was a big taste."

"It was there that we got our first taste of the continual blam-blam of shells that racks a man's nerves and drives one mad," Jim Quinn would remember. "Once you got used to that unholy din, though, you could sleep as comfortably in the mud at Luneville as in any French mud."

Once in the trenches, wallowing in rainwater and staring past the gnarls of barbed wire and ruined ground of no-man's-land, and then toward the grim German lines, the eager Americans "were disposed to start something at once," Newhall would write.

"The American artillery wanted to pound the Germans all the time. This, however, was not at all suited to the situation, and the French who were in command of the sector exercised a restraint which caused considerable discontented talk in the division.

"Three years of war had taught them the value of quiet sectors where troops could be sent to rest, had taught them to husband their resources in men and material, and had taught them not to start troubles unless there was some military end to be gained."

This, he wrote, "galled the Americans. Hadn't they come to France to fight? Weren't they at the front? Weren't those the German lines over there? Wasn't Germany itself just a few miles behind those lines?"

The prevailing attitude of the Americans of the 1st Division, he added, was that "the 'frogs' were a lot of 'boobs.' They were played out. Hadn't we come to help them? Well, why didn't they let us?"

At the same time, the let's-at-'em fighting spirit of the less-than-veteran 1st Division troops making the first rounds in those trenches was tempered by "nervousness in the face of the unknown possibilities which might emerge from no-man's-land," Newhall wrote.

"The Germans were said to be very cocky over their raid on the Sixteenth Infantry. It was reported that they had established a beer garden in an abandoned farm between the lines where they gathered every night to carouse. So persistent was this story that a patrol was sent to investigate the place and found nothing but desolation."

Otherwise, the Americans spent long nights on the edge of no-man's-land, waiting for the proverbial other shoe to drop.

"In the most approved style the men 'stood to' every morning from two o'clock on, peering out into the darkness into the barbed wire until the stakes of the entanglement seemed to become Germans creeping up to our lines. The stillness and cold would become oppressive.

"Then some man would fire his rifle or throw a grenade out into the night.

" 'What did you see?'

" 'Nothing, sir, but I thought I heard a noise in the wire.'

" 'Do you think you can hit a noise in the dark?'

" 'No, sir.'

" 'Well, hold your fire. Don't let the Germans think we have our wind up.' "

Even the officers were jumpy, Newhall wrote. "One lieutenant told how a German crawled up unseen to the parapet, placed his knees on the rifles of the two men on post so that they were helpless, and fired a pistol into the platoon commander's dugout."

The story, Newhall added, "was received with derision. An over-imaginative captain might think he was about to be attacked and call for reinforcements, but no attack ever came, and neighboring French units smiled at the excessive alertness of the Americans."

In the end, Newhall led his men from the trenches in late November, dirty and exhausted—but unscathed. If nothing else, he noted, the time in the trenches instilled confidence in the recruits.

"The men felt now that they were veterans," Newhall would write. "They had been to the front and returned safely. They knew shell fire or thought they did."

It was as a veteran of sorts that the history PhD Richard Newhall marched the 1st Platoon of Company L, 28th Infantry Regiment, back to the relative comforts of St. Amand.

6

Be Astonished

At night they could hear the muffled clanks of pickax and shovel across no-man's-land, German working parties out in the inky blue-black darkness shoring up a communication trench here, reinforcing a parapet there. It was on one of those shadowy nights that George Guest Haydock first fired a weapon out of not so much anger as curiosity, spraying projectiles and glowing red tracers out into the night toward the enemy's trenches, where under the brilliant and fleeting fizz of a Very light some slightly perturbed Germans pressed themselves closer to the walls of their fortification and cursed under their breaths at George Guest Haydock and his miserable machine.

The short burst from the British machine gun sputtered toward the German line one night in early November 1917, just days after Haydock had left school for a short de rigueur tour of the British trenches.

"We stopped at a Lewis gun post and the sentry reported a working party out front," he wrote. "He pointed the place out to me when a light was up and then let me fire a drum at them, my first shots at the hun."

The war would go on despite George's best efforts, the Germans once again putting to digging once the light fizzled.

For Haydock, the squeeze of the trigger represented a huge leap in his march to war, and a certain realization that he was in it now, that he was *of* it now; a long way from Harvard Yard, a long way from Milton,

Massachusetts, and a long way even from the docks at Le Havre. There, only short weeks before, he and Bill Morgan had first stepped on French soil, and on September 25 discovered they would be sent to the British 5th Army Instruction Camp at Toutencourt, about ten miles north-northeast of Amiens, in Picardy, and boarded a forty-and-eight filled with British soldiers returning to the front.

At Toutencourt, the Americans alit, and the heavy baggage they'd brought—"which looked like enough for an army," Haydock noted—caused the Brits to laugh. "The English officers had nothing but a roll and haversack," he added.

The group was divided by forthcoming specialty: infantry, artillery, and engineers. Haydock found himself in the infantry section, billeted in a building on which hung a sign reading ECOLE DE FILLES—"which hardly seems appropriate," he wrote.

After dinner, Haydock and Morgan took a stroll. "George and I walked through the quaint old streets of the village whose houses flanked the road with their plaster walls and red tile roofs and a large open gate opens into the courtyard into which the barn house and outbuildings faced and which is always filled with wagons, chickens and manure," Morgan recalled.

"We went past a church where old men and women and a few incapacitated men were singing. What feelings must have been in the hearts of those poor people, clad entirely in mourning for the Germans had passed through their homes three years ago and left two atrocities, one a child 2½ years old whose tongue was cut out."

They moved on to a field thick with barbed wire and trenches, from which the French had steadfastly driven the Germans from the valley earlier in the war. "We stood and looked out over the low ridge to the east which was dyed in the brilliant afterglow of the sunset while the great harvest moon hung low," Morgan wrote. "In the distance the boom of the guns could be heard and five planes soared overhead."

Even as Morgan and Haydock gazed to the east, an epic life-and-death struggle was consuming their British hosts sixty miles north of Toutencourt, in the Ypres salient. Hoping to seize high ground at the village of Passchendaele before winter, the British 5th Army suffered enormous casualties. In the coming week, the Brits would fight off five successive counterattacks in the salient and take 20,000 German prisoners.

The cost in casualties was staggering: By the third week of the offensive more than 162,000 men had been killed or wounded. The toll caused 5th Army commander Gen. Sir Hubert Gough to ask that the drive be called off.

British commander Douglas Haig would not hear of it, and while Morgan and Haydock played at war, the British drive would go on for another week in sheeting rain and almost impassable mud; by the time Passchendale Ridge was taken, the British casualty count would stand at 244,897 men killed or wounded. The count on the German side was even more ghastly; some 400,000 were lost.

Under the eye of British officers just returned from the front—"they will not kill us working because the officers here are having a holiday having just come from the line," Haydock wrote—he, Morgan, and about one hundred other subalterns began learning the British way of war.

On the first day, the class left for a bus tour nearer to the lines at the village of Albert. There George Haydock encountered the war's violence for the first time in the environs of the famous Somme battlefield, where a six-month offensive that began on July 1, 1916, left more than 400,000 Englishmen dead and wounded.

Albert had suffered from German shelling. "About 18 months ago the place was shelled, and it is pretty much a mess," Haydock wrote. "The cathedral seemed to have suffered most. It is a very large brick building and is smashed in about as much as it could be.

"There is a high tower on which was a large statue of the Madonna and child which had been knocked over and was hanging over the street at a right angle to the tower, an extraordinary freak. There were a good many buildings completely knocked down, and in nearly all of them windows were broken and the roofs damaged."

That same afternoon, they rode the lorry farther into the Somme. "We got out at a place called Poziere, which had been a town, but of which there was no sign," Haydock wrote. "Everything was desolation."

Their tour guides had been in the costly fighting, where between July and November British and French troops advanced six miles before the drive stalled to the west of Bapaume. The Germans subsequently left Bapaume and the rest of their front line to the Allies in February 1917 and withdrew to the fortified Hindenburg Line farther east to shorten their lines; they systematically leveled towns, villages, and farms as they retreated, leaving a legend written in German on the ruins of the Bapaume town hall:

DON'T BE ANGRY, BE ASTONISHED.

The next morning, real instruction began.

"They make more fuss about fixing bayonets and inspection than I have ever seen, but we learn it by degrees," Haydock wrote. "Today we drilled and had bayonet work in the morning, and then a lecture and lunch, and in the afternoon we got a little firing on a range about 50 yards. I shot well enough to get by."

Even so far back from the front, "Bosch planes" on occasion flew over. "The rumor is that they are hunting for the American bases," Haydock noted. "They have offered huge sums of money for the first American killed or captured but I understand we have doubled the reward, which seems only typically American."

Though their British hosts were outwardly polite to the Americans, Haydock noted some tones of condescension. "They think we will not be able to do much, but the more I see of them the more convinced I become that if the American army has a chance it will give a good account of itself," he wrote. "These people get my dander up, but there is no come back for us until we have a chance to make a showing, so we just have to put up with a good deal of talk that we know is not just."

Morgan, too, was taken with, and impressed by, the British. "The English drill is far more precise and better looking than ours, and the bayonet instruction which we receive is splendid," he wrote. "When you realize that the men who instruct you in the bayonet practice have charged the Huns many times, a deadly grim spirit takes hold of you.

"Most of these officers, and many of them even younger than I, have been fighting steadily for 18 months or more. From their manner one would never know that they had been to the front at all."

One captain told of being in the line for twenty-nine out of thirty months. "He was disgusted because he had never been wounded, and told how once, when he was sitting in a tent sharpening his pencil, an aeroplane bombed the camp and his tent was torn to pieces," Morgan wrote. "There he sat unscratched and he said he was sorely tempted to cut his arm with his knife."

All the talk only made Morgan more curious about life at the front. "It is strange what a fascination it all has," Morgan wrote. "The English speak of the last time they went over the top as I would speak of the last time I made a dash across Fifth Avenue. These men have taught themselves to look on it all as a great game—where some lose but many win. I haven't the least notion that I might get killed, for here we see only those who are not.

"Perhaps I shall be a coward when I come to face it. I laugh now to think what it was that I was afraid of when I left the States. Death seemed so hideous then, but now it doesn't seem fearful or hideous at all, if it should come fighting with such men."

Morgan was slowly learning to think, at least temporarily, like a soldier, and to live only in the present.

"I am gradually losing my old perspective of life," he wrote. "The future seems a mirage—far away—and it does not drag me back as it did in America where there was no direct contact with the war.

"Over here there are few flags and no cheering. It is a deep, fierce war spirit, which is after all the real stuff. It will sicken me to come back to America unless there has been a long casualty list before I return."

The war, Morgan came to see, transcended matters of nationalism or patriotism or even religion and became an entity in itself—it comprised life, just man against man.

"This war is sacred to them," he would write of the Scots and Englishmen at the camp. "The Somme battlefield, dotted with its crosses—a land where villages once stood, now absolutely barren and pitted with shell holes; what was once forests now only charred stumps; all this is holy ground to these men—ground where their best friends have fallen."

The rapture of battles not yet fought, and realities not yet experienced, seized Morgan that autumn. "I hope it won't be long before I can ram my bayonet thru the throat of one of those brutes who have turned France into such a living hell of grief," he wrote.

"How I long to lead Americans against these cursed Boches, and feel that I can hold my head up among the English and the French. Getting killed seems a small matter over here, for we are engulfed in this splendid spirit, and we lose sight of what it will mean to you at home. It seems so unlike me, and I wonder if I am dreaming when I long to kill a man—but as they say over here, 'There is only one good German (a dead one).'"

The tolling of a church bell would lift him from his gruesome reverie. "And now as I sit here," he continued, "I can hear the slow chimes in the village church, and the country is all so peaceful—fields full of poppies growing wild, and clumps of trees just beginning to turn.

"You can hardly realize the war then, the contrast makes you gasp. Indeed the world has to a certain extent gone mad. How strange to hear these men singing 'I don't want to die. I want to go home' etc. and then a little later seeing them practice bayoneting with clenched teeth—full of fight."

It was a state of mind that Morgan, at least this early in the game, hoped to acquire. "I long to get into it myself. It is all so thrilling and it never enters your head that you are the one that may be shot, and then it is such a tremendous thing to be taking part in—when you think that the ideals of the world are at stake."

His blood up and his curiosity unsatisfied, Morgan managed to obtain a pass to spend a Sunday at the front, taking a narrow-gauge railway northeast toward the British positions behind Passchendaele. When he alit, the German front was just 2,500 yards away, "on a hill commanding the whole valley."

Dozens of German helmets littered the ground where there had been hard fighting the previous year, and a snarling dogfight between Allied and German planes raged almost overhead. Freshly dug graves were thick, and Morgan stopped to pick a pansy from the grave of an English soldier.

"The grave was fresh and in a bottle was a note, 'Here lies an unknown English soldier—September 1917,'" Morgan would write. "We saw three English officers who were taking away helmets and walked up to speak to them.

"Pretty soon one of them got a bit fidgety and said, 'I say, we had better split up for this place will be a bit unhealthy in a minute or so. The Boche won't stand for five of us being out here together.' Somehow I couldn't believe that the war was so near me. I could not believe that a human being would think of actually killing us, and yet all around were graves."

Just within those few hours at the front, Morgan began to discern perceived threats from real ones—an ability that would come in handy in just a few short weeks.

"I began to get quite good at telling the caliber and whether they were German or English," he remembered. "The machine guns are [easy] enough to distinguish, for the Boche guns are slower, and when they are anywhere near you can hear a sharp 'whing-spit' as they hit the mud."

The same troubling contradictions followed him to the front. When he left, "we walked across country into the face of the most beautiful sunset, and it made *war* seem the more unreal—I can't believe it all yet," he wrote.

"A very bright new moon hung low over the fields rent with shell-holes and dotted with ruins. Behind me were the flashes and incessant pounding of guns. Can they be really killing men? Even tonight as I sit here in my hut I can hear the rumble of individual cannon as they keep on and on, hurling shot after shot into human flesh."

By Halloween, a rumor that the students were to be sent in to a front-line tour with the British 3rd Army came to fruition. They were told they would spend four days in the trenches, then return to Paris for further orders.

Before leaving, George Haydock was called in before the camp commander on November 2 and advised of the report the camp would relay to the AEF. "Fair knowledge of subject," Haydock wrote. "Very good athlete. Keen to learn and picked things up fast etc.

"He said he had noticed the same things about me and would endorse it. He said I would be a good officer and capable instructor. It may help me to get a good job. At any rate it is a good recommendation."

On Sunday, November 4, Haydock made ready to join the British 24th

Division in the lines on the Somme front. "The Col. said we were not to take our bedding rolls. I took nothing beside my toilet kit, an extra pair of socks, gas mask, tin hat, and the things I had on my back," he wrote.

Passing newly dug cemeteries holding French and English dead, the bus finally crept closer to the lines and found the 24th Division's headquarters in the pitch dark.

Here, Haydock learned he had been reassigned to serve with the 72nd and 73rd brigades, so had to "go to each Brigade H.Q. with my men to stay there and introduce them to the Brigadiers, who always asked me to have a drink, an excellent idea as it was very cold and dark. They were very nice and cordial and by the time I got through we were real clubby like."

Haydock was told he would do his frontline time with the 9th Surreys, who were located five miles away. Locating the battalion headquarters, he reported to the majors, who were "having an orgy on bully beef and whiskey. I joined them and we talked till about 2 when I went to bed.

"My bunk was in a very deep dug-out, about 30 feet under ground, and down very steep steps with lots of beams to bump one's head on. I kept my tin hat on and thus saved myself from knocking my own brains out." He would add: "The place was very dark and had lice and rats in it, other wise it was not bad."

In the morning, Haydock encountered no-man's-land for the first time, tailing along with the battalion's major on his morning tour of the lines. Behind him, within the British lines, was Hargicourt; beyond the German lines to the east, the village of Boussicourt stood untouched.

"I looked through periscopes at the sentry posts and over the top in several places," he wrote. "We stopped at various H.Q. on the way, most of them in old Bosch dugouts that had not been completed, some having only one entrance.

"While we were down there they started strafing a bit and things were a bit hot on the way in. When we were about 200 yards from H.Q. we heard a shell whistling at us. The major quite evidently had the wind up, but I did not know enough about it to be more than curious. It landed about 75 yards from us and the dirt landed near us when it came down. It was quite a close shave and we did not waste time getting under cover."

That night, Haydock returned to the front line, carefully trying to stay on the duckboards that sat atop a sea of knee-deep mud. "It was absolutely black and very tough going," he wrote. Haydock and his British escorts moved on and came to a forward post in the trench line: "The sentry said he thought there were two men just outside our wire. We watched for about 10 minutes, but could see no movement. The whole business was the most thrilling thing I have ever done."

On the way back to battalion headquarters, Haydock got his first taste of what he called "the vertical breeze," as bullets fired indirectly from a German machine gun hit the wire only a few feet from him and sparked.

"It was just one of those short bursts they fire at night as a gentle reminder that they are still on hand," Haydock wrote.

The following night, the Germans shelled the battalion on Haydock's left. "We found that night that he had scored a direct hit on the mess and knocked out the Colonel, a young fellow only 24 who has been through all the big fights of the war, the Doctor who was an American, blew both arms off the adjutant, and wounded several others," Haydock wrote.

The next day, "we moved up to the front to relieve the Surreys. While we were going up [the Germans] must have seen movement because [they] began dropping shells all around us. We were sitting in the H.Q. mess with shells bursting about 20 yards from us and making us rather windy as we had just heard of the experience of the day before."

After another day in the trenches, Haydock's short tour was over, and he and the other Americans somewhat happily rode back to the British camp by truck—"which came as somewhat of a surprise," he wrote.

Bill Morgan, too, went into line with the British, serving a few days in the trenches with the 1st Londoners southwest of Bapaume.

"Very quiet," he would write. "Germans 1,500 yards off but has advanced M.G. posts and one 'Parapet Percy' made us duck once in a while. Saw a raid on a Boche magpie nest with box barrage. Petrol shells or liquid fire which burst and threw flames and a dense cloud of smoke—a real and most vivid reproduction of hell."

His second visit to the line made him realize the magnitude of the job that lay ahead for the Americans. "It doesn't take many hours in the trenches to make you see that this is going to be a big job that we've undertaken, and a *damned* hard one," he would write.

"But the greatest thing that can happen to America will be having a few hundred thousand of our men covered with this French mud—the same mud that is on the Englishman and the Frenchman."

At the front, the British dugouts "were quite comfortable, with beds built of wood, and seats around the sides of the sandbags. As it was so quiet we could look over the top any time, and with our glasses watch the Huns walking around in their trenches. They had pushed forward a machine gun about 500 yards from our line and they used to fire it now and then, though most of the shots went too high.

"There isn't any use in dodging them for they hit you before you know it, but I couldn't help pulling my head down as they whizzed past. The sentries would duck and then laugh and say, 'There's Parapet Percy again.' "

One night, "the men in the trench on our left had a raid on a machine gun emplacement out in 'No Man's Land,' " he wrote. "I watched the artillery barrage come down around it and I can tell you that it was the most realistic bit of hell that I ever hope to see; the Germans sending up flares and rockets and S.O.S. signals—an incessant series of explosions which shook our dugouts violently; thousands and thousands of machine gun bullets whirring thru' the air, and the poor devils who went over the top were by some mistake caught in their own barrage."

Morgan himself took some tentative first steps into no-man's-land—though not too far. "A patrol was going out but the officer advised me not to go with it for the strain on the men is bad enough without having me along to add to their nervousness," he would write.

"So I only went out a little way. All of a sudden a flare went up from the advanced post and lit up all No Man's Land! I thought for a moment that a great electric light had been lit for the light is that same color of peculiar white.

"Then a few machine gun bullets clipped through the barbed wire a few yards to my right. As soon as the light went out I didn't waste much time in getting back to our trenches."

The short tour temporarily shook him, and for the first time he entertained serious doubts about his situation. "It is hell, and much worse than I can possibly describe," he wrote. "Not the sanitation etc., but the everlasting living below ground, and the endless killing. I don't know what the moral issues are mixed up in it, but I do know this war is beyond anything. I don't mind saying that I am not looking forward to it."

Upon graduating from the British school at Toutencourt, Morgan was given his recommendation by his British platoon leader: "A good keen Officer who should make a fine leader. He is of a cheerful disposition with energy and determination. He is quick to learn and with more experience should be able to instruct in military subjects but would also be a good Officer in the line."

Morgan would claim that the camp commander pulled him aside and gave him his choice of training "on this side or America. I had an awful time saying it, but I managed to tell him that I would rather stay over here. He said he was glad for they needed men over here."

As their British friends moved north once more toward the sound of the guns at Passchendaele, Bill Morgan and George Haydock took their own tentative steps toward the war.

7

Chasing the Indians

COLD, RAIN, SNOW, AND mud, and to make it worse nobody seemed to know which end was up, or how the war should be fought or even where it *was*.

They had enlisted to fight a war but instead found little but misery, a sense that the blind were leading the lame, as, operating by division, brigade, regiment, and company, the 1st Division's young officers in late 1917 tried to learn the game of warfare and impart it to their charges.

They found seeming confusion from top to bottom, even as the certainty of battle moved ever closer with each passing day.

"That was the hard winter of 1917–1918," Edward Scott Johnston, commander of the 28th Regiment's Company E, would remember. "Socks had to do duty as gloves. Shoes had to be held together with rags and string. Billets were mere barns—leaky, drafting, forbidding. There were not enough stoves. There was not enough good firewood.*

"And there was nothing inspiring in the appearance of the troops. Bristles on their faces, *vin rouge* on their breaths, mud on their long,

* Johnston's account of the early days of the AEF is from the chapter "Portrait of a Soldier" in *Americans vs. Germans: The First A.E.F. in Action*. New York: Penguin Books; Washington: Infantry Journal, 1942.

bedraggled overcoats, their noses running and their chests sore with coughing."

Not so much dissension as lethargy affected all, as after a long cold day in the field officers would retire to their warm quarters, leaving their bedraggled men, wet and tired and hungry, to the mercy of a single stove and a few frozen blankets. At the end of each day, officers and enlisted men alike wondered what the point had been and "what we were really accomplishing," Johnston wrote.

"Long sessions with the French combined with a short tour in the line had taught us something of life in the trenches. We thought we had the general idea of the trench-to-trench attack. But the actual results of our American emphasis on open warfare, as expressed in our day-to-day activities, were perplexing. To go out one day and do an imitation of a 1917-style attack—to go out the next and attack in the crowded formations of 1914—there was something not rational about it.

"When somebody said, 'I'll be damned if I know what I'm doing or if anyone else does,' he just about hit the spot."

"Each evening the junior officers would gather in one room, each bringing with him his precious small armload of wood, and while they vainly tried to get warm, they would pour out their troubles which almost amounted to mutiny," wrote Shipley Thomas, a junior officer with the 26th Regiment.

"They talked—as junior officers always do, in a cock-sure way born of youthful enthusiasm—of the uselessness of 'chasing the Indians,' of Generals who 'had learned nothing since Custer and apparently couldn't learn,' and who did not know that every German artillery shot was plotted days in advance."

Night after night, Thomas added, in the "miserable, frozen billets," the junior officers of the 1st Division "poured forth their woes over the incompetence of Generals who taught open warfare and attack, 'when any fool could see that it was the Germans, and not us, who were going to attack.'"

To make matters worse, company commanders and their junior officers became special targets of the brass.

"Higher authority was continually exhorting, hectoring, and even threatening the lower commanders and their troops, in a misdirected effort to alleviate their miseries," Johnston wrote. "Junior officers said to each other, 'Anyone can see our defects. What good does it do to lecture us about them?' Company officers acutely resented being blamed for lack of equipment which the supply services didn't produce.

"Maybe—the cankering doubt was beginning to spread—maybe the French were right. Their public comment on our situation was that the American soldiers and junior officers required only experience, but that the senior officers were incompetent."

With spring, he would add, "The business of fighting might be messed up just as badly as the business of getting us through the winter alive. No; the vanguard of Democracy was not happy!"

In late 1917, some of those concerns within the 28th Regiment were assuaged by the arrival of an unlikely leader who, as part of Pershing's purge of those officers who had "gone to seed," took over the 2nd Battalion. Though his knowledge of the military arts would prove infectious throughout the regiment and the division, his real impact would come in his ability to show his junior officers how to *lead* men in wartime.

Axel Severin Rasmussen was not an American but a Dane who had immigrated to Oregon with his brother and father, who with his six brothers had fought against the Prussian grab of the province of Schleswig in 1864.

Born in Odense, Denmark, on June 29, 1879, Axel Rasmussen grew up in Williamsburg, Oregon, and with his brother, Rasmus, joined the Army's 4th Cavalry in 1896. Both saw service in the Philippines, and while his brother afterward settled down to farm and raise a family in the Willamette Valley, Axel found the lure of distant places and wars too irresistible and moved on to become a soldier of fortune.

The famed war correspondent Irvin S. Cobb, who would encounter and befriend Rasmussen in France in the spring of 1918, wrote in the *Saturday Evening Post*: "In the Spanish war he was a kid private; saw service as a non-com in the Philippine mess; tried civil life afterwards and couldn't endure it; went to Central America and took a hand in some tinpot revolution or other; came home and was in business for a year or so, which was as long as his adventurous soul could stand a stand-still life."

He would go on to fight as a mercenary for the "Carrazanistas," leading a ragtag army in search of the bandito revolutionary Pancho Villa (and just narrowly avoiding clashes with U.S. troops under the command of John J. Pershing, also on the prowl for Villa), and afterward moved to Canada, where he "got a job in the Royal Mounted Police," Cobb wrote.

"Physically and every other way he was the sort of man that Richard Harding Davis used to love to describe in his stories about soldiers of fortune . . . He was tall and slender, as handsome a man as ever I looked at and a soldier in every inch of him."

Rasmussen had taken a wife at some point in his adventuring, but when she died shortly before the outbreak of world war he was left bereft. So he decided to return to soldiering, and wandering, and on September 23, 1915, turned up at a Canadian recruiting station in Calgary to enlist in Canada's 97th Battalion—otherwise known as Canada's "American Legion." It consisted mostly of American expats and had "troubles galore," the newspaper columnist J. W. Pegler would note: "There were bums and deserters and just plain thieves who enlisted to draw the pay through the cold winter and 'go over the hill' when it looked as though the 97th battalion was about to sail."

Amid the turmoil, the serious and experienced soldier Axel Rasmussen received quick promotion and soon found himself outranking his former commanding officer.

The 97th sailed finally for England with about 900 men—90 percent of them Americans—in September 1916. Disaster met them when they landed, as the press had got hold of a story out of New York in which one of the deserters, an officer, referred disparagingly to the battalion as the "Lost Legion of tramps."

"It took the blood and suffering of hundreds of lonely, expatriated Yanks to live down the slander," Pegler wrote.

The legion was disbanded, but Rasmussen stayed on in England and with his best friend, John Speed Manning—a native Englishman who had also served with Rasmussen in the U.S. Army in the Philippines, with the Carrazanistas, and during "raids, lectures and forays into London and Paris"—was transferred to the Princess Pats, a Canadian unit that had gained fame for a bloody stand against the Germans during the Second Battle of Ypres in May 1915.

Sent to the front in command of a machine-gun company, Rasmussen quickly was dubbed "the Flying Major" for his daring raids on enemy trenches. On March 30, 1917 he was wounded while leading a patrol against a German command post. "His party was discovered by the Boche sentries in the front line but they scurried back under a sprinkling of machine gun bullets, bringing the outpost garrison as souvenirs," a newspaper account would read.

Reaching his lines, Rasmussen realized one of the raiding party was missing, and he "crawled back through the wire alone and found him wounded." As he picked up the wounded man, a German hand grenade plunked down next to them. "In a flash, Rass seized it and threw it back, dropping flat in the same instant, to escape some of the fragments if it should go off too close by."

The grenade exploded almost as soon as he rid himself of it, and Rasmussen suffered a punctured eardrum and a wound in an arm from the flying fragments. He again picked up the wounded man and returned to the lines. "The youngster died just as the willing hands of his comrades reached out to take him from the major."

When the United States entered the war, Rasmussen and Manning—known by then in several armies as "Jock"—applied for transfers to the AEF and rejoined the Americans in September 1917. Originally slated to train young officers, each soon found a place in the 1st Division, Rasmussen as commander of the 28th Regiment's 2nd Battalion, and Manning as a company commander in the 18th Regiment.

"We were rotten lecturers," Rasmussen admitted. "I'm glad I'm going back to be with troops again because I wasn't built to fill a swivel-chair."

One affectation of the empire he did not leave behind was his battered trench helmet. "He liked to finger the gap in its brim where a bit of shrapnel chipped it as he climbed up Vimy Ridge," Irvin Cobb would write.

Rasmussen first appeared in the 28th Regiment "on one of those French wintry days so often unhappily chosen for divisional field exercises," Edward Johnston remembered. "Frozen shoes cut your flesh in the morning and the midday thaw drenched your feet with icy water. The troops moved along mechanically or stood idly, enduring dumbly and obediently, but supremely uninterested in anything except getting it over."

"They're not learning anything, they're suffering!" Rasmussen said as he watched the exercise. Instead of stopping the proceedings, though, he sent the formation flying through woods and over the snowy plains in search of imaginary Germans.

"We were at once astonished, galvanized into action," Johnston wrote. "We began to warm up with interest and exercise, and to our own surprise found ourselves in the end hunting imaginary enemies all over the winter terrain."

At the end of the day, Rasmussen ordered rum and hot tea be given to the men, per a much-appreciated tradition of the empire. "We compromised on slum and coffee, both very hot," Johnston remembered.

In any case, the men marched home happy.

It was on that day that the other young officers of the 28th Regiment learned the most important lesson Rasmussen could give: "The first thing to do is to make the men comfortable and happy."

In a subsequent flurry of activity, the regiment's noncoms were ordered to give up cozy rooms in the billets, and their stoves were spread among the larger living quarters. The billets themselves were repaired with scrap lumber; firewood parties were sent out, bedding dried, and the appearance of the rank and file improved with a shave every morning.

As well, Rasmussen instructed company commanders to stop "commanding their companies as an aggregation of squads, and using their lieutenants and sergeants as mere assistants," Johnston wrote. "There was no platoon responsibility—no platoon spirit."

Afterward, platoon commanders such as George Haydock perhaps understood their jobs better. As one of Johnston's own second lieutenants in Company E, Maurice E. Edwards, would write: "A lieutenant cannot 'pass the buck.' If anything goes wrong in his platoon, he is held responsible; he can't pass it down to his sergeants and corporals. The platoon leader has to see that his men get everything they need, whether he himself loses out or not.

"He has to censor their letters, see that their equipment is kept complete and in order, inspect their mess three times a day, see that they have shaved every morning and that they keep their hair short; he must drill them, punish them for malingering in their duties, study their adaptabilities and peculiarities to see who will make the best grenadier and who the best automatic rifleman."

As well, "he lends them money when they are 'broke,'" Edwards wrote. "I have a couple of hundred francs out in the platoon, which ostensibly went toward the purchase of tooth brushes, paste, and soap."

From that first day, "the other officers of the regiment admired him but his men, as I have reason to know, worshipped him," Irvin Cobb would write of Rasmussen. Johnston would thereafter take Jock Manning's place as Rasmussen's drinking buddy, as Maurice Edwards would note: "Madame Alleaume's back-parlor is the favorite hang-out of the officers. There they get their toddy and there once or twice our Captain Johnston has put the Major under the table with the result that we did not have to rise at 3:30 the next morning for special maneuvers—at least not the next morning."

As yet unaware of these growing pains, George Haydock and Bill Morgan returned from the British front and were told to report to AEF headquarters in Paris for further assignment; it was an order they had no intention of disobeying.

Haydock hoped to spend a day and locate his sister Louisa, who with her best friend, Penelope Parker, was working with the Red Cross. With a couple of days to kill in the City of Light, Haydock and Morgan took a room at the Continental Hotel.

"It seemed good to get back to a bed and get clothes off again," Haydock wrote. In comfort, he reflected on his few days in the trenches: "I think we learned a great deal out of our trip and it gives me a good bit more confidence to know what it is like. My first experience under fire was not nearly as bad as I thought it would be and the life, although far from comfortable, is perfectly possible and more normal than I had expected it would be."

On Saturday, November 10, he went in search of his sister, but because he had only an old address for her he had to give up the hunt fairly quickly. "It was darn disappointing because I was sure we would connect somehow and I was crazy to see [her]," Haydock wrote.

The next day, Haydock and Morgan found they had been assigned to the 28th Regiment, and were ordered to the regiment's headquarters at Trévary. They caught the noon train at the Gare de l'Est and alit at 8:00 P.M. with forty other reserve officers and reported for duty.

They found only confusion.

"Of course there were no billets for us as they had not expected us in the least," Haydock wrote. "There was no place to get food either but fortunately I had some crackers and a tin of bully beef so WOP and I made a meal of that, then we swiped the baggage truck from the station and lugged our kits about one half-mile up the hill. We found a carpenter's shop that was more or less empty and so we camped there for the night."

The next morning they were sent up the road to the 3rd Battalion's headquarters in St. Amand and drew their assignments. Haydock was put in Company L and Morgan in Company M. With their new units still in the lines at Luneville each had little to do but hang around St. Amand and wonder whether they would be able to "make good" among the regulars of the 1st Division, Haydock would write.

"I never expected to find myself in the regular army and can see that I shall have my hands more than full as we are to be shoved right in to fill the jobs with them," Haydock wrote. The regulars, he would add, seemed to think that the reserve officers just arriving "should know as much as they do and get very mad when they find we do not. It looks like a rough winter ahead of us and I begin to think I shall be lucky if I ever see the States again."

Morgan also was put off by the seeming confusion he found. "No one knew we were coming to the 28th Regiment and there were no beds left and the billeting officer was wild and all the officers stationed here mad because they now have 10 officers per Company," he wrote.

In the unfamiliar surroundings, Morgan and Haydock clung to each other. "George Haydock and I are still together and it is great to have him," Morgan wrote. "I may be a snob but somehow college men are different, more tactful with a broader education, which is more interesting for those around."

Within days, Morgan took leave of Haydock, being assigned to the 1st Division's 3rd Machine-Gun Battalion. He was happy to be out of the infantry and to have a chance to specialize. "I guess it will be pretty exciting, but don't think that it is as dangerous as people will tell you," he wrote.

He had much to learn, writing in November that in his opinion machine-gun duty would be "all the safer than the infantry, and there is very little nervous strain to it . . . There is no patrolling of No Man's Land which is the thing that wears on you. Everything is going finely, and we have a wonderful captain which makes all the difference in the world."

He had much to learn about leading the men in his platoon as well—though he expressed certainty about his approach. "These old regular army officers are so terribly indifferent with their men," he would write.

"I claim that this war can't be fought that way, that an officer must be a friend to his men, or in a pinch they won't follow you and capture a pillbox which is holding up the attack of a battalion and when you most need them they'll say they will be damned if they will help you."

His experience with the British Army, he thought, had taught him a better way. "I saw how those Tommies loved their officers and how many an officer gave up little comforts in order to look after the needs of their men before thinking of themselves. I pity officers who do not understand their men."

Morgan also had little sympathy for the old army regulars who, to his thinking, failed to grasp the new "science" of the war. "This war from start to finish is a tremendous science, and even after the science has been worked out a man must have a mind like lightening and all the qualities of leadership," he wrote.

He found little spark among the older officers. "In the first place some of the officers are either old men who would fare badly in the trenches, or old army sergeants who have been given commissions and who are entirely unfit for their jobs," he wrote. "One jolly old Irishman admitted that 'even a monkey can think and I can't do that.'"

As had Newhall, he would complain that the army chiefs cared less about a man's initiative and thought process than they did about mindless drilling. The efforts of the young and educated officers filling the ranks of the AEF, Morgan would write, were unappreciated by an army dominated by higher-ups still fighting the last war—a problem that was noted at the top.

"We had . . . once excellent officers of higher ranks, who had gone to seed in the doldrums of peace and could not shake themselves loose from the cut-and-dried methods of the old Army," Gen. Hunter Liggett, himself sixty and overweight when war was declared, would write.

Liggett showed enough hustle and ability to impress AEF commander John Pershing, but many other would-be divisional commanders were deemed physically unable to endure the hardships they would encounter at the front. In France, Pershing would recommend that seventeen generals be relieved of duty and shipped back to the United States, leaving the AEF to accelerate the promotions of younger, more fit officers.

It wasn't a move up the ranks that Morgan sought—just a little respect. "I really don't give a hang about promotion, in fact none of these reserves do," he wrote. "It is obvious we didn't come in for that by any means, and we don't intend to stay in the army a day after peace is declared."

Each night, Morgan and his restless and know-it-all peers were lectured on what they considered arcane and boring details of running a company. "I ain't had a college education, I ain't as fortunate as you, but what do you know about providing for the messing of a company?" one old-time officer would ask.

"And from the back of the room came, 'Winning the war,' accompanied by much laughing," Morgan wrote.

Morgan was sent on to machine-gun school at Gondrecourt, where he was instructed in the peculiarities of the weapon that, more than any other technological advance, had changed the nature of warfare and by 1917 was perhaps warfare's most exemplary example of the use of science.

The German Maxim, the French Hotchkiss, and the British Lewis guns would be described by the English major J. F. C. Fuller as the "concentrated essence of infantry."

Where a skilled infantryman could shoot fifteen accurate rounds a minute, a machine gun could shoot six hundred rounds in the same time, and just a few well-placed and well-sited guns could break an attack and inflict staggering losses on an advancing foe.

The concentrated fire brought the infantry back to its role in the eighteenth and nineteenth centuries, before long-range rifles changed the nature of battle but made infantrymen "erratic agents of death," the military historian Sir John Keegan would write. "Unless centrally directed, they will choose, perhaps badly, their own targets, will open and cease fire individually, will be put off their aim by the enemy's return fire, will be distracted by the wounding of those near them, will yield to fear or excitement, will fire high, low, or wide."

The machine gun, Keegan noted, "put back into the hands of the regimental commander the means to inflict multiple and simultaneous wounding by the giving of a single word of command."

The most important thing about a machine gun, he added, was that it was "a machine," easy to operate and able to perform its functions "with the minimum of human attention, supplying its own power and only requiring a steady supply of raw material and a little routine maintenance to operate efficiently." The machine gun "had not so much *disciplined* the act of killing . . . as *mechanized* or *industrialized* it."

The guns' lethality had shown itself across the Western and Eastern fronts since 1914, on which many an advancing battalion or regiment had been mown down to lie as neatly as a row of crosses. Because of its effectiveness, its operators would also become the first and special targets of an enemy's artillery prior to leaping from the trenches.

In the AEF, three machine-gun battalions comprised of four companies each were formed in each division. In the 1st Division, the 2nd Machine-Gun Battalion was assigned to the 1st Brigade, the 3rd to the 2nd Brigade, and the 1st Machine-Gun Battalion served as a divisional reserve. In battle, one machine-gun company was assigned to each regiment's three infantry battalions, and the fourth served at the disposal of the regiment.

The work required some knowledge of mathematics—chiefly the computation of angles and distance when laying indirect fire, in which gunners sprayed bullets into the air like deadly rain on areas where the enemy, unseen to them, was expected to be concentrating for attack.

"An enemy, upon being subjected to indirect fire, becomes more dismayed than if direct fire were used, for he cannot see the hidden machine guns that are decimating his ranks, and is consequently unable to return an effective fire," the 1917 American book *Machine Guns* would note.

Although its practitioners were painstakingly sought out by enemy artillery, the work afforded more protection than advancing infantry had, the gun crews laying their indirect fire from sheltered backline positions.

There was also a flip side to the work, however. "In no case should a machine gun detachment abandon its post," one military expert would caution; "if need be it will permit itself to be besieged there and will defend itself to the last. The tenacity and heroism of a few machine gun men has often enabled the retaking of lost positions."

Even in the worst case, one not dwelled upon by the young lieutenants considering the branch, it offered the promise of some enduring glory—and Morgan became engrossed in the work of figuring the details of direct and indirect fire, even as what would be one of the worst French winters in years had settled in, adding to the misery.

"Snow all over the ground and cold roaring wind," Morgan wrote. "It is hard to describe how uncomfortable we are because the stoves in the buildings are inadequate. We are ordered to rise every 30 minutes in recitations and do the double quick standing still, and at night no one can study in the barracks so they cluster around the stove, or go to bed, or down to the cafes which I have had to do in order to study."

Thanksgiving eased some of the pain, as the army provided a full feast—"turkey, stuffing, sweet potatoes, pumpkin pie, 2 kinds of cake etc.," Morgan would note. After dinner, he went to the billet of a Harvard pal in a farmhouse just outside of Gondrecourt, where he and 2nd Lt. Alexander McKinlock enjoyed "beaucoup wine and cognac during all afternoon and evening.

"We sat in the big room of the farmhouse, around a stove. It was really almost a barn, cows, horses, and chickens in the next room, and all the walls and floor were of rough boards. We sat and talked with the old woman who owned the house, and she was so interesting."

Even in the relative comfort of that rude billet, Morgan remained aware that a war raged not far away—and that one day it would find him. "Every day I am over here makes me more and more lose sight of peace. Everyone is so active in the war, and no one thinks of anything else. The war is a background for everything you do and see. Everything else seems like wasted time—so unexciting and trivial."

The big question—whether he would hold up when under real fire for the first time—continued to haunt Morgan.

"Things are pretty hard sometimes over here, and often I am almost afraid of my nerve, and I wonder," he would write.

"There is so much wondering over here."

8

The Possibilities

He's a bit of a mama's boy, still, though he's passed his twenty-fourth birthday, has graduated—barely—from Harvard, and is serving as a second lieutenant in the United States Army as it not so much revs up to speed but lumbers, an ungainly and sputtering machine beset by the tug and pull of the Allies who would tear it to pieces if only John Pershing would let them.

Before it's all over this one will be called a hero and come to the attention of the same Pershing. Right now, though, he's just another fumbling second lieutenant, albeit one with a leg up on most of the others on account of fame won on the gridiron with the Harvard eleven, and by all appearances the influence of a doting and somewhat domineering mother, who is in belated fashion tracking his movements across France on a pin-studded map in the family's fabulous mansion in Lake Forest, Illinois.

"It was almost fun," George Alexander McKinlock Jr.'s mother, Marion, would later say of living her son's great adventure vicariously.

Though there's a war on, she doesn't focus much on the peril Alexander faces. Instead she simply waits for him to return to Lake Forest and assume his rightful throne as the heir to the Central Electric Company, which has made his father's fortune.

"We knew the possibilities," she would say many years later, "but the twentieth century loomed *huge* with possibilities. France in the atlas was just one musty map with too many hyphens and odd consonants. It seemed to hold so little destiny."

Alexander McKinlock was born with the proverbial silver spoon in his mouth. He counted among his playmates the offspring of the city's wealthiest families and industrial giants—"the Dicks, the Swifts, the Armours, the Meekers, and the Mortons, the Durand Smiths, the Cummingses . . . the Forgans, Spragues, Carpenters, Kings and McLaughlins, and the Bigelows," all of whom had "devoted one part of the family estate to something of the especial interest of the children," the *Chicago Tribune* would report in 1907.

Not far from where faceless and nameless immigrants slaved in the South Side meatpacking jungles of those Armours and Swifts, Alexander's days were filled instead with riding horseback at the exclusive Onwentsia Country Club and roaming the broad lawns on the family estate, called Brown Gables. There, his whims were tended to by a bevy of servants, while his father saw to business and his mother to her place on the Chicago social register.

As with W. O. P. Morgan, the military was well represented in Alexander's bloodline. His great-grandfather, John McKinlock, "was private secretary to Commodore Vanderbilt," one family history says; *his* son, another John, was born in New York City in 1834, and a few months after the outbreak of the Civil War helped raise a regiment of volunteers in Oswego County, New York.

After the war, the captain brought his family west to Detroit, then in 1890 moved to Chicago and began an electrical-supply company that would grow into the Central Electric Company. In 1912, a history of Chicago would include him as one of the city's great builders and note that he was "still active in that field, although seventy-seven years of age, and such a good record should put to shame many a man of younger years who, grown weary of the struggles and responsibilities of business life, would relegate to others the burdens that he should bear."

George Alexander McKinlock, the eldest son of John, was born in Oswego in 1857, was educated in the public schools there, and at the age of twenty became the business manager for the American District Telegraph Company in Detroit. He followed his father to Chicago and helped organize the family business, which supplied materials for the electrification of the city, still rebuilding and expanding following the great fire of 1871.

George McKinlock quickly became both quite wealthy and one of the most eligible bachelors in the burgeoning city. Not long after his arrival, he met and courted Marion Wallace Rappleye. On December 2, 1890, they were wed at her father's home.

"The bride's dress was of white faille mousseline de soie, with diamond ornaments," the *Chicago Tribune* reported. "Mr. and Mrs. McKinlock left for New York, whence they will sail Saturday for Europe, to be absent a year."

For the new Mrs. George Alexander McKinlock, marriage brought a huge leap in social standing—as well as closure to an upbringing shrouded in scandal, which had begun with the seduction of her maternal grandmother, Jane Slover, who had in 1844 been a teenaged live-in maid in the home of John Seeley Wallace, a wealthy businessman in Valparaiso, Indiana.

Jane's child, Cythera, married the Chicago businessman Nicholas Rappleye and gave birth to daughters Maud in 1865 and Marion in 1870. Nicholas Rappleye's real estate business was booming, and he seemed to be on a path to great wealth—until in 1873 he agreed to act as guardian and trustee for the three children of an attorney whose wife died in November 1871.

Rappleye instead spent the money in the trust as if it were his and, after having his name dragged through the city's newspapers, ultimately narrowly escaped being sent to prison for fraud. Still, the affair ruined the family's finances and left a stain on its once-notable name.

Amid this scandal and drama and ruin, Marion Wallace Rappleye grew up with her older sister in the family home at 2020 Wabash Avenue. She attended the Dearborn Seminary and Wells College before meeting George McKinlock. Though no great beauty, she was as smart and as ambitious as the thirty-three-year-old bachelor McKinlock; in each other they found a perfect match.

George McKinlock, preferring to stay out of the papers, allowed Mrs.

George A. McKinlock to handle all social duties and to be the public face of the family while he remained in the background.

Following their long honeymoon in Europe, he returned to business, while Marion McKinlock entered the whirl of Chicago society, glad to have left her family's trials and dramas and uncertain prospects behind her and to have taken up residence on the very fashionable and exclusive Astor Street on the city's Near North Side.

She soon began drawing plans for the ultimate symbol of status in turn-of-the-century Chicago: a mansion to be built thirty miles up Lake Michigan at the corner of Waukegan and Deerpath roads in Lake Forest. There, the McKinlocks truly arrived, building their beloved "country home"—Brown Gables—set far back along a winding driveway from the prying eyes of the less fortunate, the grounds surrounded by the similar grand mansions of such Chicago giants as the Ogden Armours and the Cyrus McCormicks.

It was here, among the broad lawns and sweeping views of Brown Gables, that Alexander McKinlock would spend many a happy summer's day, laughing and running and riding a series of ponies under the doting eye of the former Marion Wallace Rappleye.

He was born on May 16, 1893, and his mother allowed him as free and unencumbered a childhood as was then possible. Though pampered and indulged with every excess when it came to toys and privilege, Alexander grew to be a sturdy and rambunctious youth, a force to be reckoned with whether chasing a ball across the lawns or galloping horses at the nearby Onwentsia Club, at which Marion and he spent many summer days as he grew up, surrounded by the equally privileged offspring of Chicago's Gilded Age.

"Near the great porches and on the beautiful lawns are seen the little chairs and strange wild beasts of baby animal land, left out and forgotten," a *Tribune* reporter would write in a turn-of-the-century article about Lake Forest's wealthy progeny titled "The Paradise of the Children of Chicago's Millionaires."

"Louis Swift, with every kind of a bird or animal that can be domesticated on the place, cares most for his horses. Alexander McKinlock is one of those boys that are fond of horses, as was seen by his honors at the horse show."

His carefree childhood was reflected in what one friend would remember as Alexander's "wonderful smile, radiant, unbounded, comprehensive; an epitome of untainted, strong boyhood, full of the wind and sun of open air, too young and too babbling for care and suppression; a provoking, beckoning smile that called you out to play—and you smiled back, and went with a rush.

"His eyes were brown as beech leaves at the bottom of a brook pool; they reflected the sun of his smile. But in them, too, were sympathy and a wistful look, as you found on better acquaintance."

Marion McKinlock kept her son at home until he was ten years old before reluctantly packing him off to the Fay School in Southborough, Massachusetts. After three years at Fay, Alexander at the age of thirteen was sent on to St. Mark's School, also in Southborough.

Alexander quickly proved himself a leader, playing the next three years on the school's football team under the tutelage of Daniel Woodhead, a twenty-something Englishman who had emigrated to the United States at the age of ten with two siblings and gone on to play fullback for the Wesleyan University football team.

Woodhead and Alexander quickly bonded, and whether because of Alexander's gushing letters home or the elder McKinlocks' own favorable impressions of the young football coach, Woodhead in 1909 was offered a job in the family business—and he left Southborough to move to Chicago and work as a salesman for George McKinlock.

At St. Mark's one schoolmate would characterize Alexander as being "strong, restless, affectionate, conscientious, humorous and serious at once." Yet his interest in schoolwork apparently did not match that of the football field.

"I was always aware he had far greater ability than he showed in his schoolwork," St. Mark's headmaster, the Rev. William G. Thayer, would remember. "This ability did not find full expression until he was well along in his college life."

In 1912, perhaps due more to his parents' social standing and money than to his grades, Alexander, by then a stocky 5′8″ 169-pound nineteen-year-old, was accepted at Harvard University.

There's a sense that the long first decade of Alexander's life, in which he was afforded nothing but playtime, turned him into something of an eternal child, unable to cope with the boring, day-to-day need to focus. Or it may have been that certain loneliness that can come with being an only child and not having a sibling with whom to roughhouse.

"There was always something playfully bothering and quarrelsome about him," one friend remembered. "He was in every rough-house those days, at the bottom of many, and day in and day out engaged in personal combat of the most ridiculous and amusing nature."

In the summer of 1913, even as the first storm clouds were gathering in Europe, Marion McKinlock took her twenty-year-old son to Germany to study the language. For six weeks, they toured Bremen, Berlin, Dresden, Heidelberg, Bad Manheim, Nuremburg, and Munich and also made it to Paris and Zurich.

The young McKinlock was, overall, unimpressed with the state of the average German. "The people, especially the women, are coarse, poorly dressed, and pasty faced, with the exception [of] those whose faces are bright scarlet," he wrote his father. "They appear to have no interest in athletics. The men drink lots of wine and every after noon have coffee and Kucken an assortment of cakes."

His less than enthusiastic appraisal of the country and its people was not so much original as a reflection of a prevailing and denigrating European opinion of Germany—an opinion that would find a response in the rhythmic clicking of thousands of hobnailed boots marching across neutral Belgium in just a year's time. Whether the irony ever occurred to Alexander McKinlock is unknown—but he would ultimately find himself dealing with Germans in a much different manner than he had in that easy summer of 1913.

By his junior year at Harvard, Alexander made the varsity football squad and played alongside the legendary Eddie Mahan, the original triple threat in passing, running, and kicking the ball. Though not a star like Mahan, McKinlock held his own—and on October 9, 1915, he intercepted a pass and ran it back for an eighty-yard touchdown against Carlisle.

In the spring of 1916, on the cusp of graduation, he was one of those young men in the Harvard Regiment drilling there in Harvard Yard, even though, it appears, his graduation was in some doubt. A degree, and the gift of a car from his parents, hung in the balance; nonetheless, Alexander felt optimistic enough that he picked out a color for the automobile and would write his father on April 7, 1916:

"Since all the returns from the hour exams are not in, I don't know whether I am relieved of my probation standing, but I can at least say that the mark I have heard of is better now than it was, for I had A- in German sight translation part and a B in the prepared reading of German 32 exam.

"I must close now since I have to study (these last few lines are so ingenuous and convincing that I fully expect a blank check with a 'Go as far as you like my boy, I am proud of you, yours is the spirit that wins out. Only remember, which I am sure you will, that anything is possible to him who wills.')"

In the summer of 1916, Alexander joined Richard Newhall, George Haydock, and the thousands of others at the Plattsburg camp. His mother, meanwhile, tried to match her son's zeal and joined some of her wealthy women friends and a bevy of college coeds at the National Service School Camp Number Three in Lake Geneva, Wisconsin.

She was instantly named brigadier general of the camp, which was all the rage in high society that summer. While talk of war and talk of preparedness dominated the conversations of husbands and sons and brothers, Marion McKinlock and each of her society friends turned out because they, like their men, were willing to offer their services "if the country needed them."

Operated by the Women's Section of the Navy League, the schools were intended "to train American women for the duties which come to them in war times and in other great national disasters." Such duties included "nursing the sick, feeding the hungry, making bandages . . . , and comforting the sorrows and relieving the necessities of those dependent upon the defenders of the Nation at the front. It is . . . one of the greatest movements among American women today," the Women's League would say.

With help from the military and the Red Cross, Marion McKinlock and her cohorts for two weeks attended such courses as Elementary Hygiene and Home Care of the Sick, First Aid to the Injured, and Preparation of Diets for the Sick. As well, there were lectures on Good Citizenship, American History, National Preparedness, and the Americanization of the Foreign Born.

The camp, for Mrs. McKinlock, went off without a hitch—except for one small hiccup duly reported by the *Chicago Daily Tribune* on August 24, under the headline ROOKIE OFFICER MAY STEP OUT? MRS. GEORGE MCKINLOCK, BRIGADIER GENERAL, FAILS TO GET LEAVE; "PEEVED."

"There was a partly empty table where Col. Lolita Armour sat down to her birthday dinner in camp tonight. Brig. Gen. Mrs. George McKinlock, Gen. Eleanor Countiss, Chief of Staff Vylia Poe Wilson, and Commander Jeannette Moffett were in conference.

"The party was half over before Gen. Countiss arrived with all her staff except Mrs. McKinlock, and the birthday feast went on without her. The reported resignation of Mrs. McKinlock has been talked about, it appears, at a most inopportune time. She remained in her tent. Explanation of Brig. Gen. McKinlock was that she sought leave to go to Lake Forest to her home and didn't get it."

So while the others enjoyed dinner and a celebration of the twentieth birthday of Lolita Armour—the "petted" only child of Chicago slaughterhouse magnate Louis Armour—the peeved and petulant Marion McKinlock on August 24, 1916, sat and stewed and fretted over the denial of her simple request for one night's leave to return to Brown Gables. In the end, Marion McKinlock remained at the camp, to learn to knit socks and sew bandages and to gain, it was hoped, "a certain power of self-effacement and an understanding of how superfluous are many of the things we have for a long time considered the ordinary necessities of life."

It would be when war came the following April that her largest sacrifice would be made, as she said good-bye to her only son, her only child, George Alexander McKinlock Jr., who on May 15, 1917, left the employ of his father's company. The elder McKinlock had insisted his son—despite, or maybe because of, the fact he was the boss's kid—begin his career at the bottom of the ladder.

(Their relationship, in fact, seems not to have been as cozy as that Alexander enjoyed with his mother. "It is unfortunate that you don't like to write letters," Alexander wrote to his father from France in May 1918, "for you see I have inherited that characteristic from you, and therefore do not keep very close touch.")

Where Richard Newhall and Bill Morgan would leave some sense of their motivations for enlisting—that vision of a better and unified world once rid of the rottenness—McKinlock, it appears, joined out of a sense of obligation, or simple duty. Like most of his peers, however, he had no interest in starting from the bottom in the army and set his sights on the officers' training camp at nearby Fort Sheridan, at which he was accepted.

"Many young men were drawn by the love of adventure and the excitement of getting into the fight," the Reverend Thayer would write. "McKinlock much preferred peace and the opportunity for other kinds of service, but nothing could keep him from fulfilling his obligation.

"From the moment his life began in the training camp . . . he entered heart and soul into the task before him using all his energies, physical, mental, and spiritual, in full measure pressed down and running over."

Marion McKinlock, perhaps finally realizing how truly "superfluous" the trimmings and finery of Brown Gables were amid the reality of sending a son to war, vowed to do her own bit and accepted the post of canteen commandant for the Red Cross in Chicago.

"In our time, if you lived on Deerpath Road, you lived a certain way," she would recall. "No lying in bed until 10 A.M., no reading stacks of novels."

Instead, "with a number of women, most of them social leaders," Marion McKinlock set up shop in the Chicago railroad yards, ministering to the boys heading east via thirty-seven railroad lines with hot coffee, cigarettes, jam sandwiches, and, before too long, fresh dressings for the wounded headed to western homes and hospitals. "At any hour, we were ready for road convoys or passing trainloads of soldiers," she would remember.

Alexander, meanwhile, went shoulder to shoulder with Bill Morgan and the many other well-heeled scions of Chicago industry at Fort Sheridan. The former football hero perhaps for the first time put his full energies into something other than sport, spending days and nights in the faux trenches and in war games, learning to use his powerful muscles to dig revetments and his football-groomed legs to march and drill under a hot July sun.

When August 15 came around he found that he, like Morgan, had the stuff of a second lieutenant. On September 9, 1917, Alexander McKinlock sailed for France, and whatever fate awaited him there.

"We didn't have a smell of a submarine," he would write of the crossing. "I don't think so much of the *unter-see-boten* [submarines]. Either the Germans are not making use of it, through lack of supplies, or else it's not an omnipotent weapon, but one which can be fairly well foiled by proper protection."

Arriving in England, McKinlock had a wait of a day and a half for a troop train to take him to Southampton. Once across at Le Havre, he rented a room; that night he took in a local theater and then invited "seven French officers for supper . . . in an upstairs room in the hotel." His French shaky, he found he could converse with one of the officers in a common language: German. "Rather odd to talk to my first ally in the enemy tongue," he wrote.

Unlike his Harvard cohorts, McKinlock bypassed a training stop with the British and instead was sent straight to the 1st Corps School at Gondrecourt. The army, it seems, had special plans for him, and whether because of his family's status and social connections or some inkling of higher ability—so his commanding officers would all say—he was put on something of a fast track at the school. If nothing else, he was offered a better chance to rub elbows with staff officers as he trained, and perhaps a better chance to be noticed when the time came for assignments and promotion.

That was where he found himself on October 22, 1917, writing Marion McKinlock to tell of his deprivations since leaving the United States and arriving at Gondrecourt, where for the time being he was billeted with other Americans in barracks.

"It was a relief to settle down even though the accommodations aren't any too dry," he would write. "The sleeping bag with waterproof cover has been just the thing, for during the first week there were three leaks in the roof, but now I have moved to a dry spot."

Like many young American officers billeted in the towns around Gondrecourt, he had struck up friendly relationships with several families near his leaky billet.

"I have been taking an hour's French at seven P.M. from a middle-aged woman in the village," he wrote. "This evening I walked down to the Flaubert's, a French family, who do my linen. I spent an hour in the kitchen, talking and explaining the advertisements in the *Saturday Evening Post*. We buy grapes, apples, figs, chocolate and English walnuts at these tiny little shops run by a mother and a daughter.

"There are few men and everyone looks new to us. There's a general feeling, felt more than expressed, that they would have closed shop over here if we hadn't come in. The grey color which one sees everywhere is monotonous and rather depressing; it would be even more so if it were home and we had three years of it."

Still, he would write, "we are gradually getting used to the rain and the mud. The last ten days have passed quickly and soon our term over here will be over; what will happen then, none of us know."

9

Damn This War

He wants to do well but he's just too, well, too damn *nice*. The men sense that he's in over his head, just a kid out right out of college while some of them have knocked around the army for years and know the drill inside and out. Now, they try not to laugh at him, some of them, but for Christ's sakes he's so nervous his knees are knocking, his lips trembling, and he doesn't bark his orders so much as issue them as pleas.

He has a lot to learn, does 1st Lt. George Guest Haydock.

"The trouble is I don't understand the men and they don't understand or give a damn for me," Haydock would write in November 1917. "I am too polite with them and suppose I will remain so till I really get mad some time and start to treat them like brutes, which seems to be the proper way to handle them. It is what they expect, and something certainly unnatural for me and I feel now as though I never could learn to talk to them properly and give them the right kind of dressing down.

"It really is a joke to try to cuss out a good hayseed tough from Texas and I consider that I have done a good job if I can get away before they laugh at me. Being naturally kind hearted and not a born hard guy it strains my bluffing powers to the limit to tell a big thug he needs a bath or that his bunk is dirty."

They might have told him at Plattsburg there would be days like this, but they didn't. Plattsburg was all about potential, the actual art of leadership being left to be learned through experience, if at all.

Of course, some were born leaders and innately understood the delicate mix of hard authority and occasional and limited compassion that comprised leadership in the army. For the Quaker George Haydock, raised to see the good in all men, taught in the school in Germantown that he was no better than anyone else, barking orders and getting into the faces of the hard-bitten regulars of the 1st Platoon of Company L, 28th Infantry Regiment, U.S. 1st Division didn't come easily.

Still, he was happy to have the job, or *any* job after sitting idle for eight days after reporting to the 28th's headquarters at St. Amand, awaiting the return of the company from the trenches and stewing over his predicament as an unattached officer.

Finally, on November 20, Haydock and a group of new men were ordered to help arrange for the return of Company L. "When we arrived we found one Lt. from L Company and after bickering with the mayor for a while were finally told that we would be billeted in the hospital for the time being," he wrote.

Unable to find a cot, he spread his blanket on the hospital's stone floor. A squad of new recruits was sent on to a loft in a nearby barn. "They billeted one squad in the loft of a barn and the thing collapsed dropping the whole bunch," he wrote. "It is the original mess if ever I saw one, but it has the redeeming feature of being amusing because it does seem so absurd."

He would note the inevitable speculation that swirled within the regiment. "There are the most wonderful rumors floating around having us spend the winter anywhere from Italy to Bordeaux, in the trenches or here, but the latter I am afraid will be the case. The latest is that the division will take over on Jan. 27.

"I think I shall start one that we are going home."

That same night, the 28th's 3rd Battalion returned from the line. Haydock, after spending the night in the hospital, reported to the battalion's commander, Maj. Francis H. Burr, a Massachusetts native who, after graduating from Norwich University in Vermont, had been commissioned as a second lieutenant on October 28, 1902, at the age of twenty-one.

The former second lieutenant seemed more bemused than angry at having to dispose of more than a dozen George Haydocks crowding his headquarters.

"Like all others he expressed surprise at finding some 15 new officers dropped out of the blue into his battalion," Haydock wrote. "Nevertheless he was much more civil to us than the others had been and told us to report to our companies at about 9."

At the assigned time, Haydock and two other officers—Earle Carrothers and Edmund P. Glover—reported to Company L's commander, Francis Van Natter. Haydock's first impressions of the Hoosier were favorable.

"He seems to be very nice and to know his job," Haydock wrote. "He was surprised to see us too, and said he now had 11 officers so I am afraid we will not have much to do here either."

Haydock and four other neophyte officers—Glover, Carrothers, the Georgian John Glascock Mays, and the New Hampshire native Arthur McKay—finally found billets on the first floor of a dank farm home they would dub "the Cave," where they were introduced to the peculiarities of the rural French.

The rooms were "dirty and damp," Haydock would write. "There is a manure pile and canal at the front door, and an occupied pig here in our immediate rear, in fact he can look right in the window at us. They have a damn funny way of living in this country, the cow or pig has the front room which is usually the best, and the people live in the back room."

He was amused by the home's great hearth and its funnel-shaped chimney. The spare living conditions included "a large and extremely dirty bed built into the wall. There is a really fine old wardrobe that I would like to swipe, but as it fills up about one quarter of the room I am afraid I could not get it into my two by twice locker."

The French inhabitants, meanwhile, had "adjourned I think to the attic, although as yet I have not been able to catch them there. They consist of an old man and his daughter. The old man is only 81 and his daughter I should say was about 70, although that does not seem quite right.

"The old man says he fought in the Napoleonic wars and so he gets very clubby with us. He comes in and jabbers at us a mile a minute and always ends up by asking for a cigarette. Yesterday he came in when I was out and sat down on my cot much to my regret for as I found out last night when he departed he left some of his smaller inhabitants in my care."

As for the pig, "he has a promenade in the backyard but takes his meals indoors and is very noisy about it," Haydock wrote. "His chief amusement is to climb up on the manure pile outside the window and look in on us and make what we were sure were nasty remarks, so to get even with him we had the old man move said pile, which he promptly placed on the front doorstep, causing a storm of bad French and most expressive English."

Still, he added, the old man "works very hard to get on the right side of us because he wants us to provide meals for his live stock, and he has a rooster he thinks would look well on the officers' mess table. The result is we are now furnished with a table and a park bench which is indeed a luxury.

"Our chief trouble now consists in trying to keep the pig and some chickens out of our room, but I think we have got the upper hand now and believe me we intend to keep it. It does not take long for certain of one's pet ideas to vanish into thin air in these parts but I still object to sleeping with a pig and have been very successful in making him keep his distance till we are properly introduced."

The 3rd Battalion's men, meanwhile, went through delousing to remove the pets they had acquired in the trenches. "This morning they inspected the men who came in from the line last night for bugs, and found 128 of them" had lice, Haydock wrote. "They are isolated, given a bath in gasoline and their clothes put through the steam sterilizing cart which looks like an extraordinary form of water wagon. Watching the men scratch has made me feel bugs running all over me and it has almost convinced me that I have them too."

The spare conditions, which included at that moment a lack of food on top of the damp and dirty environment, led one young lieutenant to remark that "it was something like Valley Forge, but I am sure it is more amusing," Haydock would write, "although it begins to get on my nerves a little having nothing to do.

"They say we are likely to be transferred at any moment and that everything that goes on is entirely experimental, and we are the goats."

By November 25, things were looking up for George. Each officer was assigned his own "striker," or orderly, and Haydock was given the task of holding reveille in the morning and retreat at night.

At inspection, Haydock was told to make sure Company L's 1st Platoon members were "clean and uninhabited" by lice—and was instantly intimidated by having to ride herd on a group that included some hardened veterans.

"I may state that there are moments in my life when I have had the wind up, but the first time I ever had an honest to God job, to have it with regulars was a little more than I was looking for," he wrote.

"Fortunately I had just read it up in the drill book or I should never have known what to do, but I think I got away with it though I could feel my knees knocking when I got out to the front of the platoon."

He intended "to bluff my way along as much as possible and try to get away with it. Being with regulars all work is really much easier because the noncoms are fine and the men of course all know what they are doing a great deal better than I ever thought of knowing it, and if I am careful they may make a soldier out of me yet."

He quickly learned the importance of relying on a few veteran and able noncommissioned officers to show him the way. "The only saving grace in my case is the good noncoms," he wrote. "If they will help me all will be well."

It was also good fortune for Haydock that he had the sympathy of some regular officers who were willing to make sure the newly minted first lieutenant didn't fall flat on his face. Among these was the former noncom and recently promoted 2nd Lt. Charles Mord Stromberg, whose varied pedigree echoed that of Axel Rasmussen, and who took pity on Haydock that November.

Stromberg, who would become great friends as well with Richard Newhall, had come to the army late in life, after years of aimless bumming around Canada, Cuba, Mexico, and the United States. Born of Swedish ancestry on Prince Edward Island in 1870, he had an older brother, John Alexander, who was a noted composer and bandleader in the latter part of the nineteenth century and who churned out such hits as "My Girl's a Corker" and "Hoity Toity."

John Alexander—though born Strambergs, he and Charles would take the surname Stromberg—ultimately found huge success as the musical director of the Weber and Fields Music Hall in New York City, where "the company included Broadway's brightest talent with the most radiant star of all, Lillian Russell," one account of his life says.

Charles Stromberg, meanwhile, had been on the move since he was just eight years old, growing to a towering 6′7″ on a slight 151-pound frame while taking up with various relatives in Canada, then seeking his fortune in the United States. "It seems my fate that I shall never live more than three years in one place at a time," he would write.

In 1887, he left Canada for New London, Connecticut, where he "started to travel as a companion to a rich old invalid; we traveled over pretty nearly all of the Eastern States and finally he died in Toronto, Ontario." He went on to Mexico, where he worked on the national railroad, and then drifted north to Kentucky, where he spent the summer of 1892 in similar fashion. After a few years in New Jersey, Stromberg sailed for Cuba in the spring of 1895.

In Cuba, he apparently fought and ran guns for the rebel army. "I did not receive a scratch although I was under fire several times, but I was terribly sick," he would write. "I strayed away from the band I was with one time and got lost in a swamp and took the fever, I don't know whether it was the yellow fever or not, but I was delirious for I don't know how long."

Two girls "whose brothers were in the rebel army found me lying unconscious, and dragged me to their home on a sort of a sled drawn by a jackass. I don't know anything about it but what they told me afterwards.

"The first thing I remember is, that an old priest was at my side, I think he was going to administer the last rites of the church; at this time I am very sorry to say I swore horribly, in English, and the good man did not understand me. He said to one of the girls, 'The poor young man still lives.' I then said to him in Spanish, 'I am much obliged to your reverence for your kindness but I am a Protestant.'

"He left on hearing that but the women were just as good as ever."

By August 1896 he had changed his name to Charles Hudson and left Cuba because "the climate was so severe on me." He wandered on to Ventura, California. "I have a good job here now, working as a gardener for an old Spanish lady who does not speak a word of English," he told his sister Elizabeth in a letter.

He would say of his ramblings: "During all my wanderings I have never begged or stolen and have always kept sober and have never seen the inside of a jail and always keep respectable company."

In May 1901 Stromberg enlisted in the United States Army, in which he would finally find a permanent home—and one that satisfied his wanderlust. He listed his birthplace as Mexico City, for whatever reason, and before long found himself in the Philippines.

He was cited for distinguished action in a skirmish with the Moros at Mange Swamp on November 16, 1903. April 6, 1917, found him serving as a sergeant with the 28th Regiment on the Mexican border of Texas—and at the age of forty-seven, Stromberg was one of those regular non-coms who would quickly be granted an officers' commission as the army tried to fill its ranks with leaders.

Worldly, calm, instinctively friendly and unflinching, he was assigned to Company L while still in Texas, and his wanderings would end in furious battle at the Paris-Soissons Road in July 1918.

"When the bullet struck him he had his pipe in one hand and tobacco in the other," Sgt. George Hunsiger would say of Stromberg's demise. "He had said several times that: 'When you see me in the battlefield I will be smoking my pipe just like this.' "

That would be some months after George Haydock, to his great relief, found the former soldier of fortune Stromberg serving as officer of the day on November 26, when Haydock was named officer of the guard.

Haydock struggled with the duty. "I had retreat first, and then after reporting the Co present to the O.D. went on down to get the new guard from K Co.," he wrote. "I was supposed to act as O.D. and inspect the guard, and then march them to the post.

"When I got about halfway way down I met the guard all ready formed coming up. I asked the sergeant if he had inspected them and he said they had been at retreat so that is how they got away so soon.

"I told him I was officer of the guard and thought he understood so I marched them around, got them into line by the old guard, and then the sergeant gave them present arms. I did not know just what to do, but Stromberg who was the new O.D. came to my rescue and so I carried on. There was one prisoner, so I verified him and took him to his place and told the sergeant to carry on with the posting."

That night, George was to inspect the guard every two hours. On one visit, he found that "one man was off his post, but Stromberg was out at the same time and we both found him together and I proceeded to bawl him out in good shape. I caught on to quite a lot about the way things are done and will be able to get away with it again O.K."

For the rest of the duty, Haydock censored soldiers' letters home—which "were as a whole rather cheerful, some of them rather pathetic and all very much the same."

Mocking their simplicity—to be fair, censorship forbade saying where a soldier was or what he had been up to—Haydock wrote: "I will now take this opportunity to write you a short letter in reply to your welcome letter received two weeks ago. Tell Mary hello for me. Is my old hog fat yet. Tell Jane to send me her photo and if she wants mine ask brother Jack to send it to her."

Haydock's duties quickly expanded when on Monday, December 3, he was put in charge of Company L's 1st Platoon. Second Lt. Howard E. Hawkinson, a Syracuse, New York, native who had enlisted in the army in 1916 and completed his officers' training at Fort Leavenworth before being assigned to the 28th Regiment while it mobilized on the Texas border, was made his second in command.

Haydock quickly realized he was still in over his head. "In the afternoon came my downfall," he would write. "Got away to a very poor start with the platoon. We had company drill and I made a lot of bad bulls and got in wrong with both the captain and the men, so I am in for a hard job to get into favor. I learned a lot of things *not* to do and seemed to forget everything I ever knew about drill."

He would eventually learn Axel Rasmussen's axiom and first make sure above all that his men were comfortable and happy, but, flailing around in the cold of that early winter, Haydock continued to try to strike an equilibrium between the chummy relationship between officers and men that he observed in the British Army, and the more detached, disciplinarian role expected of him among the Americans.

"Nearly all the other U.S.R.s are experiencing pretty much the same thing except for the really hard guys who get along splendidly with the men and get results beside, chiefly due to the fact that they can talk to them in their own language," he wrote.

"The whole idea of ordering people about is a strange one to me, and I certainly have a large order to be with this bunch, who . . . seem to be the ranking regiment of the First Division, and therefore probably as good as any regulars in our service."

The task was "the hardest I have ever run up against in my life, and I can fully say that I do not relish it one little bit. In fact I look forward to taking charge of my platoon for company drill about like a night-mare.

"DAMN THIS WAR ANYHOW!"

If he was looking for sympathy or respite from the burdens of leadership, he didn't find it at night in his officers' quarters. "There are five of us in this billet and we spend an hour every day expressing perfectly frank opinions of each other and usually end up getting so mad that it is funny, so we really get along fairly well."

On December 5, the 28th Regiment was ordered to Gondrecourt to be inspected by Pershing, Gen. Tasker Bliss, Woodrow Wilson's adviser Col. Edward M. House, and several staff members and aides.

The "proceeding . . . was the cause of a great deal of trouble on our parts," Haydock would write. "In the first place we had to get up at 3:30 in the morning when it was cold as Greenland.

"We had breakfast and got started by 5 o'clock. It was still as dark as could be and stayed so until about 6:30. The whole regiment marched to Gondrecourt about 15 miles, with tin hats, overcoats and light packs. My opinion of the general immediately dropped considerably, but there was nothing for it but climb out and hike."

Through snow and cold, "we made almost 10 miles before daylight. When just about 3 miles from [Gondrecourt] we had two waits of an hour each while it snowed very hard. The roads were not very good because they were frozen and slippery, but it was a relief to get away from the mud."

In Gondrecourt, the 1st Division "lined up our lines on either side of the street with the colors. After waiting for about half an hour the generals march was played and we stood at attention for about 10 minutes then present arms and we saluted while the party walked slowly the whole length of the regiment. I thought my arm would break for it took them nearly 15 minutes. The tin hat, however, proved its usefulness, because since it had a stiff brim I was able to hook my fingers on it and get a little support."

Fortunately, the review over, the regiment was allowed to ride back to St. Amand in trucks. Because of the nasty conditions outside, Haydock and the other platoon commanders found themselves lecturing their men inside the dank billets, usually nothing more than a straw-smattered barn.

The 28th's commander, Col. Hanson Ely, had issued orders that in the event of bad weather "platoon commanders will assemble their non-commissioned officers for talk on care of clothing, equipment and arms."

Haydock's talk went beyond clothes and weapons, drawing on any source of entertainment he could think up. "I had to lecture my platoon for four hours, keep them interested and warm on a very cold day," he wrote. "It was a good deal of a strain but I lived through it and kept them fairly interested by getting off about every wild tale I had heard when at school."

The next day, Company L once again took to the snowy surroundings for the beginning of what would be three days of maneuvers in "open warfare," each day beginning at 3:30 A.M. and ending at 3:00 P.M., when, cold and tired, the men returned to their billets.

"Of course our company got the most work to do," Haydock wrote. "Each day we would hike from 10 to 15 miles and take up a position. We had to run up and down every snowy hill in sight and believe me they are numerous and steep.

"It is the first time I have ever had to handle men and after being liberally cussed out learned a great deal. I am afraid I am too polite to be a soldier, it is not in me to bawl men out the way it should be done, but I learned a lot through rather bitter experience.

"I am getting a little more brass but feel a good deal like a fish out of water. I am glad tomorrow is a holiday because they did their best to walk the legs off us and keep us working most of the night and day. We are all good and tough now."

Throughout December, as thoughts of Christmas and warm billets occupied the men's minds, the 28th Regiment once more engaged in maneuvers. The training was intense, and so were the snow, rain, and mud, as the 1st Division tried to catch up with the war. The large-scale maneuvers were performed at "Washington Center" near Gondrecourt, where a full battle line with frontline, support, and reserve trenches had been dug, and strings of barbed wire laid, Maurice Edwards would remember.

The days were long, the conditions brutal.

Rising well before dawn, "the day goes through like clock-work, sometimes with close-order drill and sometimes with special maneuvers till 10 or 11 P.M., Sundays included, Edwards wrote.

"At night the platoon leader must see that all the platoon bathe their feet in cold water and rub them, for fifteen minutes thereafter, to prevent trench feet . . . We have to prepare for serious business by crowding a year into six months, and so we're fatigued by any number of maneuvers in order not to be wiped out by ignorance."

During the maneuvers, "every detail is carried out as in an actual offensive on the front. The men go at it with earnestness and purpose. I heard one of them the other day say to a buddy, 'I wish we could get through educating these officers.'

"On maneuver day, we leave our billets during the night, and dawn discloses long columns of artillery with the horses straining up the steep hills or slipping and falling on the sleet-covered roads. Then come the masses of infantry moving along silently as if the outcome of the 'battle' depended upon their getting in position on time. After it is all over, the men, wet, cold, and hungry, march back to the billets for the only hot meal of the day."

The 1st Division's commander Gen. Robert Lee Bullard, appreciated the trying conditions. Nevertheless, with the expected German spring offensive, the work had to go on even in the worst of the winter weather, Bullard wrote in his 1925 book *Personalities and Reminiscences of the War*:

"There was nothing for the Americans to do but continue their training no matter what the weather or what the suffering," he wrote. "In the last two weeks of 1917, in cold, hard December weather, the 1st Division were executing manoeuvres which required camping overnight, sleeping upon the ground, and standing in the open during hours and hours of waiting, chilled by winds after being wet with rain."

The 1st Division, he added, had no choice.

"If they failed the world would say that America would fail. For this reason the drill and training were probably made the hardest that ever American troops were put through. No consideration of the peculiarities of officers, no personal considerations were allowed to interfere with the plan."

If it was any consolation to George Haydock, "it had been decided by General Pershing that the very best officers that could be made available should be given to the 1st Division," Bullard added. "Therefore this training was made a severe test of officers and non-commissioned officers."

The training schedule outlined in the division's records for the week leading up to Christmas left little room for relaxation:

17th—Company in open war—Advance and Rear Guard, patrols, scouting, in attack and defense.

18th—Brigade problem.

19th—Battalion against battalion in attack and defence.

20th—Company and platoon, close order. Target practice.

21st

22nd—Division Maneuvers.

23rd

24th—School of soldier, group, platoon, and company, extended. Target practice.

Within the broader scope of training there were smaller problems to solve on a squad level, including raiding and holding enemy trenches. Maurice Edwards would describe one such exercise, which involved raiding dummy trenches dug in the fields near Gondrecourt and labeled on maps and aerial photos as Essen, Potsdam, Bremen, and Coblenz:

"Squad A will take and occupy the Essen trench. Four men and a corporal will establish a barricade at *a*. Another barricade at *b* will be held by four men. Squad B will get into communication trench Potsdam and will go to trench Bremen . . . Squad C will get into Coblenz trench and will establish liaison with Squad B at *d*. A team composed of four grenadiers and two rifle grenadier men will establish a barricade at *e*. The rest of the squad will blow up dugout at 18 . . . The commanding officer goes with squad B as soon as liaison is established with squad C. He carries with him a Very pistol with two yellow rockets, the signal for return."

That wasn't all the commanding officer would carry. In what reads like a passage from Tim O'Brien's *The Things They Carried,* George Haydock would describe the layers of his accoutrements while on drill in the bitter cold:

"Starting at the bottom I wear the heaviest underclothes I own, flannel shirt sweater and uniform, either my big boots or heavy shoes and spiral putties. Over this I wear my sheepskin coat, carry a pack with two days' rations, blanket poncho, shelter tent and an extra pair of shoes and mess kit.

"On my belt I wear a canteen, first aid packet, automatic and two extra clips, a Veri pistol, which is a modified form of shotgun to fire rockets with, around my neck I wear an English small box respirator which is a gas mask with a box to take air in, and is about a foot square.

"On the other side I wear a French gas mask which is smaller and not so good, to be used only in case the English one goes bad. I also have a dispatch case containing note books, papers, compass, pencils etc. and am supposed to have field glasses beside them to crown the whole business."

Also, of course, there was his "tin hat, which resembles a coal scuttle, and may be used for anything from a rocking chair to a wash basin. After getting us dolled up like this they march us anywhere from three to five miles, stage a fight, and march us in again. We carry one small sandwich for lunch and think we are lucky if they do not pull us out of bed at 3:30."

He would add: "They surely are working us fit to kill now, and we are getting to be pretty tough animals. They have gotten the bad idea that we must not move without full packs so I disguise myself as a Christmas tree before going out to drill just to give them an idea of what we look like."

The men underwent two types of exercises—either open or trench warfare. "If open, we go anywhere from two to five miles across country over the darnedest hills I have ever seen, they are nothing less than cliffs," Haydock wrote. "The trench variety is not quite so strenuous but more confusing and very cold as we invariably have to do a lot of standing around after a hot hike."

On December 21, another maneuver was announced, and Haydock and his platoon "packed up our bedrolls and packs, and prepared for what might come." During the exercise, the 28th's 3rd Battalion was held in reserve to "defend" St. Amand as the other units moved out—"and the result was that we stood from nine in the morning until six at night, ready to move at a moment's notice."

At 6:00 P.M., Company L was sent forward to act as guard for the 2nd Brigade for the night. "That came as a blow," Haydock wrote, "as I had visions of sleeping in my billet. We had a few minutes to get an egg and piece of ham for supper, and were then shown what part of the world we had to cover. I was given about fifty men to cover approximately three miles on the extreme right flank, and we were told that a brigade of the enemy had been advancing on us and were occupying the next town."

At 7:00 P.M., Haydock moved his men out and set up four outposts, two of which were in shacks and two of which were in the open—meaning no fires could be lit. After walking five miles to get the men posted, Haydock chose a spot in the center of the men on "a high ridge with the coldest wind I have ever known blowing about thirty miles an hour straight on us," he wrote.

He had packed up much of his extra clothing in his bedroll, which was left behind on the company wagon, leaving him with one blanket, a towel, a shelter half, and two days' rations.

"I found a place where the grass was sticking up through the snow, and told the men with me (about fifteen) they could settle there or in a clump of woods nearby," he wrote. "I chose the grass, opened up my pack, and to start with was fairly warm, as I had walked about five miles to get the sentries posted.

"It was a beautiful, clear, moonlight night, and I smoked my pipe to try to kid myself to sleep; and just as I was dozing off the Captain came around to see my disposition of the troops, and after he left I slept for about an hour and woke up half frozen; so I did the rounds to inspect the outposts and sat by a fire until I was thawed out."

Every two hours, he would check the outposts "and managed to sleep a little between times. At eight-thirty in the morning, having had no breakfast, I was told to prepare to act as rear-guard for the brigade when they came through and in the meantime to cook what we could from our iron ration. A few minutes later the head of the column started to come through, so we had to hurry to get anything to eat."

At 9:30 A.M., the tail of the brigade passed by, and Haydock and his platoon marched at its rear until noon. The brigade then simulated an attack—which rambled nearly five miles through the woods and "over hills and streams and anything that happened to be in the way.

"It developed into a pursuit, so we had to keep going ahead just as fast as we could hike, till about four, when in all we had gone about ten miles. The General then decided we had won a decisive victory (I never saw the enemy), and that we could go home.

"I was sure glad to see my bed, and rolled into it as soon as I got some beans to line my stomach with. The men went through it all without growling as much as they do during an ordinary drill, and I think in all we made a pretty creditable showing. Our Company had the hardest jobs to do, and were the only ones to spend the night in the open; they always seem to pick on us."

Thoughts of the impending Christmas holiday only made George depressed. "I haven't had a chance to get the spirit yet," he lamented to his mother. "It makes me mighty homesick to think of the carols in Boston.

"Thee said thee guessed a quiet life would never appeal to me again but as soon as I strike home it will take more than dynamite to move me, and that is no joke. When I come home I am coming to stay. Not even the charms of North Andover will drag me away."

Christmas brought snow—and a day of respite and reflection.

"Yesterday one of the other officers billeted here and I got talking about where we were a year ago," Haydock wrote, "and we decided among other things that it would not be Christmas without stockings, so we agreed to fill each other's.

"After supper we started out to do our Christmas shopping. We went around to little different stores in the town, and bought sticks of candy, nuts, mandarins and such little things and managed to get quite excited doing it."

He slept late, "and woke to find that it had snowed some more and it was a real white Christmas. In my stocking I found some Bull Durham, tooth powder, nuts, chocolate, chewing gum, cigarette papers and in the toe as always a mandarin.

"I have just eaten a most wondrous dinner with turkey and all the fixings brought all the way from the States. It was a regular blow out, and to celebrate we had a fire in the mess room so we did not have to keep our coats on. The whole company had the same dinner that we did and I am sure they were well satisfied."

In the afternoon, the YMCA put on a pageant for the children of St. Amand. "All the kids of the town less than 12 years old were invited up with their familys," Haydock wrote. "The hut was nicely fixed up, a great big Christmas tree filling up one end and the rest decorated with streamers, paper flags, and anything that could be gotten to add an air of festivity.

"The tree was covered with toys and lit up with candles and there was a great pile of things under it. The Mayor was present all dressed up like an Easter egg, and as he read the names each child stepped forward and was given a toy, some candy and nuts.

"The kids' eyes were fairly popping out of their heads and they were very cute as they retired laden down with rocking horses, dolls, or some kind of a game. The men enjoyed it as much as anyone, and I guess it was a better Christmas party than most of the youngsters had ever seen before."

The next day, it was back to work.

"I guess from now on it will be the real thing," Haydock would write, adding that the work "consists largely in marching or standing around in the cold. We marched to Abainville which is just this side of Gondrecourt, a hard four hour march concluded by standing around for an hour and a half waiting to be billeted.

"I got cold as the devil and had a peach of a chill after I got into bed. We had a fair but awful cold billet but a very good officers mess. Some of the men had to sleep on concrete floors with almost no straw and it sure was cold."

The following days brought more standing around in the cold and snow—and the expectation that they would soon enter the trenches. "I have gotten the frame of mind where I would be glad to go into the line, anything to get away from this place and this business of stalling around. It all seems so futile, and I think it is," Haydock wrote.

Like many a young lieutenant, Haydock was skeptical as to whether the exercises had imparted any practical knowledge.

"I have not learned anything very valuable and I am quite sure the men have not," he wrote. "However they say that the generals are getting experience in handling large bodies of troops. If they are it is worth while to stand around and freeze if they are going to be able to run us better when we get started."

He appreciated the "argument" that "they have been knocking us around like this so we would be glad to get a chance to fight. I think it has had that effect on many of us."

Ever the fatalist, Haydock would add: "I should like to go up and get a good blighty right away. That would be very convenient and save an awful lot of bother.

"What will happen though," he added cynically, "is I will get along O.K. till the day before they call the war off and then get checked.

"It's a bonne war."

10

Don't Worry

THIS ONE IS UP late this night in his sparse billet, taking a quiet moment to consider and reflect upon the possibility of death, his own death, which seems reasonable given that there's a world war on just a few kilometers away, and given that at its base the reason he had been sent to France was to kill or be killed by Germans, or both.

Thus it is with great interest that on this evening George Buchanan Redwood finds himself paging through *A Student in Arms,* written by the British soldier Donald Hankey, pausing at the chapter titled "Don't Worry."

Hankey, born four years before Redwood, had spent four years as a soldier before resigning to attend divinity school at Oxford. He reenlisted in August 1914 and was serving as a lieutenant when he was killed in action on October 12, 1916; in 1917, his writings from the front lines were collected into *A Student in Arms,* which found much resonance in Redwood.

"The whole teaching of the Gospels is that we have got to find freedom and peace in trusting ourselves implicitly to the care of God," Hankey wrote. "We have got to follow what we think quite recklessly, and leave the issue to God; and in judging between right and wrong we are only given two rules for our guidance. Everything which shows love for

God and love for man is right, and everything which shows personal ambition and anxiety is wrong.

"What this all means as far as the trenches are concerned is extraordinarily clear. The Christian is advised not to be too pushing or ambitious. He is advised to 'take the lowest room.' But if he is told to move up higher, he has got to go. If he is given responsibility, there is no question of refusing it. He has got to do his best and leave the issue to God . . .

"As for personal danger, he must not think of it. If he is killed, that is a sign that he is no longer indispensable. Perhaps he is wanted elsewhere . . . Every man who goes to war must, if he is to be happy, give his body, a living sacrifice, to God and his country. It is no longer his. He need not worry about it."

"Strange to say I have been feeling utterly careless and irresponsible for some time," Redwood writes upon reflection, "and it was just as I was beginning to be smitten with the fact that I ought to take things more seriously that I struck the 'Don't Worry.'

"I think Hankey's idea is the right one so long as one is conscious of trying to do one's best and sticking at one's work. I regret to say, however, that I have not put in the time that I should in studying my profession of late, and I must get busy."

George Buchanan Redwood has heard the war calling out to him for years and has struggled not to answer, struggled to remain at his desk at the Moffett-Lynch Advertising Company in Baltimore ("Our Bedrock Policy: We will never—regardless of possible profit—prepare or place Unclean or Dishonest Advertising"), while covering cops and real estate at the *Baltimore News,* and while attending the Plattsburg camps in 1915 *and* 1916.

He had longed for war his whole life, ever since he had spread his lead soldiers on the floor of his parents' home and marveled at the pomp and panoply of his arrangement; and the war had waited for him, even as he puttered in this job and that for seven years following graduation from Harvard in 1910.

"He was the only boy I ever knew whose main interest was almost *exclusively* warfare," one childhood pal would recall, and some of that interest surely coursed through young George Redwood through his family line, which included his distant relative Capt. John Chowning, who served throughout the Revolution in the Virginia Cavalry, and a great-grandfather, Col. James Chowning, a gallant officer in the War of 1812.

As well, three of his uncles on the Redwood side—Allen Christian, James William, and Harry—left their father's home in King George County, Virginia, to serve with the Confederacy in the Civil War.

Allen, in particular, had had a colorful war, serving with the 55th Virginia Infantry in the Army of Northern Virginia, in which he saw action in the Seven Days battles, at Fredericksburg and Gettysburg, at Second Bull Run, and in other places before being taken prisoner; he remained incarcerated until the conflict ended in 1865.

Afterward, Allen Redwood became a prolific author and illustrator of the Lost Cause, writing articles and books—a memoir of Stonewall Jackson, a biography of J. E. B. Stuart titled *Following Stuart's Feather*—and painting and drawing scenes from First Fredericksburg, Second Manassas, Gettysburg, Marye's Heights, and other battles he witnessed firsthand. His words and paintings documenting the Confederate effort appeared in magazines such as *Harper's* and *The Century*.

Born in 1856, George Redwood's father, Francis Tazewell Redwood, was too young to be gloried in the War Between the States. He instead left the home of William Holman Redwood for Baltimore and entered Loyola College. As a young man he went to work for the banking and brokerage firm of Brown & Lowndes in Baltimore, "and his talents and close attention to business soon won the regard of his employers," his obituary says.

He took to the turn-of-the-last-century life of the nouveau riche with panache, purchasing several yachts, becoming a charter member of the Baltimore Yacht Club, being quickly accepted into the Baltimore Club and the Baltimore Country Club, and serving on the board of the Maryland Club. He had other interests beyond mere social climbing, however, and was "an enthusiastic huntsman and often went on hunting trips to the lodges of the South."

In 1887, Frank Redwood settled down with Mary Buchanan Coale, and on September 30th, 1888, George Buchanan Redwood made his appearance. While Frank made the money and enjoyed the manly life of a sportsman, Mary doted on her young son. Through his life George Redwood would call her "Mom-Mom"; for reasons unknown, he was given the moniker "Koots."

It was Mom-Mom's cherished mother, Caroline Coale, who became George's "greatest influence," the one most responsible for George's "deep abiding faith, and the tenderness of heart and high ideals which characterized his whole life," Mary Redwood would write.

Caroline Coale, she added, "was a woman of keen intelligence, wide reading and broad sympathies—an ideal companion to guide and encourage his imaginative, sensitive nature. From . . . early talks and childhood books [George] was led by his grandmother through many old English ballads, stories of heroism, Kipling and the Ingoldsby legends. Dana's Household Book of Poetry and other collections of verse were well loved and many of the poems were learned from their pages."

The tales of chivalry apparently took hold of his imagination at a young age, and Caroline Coale also instilled in George, wrote Mary, "his deep interest and love of the Church and his real enjoyment of the services."

There's some sense, though, that the coddling he received at the hands of Mom-Mom and Grannie Coale in the home at 918 Madison Avenue left him unprepared for the realities of the outside world. Perhaps out of loneliness he acquired a make-believe friend he named Ned; this Mom-Mom would take as a "quaint" example of George's imagination.

The introverted boy let his imagination loose in writing and illustrating; while at Baltimore's Country School for Boys he penned such tales as "Khih-ch-ou, the Dragon: The Tale of a Sneeze"; a story about a German-American family called "Uncle Franzl's Resurrection"; a morality tale titled "Company Manners" ("Well composed," Redwood's instructor would write, while giving him an A-minus for his effort), and, keeping true to his interest in war, a fictional account of a Spanish-American War naval battle called "The Fight off Sandago."

It wouldn't be until he was sixteen years old that George Redwood gained a sibling, his brother, Francis, entering the world in December

1904. Two years later, George left for Harvard—and late that same year, tragedy found its way into the Redwood home.

In November 1906, Frank Redwood, just fifty years old and ever the outdoorsman, was traveling by train as a guest of Samuel Spencer, the president of the Southern Railway. On its way to a hunting preserve in North Carolina that was owned by Spencer, "the private car was attached to the Jacksonville Express, which broke down," Frank's obituary reported.

"The Atlanta Express, following closely behind, plowed into the Jacksonville train, killing all four of the friends in Mr. Spencer's car, as well as two Negro porters," Jack Redwood, Frank Redwood's nephew, would relate in his memoirs.

Frank Redwood apparently left a tidy sum behind when he passed, as a future employer of George would note that "it was not necessary that he should toil." However, the same source—the former city editor of the *Baltimore News*—would write: "Many a young man in his position has despised the indignity of work and squandered a fortune in idleness and prodigality. Redwood wasn't made of that sort of stuff. He wanted a busy, useful life."

Though away at school when Frank Redwood died, George made a special effort to keep tabs on Francis. He wrote letters and postcards filled with drawings of soldiers and weapons and trains, addressing Francis as "Sir" and "Master Francis T. Redwood." Francis would later say of his late father, who died when Francis was just one year old: "I don't miss him, George is a father to me, and a brother, too."

At Harvard, Redwood's dual nature of being seriously religious on one hand and an inveterate and irreverent wit and prankster on the other was revealed. "I used to get quite annoyed with him in college because he seemed to feel no obligation to support anything merely because it was religious," a classmate, the future Rev. Floyd K. Tomkins Jr., remembered.

"He nearly broke up our little Brotherhood of St. Andrew by a wild and whirling joke of his own devising, the 'Brotherhood of St. Charles.' He didn't care a snap for the fact that we were pious and well-intentioned persons—he just sailed in with his slap-dash horse-play as gaily as if he were breaking up a literary coterie of high-brows instead of an earnest bunch of young Christians."

After graduating from Harvard, where he became friends with George Haydock's older brother, Robert, Redwood indulged an interest in Germany, studying its language and its military and attending the Passion Play in Oberammergau. Returning, he briefly took a position as a broker in Baltimore but found no calling in stocks and bonds. Instead, he indulged his interest in writing and in the "eccentric types of human nature" by landing a job as a police reporter for the *Baltimore News*.

While the era conjures the images of sob sisters, sensational crime stories, and cutthroat competition as portrayed by Ben Hecht and Charles MacArthur's Roaring Twenties farce *The Front Page*, the *News* under general manager Stuart Olivier prided itself on being "ever vigilant on behalf of the best interests of Baltimore, keeping pace with the most modern ideas of the journalistic world, and nothing of a sensational nature is allowed within its columns," *Baltimore: Its History and Its People* would proclaim in 1912.

Still, a good crime story remained a good crime story, a good fire a good fire, and Redwood reveled in chasing stories all over Baltimore, gaining his first good look at life across the tracks.

Plagued by a stomach illness that caused his weight to drop to 138 pounds, Redwood took a break from journalism and spent the winter of 1912 and 1913 in Asheville, North Carolina, hoping the mountain air and exercise would help restore his health. For a short time he worked for the *Asheville Citizen*, making thirteen dollars a week.

After leaving the newspaper in March, Redwood for a short time indulged in the "idleness" he abhorred. "Besides my hour's drawing I have been doing nothing worth while here at all save stroll about, sleep, and absorb milk and eggs," he would write on April 26, 1913.

In Asheville, Redwood was confirmed in the Protestant Episcopal Church. He was no fire-breathing Harry Hairshirt but, according to all, felt his faith quietly and deeply and as passionately as his interest in the military.

A friend from Harvard, J. G. D. Paul, would write that Redwood's "preoccupation" with war and the military matched his religiosity and was "only a manifestation of the fundamental elements of Redwood's character, which, in their blending, seemed to many of his friends a fitter expression of the spirit of the crusading Middle Ages than the day in which we live."

Paul would also write that Redwood had "an indifference to the material standards of school, college and the larger world verging on asceticism; a completely democratic nature which unlocked to him the freedom of unconventionality.

"Taking into account the intensity of his nature, this last might have led him far afield had it not been for the ever-present restraint of his religion and his high sense of honor."

He was definitely not his father's son. "We all agreed then that one of [Redwood's] characteristics was his gentleness, a sensitive scrupulousness, that was almost feminine, in contrast to his father's robust masculinity," an "old friend" of the family would write.

"I have always seemed to see something of this same characteristic whenever I saw him later, and saw that he had developed into a cultivated, observant, studious young man. I thought he was marked out for a literary life, an author's, never a man of affairs, like his father."

His religious passion led him to consider entering the ministry, and perhaps go on to become a missionary in China, his younger cousin Jack Redwood would recall.

By the time world war erupted in August 1914, however, Redwood was back in Baltimore and working for the Moffett-Lynch Advertising Company. As the Germans stormed across Belgium and into northern France, the duality of Redwood's urges was revealed again, and his first impulse was to enlist with the Canadian or British army, as would so many of his Harvard brethren

It was Mom-Mom who dissuaded him from either course, according to Jack Redwood, and so Redwood was left to quench his thirst for military experience at the Plattsburg camp for tired businessmen in the summer of 1915 and the more sprightly and rigorous camp in 1916, at which George Haydock, Bill Morgan, Richard Newhall, and Alexander McKinlock also played at war.

While at Plattsburg for his second go-around, Redwood considered enlisting in the regular army but was advised not to by the regular officers assigned to drill the attendees. Though he felt he had "practically no chance" of passing the examination to become a commissioned officer in the reserve, Redwood took it anyway—and was successful.

He rejoined the *Baltimore News* in early 1917, and that April the war finally landed on his doorstep in the form of a telegram. Redwood received orders to report to officer's training at Fort Myer, Virginia, and he left his job and prepared, finally, to become a soldier.

His departure for the army, and perhaps for the war, caused some snickering in the newsroom, where, despite his long interest in the military and his stints at Plattsburg, a few of Redwood's co-workers were dubious of his military potential.

"I worked 'against' George, but really with him, for a mighty long time," Baltimore *Sun* reporter George Jenkins would write. "Every day, six days a week we were together more or less and I can't remember a time when he was not bubbling over with witty and cheerful foolishness."

Jenkins added that he and other reporters "often joked about him being a soldier. . . . He was really so unassertive and so utterly lacking in chestiness that you just couldn't picture him in khaki.

"You never can tell about these mild-mannered boys."

Redwood began his real military career inauspiciously enough as a supply sergeant, and also served as the camp's information officer—an assignment that was undoubtedly connected to his newspaper experience.

By the second week of training, Redwood found himself already behind the others because of his supply work—on top of which he was given the responsibility of leading a platoon. "I am trying to catch up with the semaphore signal code and the manual of interior guard duty," he would write on May 29.

"All last week I was not only a supply sergeant but commanding a platoon. Saturday we had a test, each platoon by itself under the eye of our regular Army instructors." Throwing a monkey wrench into the deal, "they gave each platoon leader a different platoon from that he had been drilling before to try him out."

The usual training—drilling, digging, target practice—took up the rest of the summer. Redwood worried, as had Newhall, that he wouldn't retain his commission—until he received a piece of camp gossip in early July that gave him hope.

"This is in strict confidence," he would write Mom-Mom on July 7. "Capt. White told another man named Nicol that when the transfers were made from the 10th Co. on June 15 Capt. Doig graded the men A, B, + C. We were both B grade, he said, Nicol and myself."

Otherwise, he tried to enjoy himself. Like Newhall, he found his greatest pleasure in field exercises.

"Yesterday and the day before," he wrote on the same day, "we had experience as part of a battalion in advance and rear guard. The first three squads of our company (I am in No 3) were told . . . to simulate a machine gun company, each squad acting as the crew of one gun.

"We had lots of fun, two men in each squad simulating mules—I was one of them the first day. My only duty was to look out for semaphore signals to our squad—rather a peculiar one for a mule I think.

"Next week we have periods of trench construction two mornings and on each of the following three mornings an hour's march and practice in throwing hand grenades. We have had some of it already and it is very far from being as easy as it looks."

Though he should have had an advantage on account of the two Plattsburg camps, and his having already been commissioned, the competition was turning out to be tougher than Redwood had anticipated.

"Everyone here, almost, is in suspense as to whether he is to be among the fortunate ones or not," he would write. "Our instructor has made his selections, but will not make them known until after they have been passed on by the board. The fact that some of us got our commissions previously is no guarantee that we will keep them after this camp. The sorting out is to be without favor."

In the end, Redwood passed easily and was commissioned as a first lieutenant. Typically, he made tentative plans to spend his coming leave "near some Canadian training camp and if I could get the entrée to the lectures and instruction etc. I might obtain some valuable information before I was called to duty about Sept 1.

"All this is pretty problematic for I am like Br'er Rabbit 'not knowin' what moment's gwine ter be de nex'," he would admit. "Still I thought if I did have two weeks leave and could get the chance to put it in to such advantage it was an opportunity not to be missed."

However, by early September, just weeks after learning he would retain his commission, Redwood received orders to report to the docks at Hoboken for transport to France. He sailed on September 7, in the same convoy as Haydock and Morgan, and at the rest camp outside Le Havre learned of his fate—joining about twenty other Americans at the British 4th Army School for Scouting, Sniping, and Observation outside the village of Bouchon.

"A group of us are quartered in a queer picturesque out-of-the-way little French village, billeted in the houses of the people, my billet is a very good one indeed," Redwood would write on September 28.

In letters home, he avoided talk of military matters and instead dwelled on his peaceful surroundings, the writing ability that had served him well on the *News* in full flower.

"The village is quaint with [a] gray church and red roofed houses, half-hidden by shade and fruit trees and the country is lovely. Autumn is only noticeable in a breath of freshness in the air. Wide stubble fields, flecked with blue chicory, ragged robins and flaming poppies surround us varied with stretches of ploughed ground and bright woods barely touched with brown.

"Here and there stand great yellow hay-stacks with trim conical tops and occasional groups of red or black cattle wander about, conspicuous against the sunlit grass. Everything is fresh, and sweet, and pretty as it can be."

His hosts were "an old couple who are comfortably established and keep everything as nice as can be, tile floors swept, clean sheets on my bed—(the way it was built up made me think of the picture of the princess on a pile of mattresses in the fairy story)—and fresh water in my pitcher.

"They are cordial and though apparently of the peasant class the man was talking to me the other day about the Latin Classics, Virgil, Horace and Ovid, which he had read!"

Redwood had already also encountered some of the enemy. "I have seen some batches of German prisoners and it was rather interesting," he wrote. "In one place there was a camp in which were men that had been captured at different times—some as far back as the spring of 1915. They were of varying height, some tall fellows, and generally of fairly sturdy build.

"Yesterday in a town near here I saw a party newly arrived from the front, their appearance was noticeably different. They were either young or undersized. I believe I could have looked clean over the heads of almost all of them."

Redwood also enjoyed the semicelebrity status the French conferred upon the Americans in the camp. "This afternoon when our lessons were over I walked to another town near here to get a haircut and I was an object of great curiosity wherever I passed," he wrote on October 6.

"If a full grown hippopotamus had walked down the street it would hardly have caused more excitement. There was always a shout of 'American' and heads popped out of doors and windows right and left. They always recognize us by our felt hats, which are different from anything in either the French or British armies.

"The children we pass in the roads greet us with a 'Bonjour M'sieu!' and the grown-ups smile and bow. There is a comparatively small group of us quartered in this particular place and the novelty of our appearance has not wholly worn off."

Though he attended the same school and was billeted in the same village as Richard Newhall, they did not mention each other in their letters home that fall. Interestingly, it was Redwood, and not the historian Newhall, who would instead mention an "old Roman camp" near the village, adding some historical context that surely would have brought an appreciative smile to Newhall's face: "It seemed queer to think that men had been camped there between fifteen and twenty centuries back as part of a garrison to hold Gaul against the Huns and that we had just come from across the Atlantic for substantially the same purpose."

In mid-October, the two-week course at the British school ended. The entire group of Americans, about twenty in all, was assigned to the officer-hungry 1st Division; five of them went to the 28th Regiment—Redwood, Newhall, Jim Quinn, Charles G. Starkey, and Jerome Brown.

Redwood on October 23 found himself being assigned to Company I, commanded by Charles Senay, himself still just a first lieutenant.

"The American officers with whom I have been thrown are a mighty nice lot, generally speaking, and those of the regiment to which I have been attached have been very decent about showing me the ropes," Redwood would write to his friend Stephen Luce on October 26.

He would finally mention Newhall, a Harvard acquaintance of Luce's. "By the way, there is another Reserve officer attached to this regiment whom I have seen a good deal of and who asked me to give you his regards when he heard that I was writing to you," Redwood wrote.

"He is one Richard A. Newhall, who has just come from Harvard, having taken a Ph.D. there, I believe, and been an instructor in history. We often speak of . . . common acquaintances of college world."

Redwood and Senay were barely able to become acquainted; after the 3rd Battalion's tour of duty in the trenches in the Luneville sector, Senay—affected for months with chronic diarrhea—was ultimately diagnosed with amoebic dysentery and sent to the Johns Hopkins Base Hospital near the AEF headquarters in Neufchâteau.

"I took quantities of camphor and opium pills and was kept in bed on a limited diet," Senay wrote. He would spend almost four months of his war in the hospital before finally feeling well enough for duty and taking command of the regiment's Company C in March 1918.

Redwood, meanwhile, took over a platoon and billeted in the village of Demanges with another new arrival, 2nd Lt. John Stuart Morrison, twenty-seven, the son of an itinerant newspaperman.

Morrison had been born in New Orleans but was living in Yonkers, New York, when war was declared. In striking contrast to the mostly carefree and single junior officers in the regiment, Morrison by the age of nineteen had married and had a daughter, Edith, who was just seven years old when her father, without the benefit of a college degree, applied for training at Plattsburg.

His marriage to Ethel, it appears, was rocky; his leaving for France may have been the better part of valor. Despite their differing origins, Redwood and Morrison became fast friends, and their billet in Demanges became an after-hours hub of activity for the young officers of the 3rd Battalion.

Among the revelers was Richard Newhall.

"They called me 'M. Bois Rouge,'" Redwood would write of his hosts, yet another "old lady" with an "infirm husband" and two children. "Lieutenant Newhall had to translate himself as 'Salle Nouveau.'"

II

A Man's Job

For a few days there was no war, just the pleasures of Paris, the art shops on the rue Bonaparte, the wonders of the stained glass in a Gothic chapel, a performance of *Faust* at the Opera House, and baths—four baths in just those few days, during which the layers of bitter mud from the trenches were washed from his body and swept down the drain like bad memories, memories of filth, and cold, and long nights watching and waiting there in the front lines for the Germans to come over and do unto Company L as they had done to Gresham, and Hay, and Enright.

"Airs from 'Faust' have been running through my head, and the recollections of four baths have wonderfully stimulated my morale," Richard Newhall would write on December 23, 1917. "Indeed the latter was sufficiently high to make me change my clothes, put on my new uniform, generally scrub up, and go to church."

Returning from the trenches on November 22, Richard Newhall almost immediately found himself on his way to the 1st Corps Infantry School at Gondrecourt for training in "bombing."

"I had shown no special aptitude along this line," he would write years later. "My name was drawn out of the hat."

He would describe the school as "a sort of post-graduate Plattsburg where we learn about the novelties of the present war—including the new-fangled tanks and other machines that were trying to make their mark.

"This going to school business is quite in my line, I suppose, and it was a compliment to be detailed to go, but I am rather sorry to be separated from my platoon.

"I was beginning to learn how to handle it, what to look out for, who the men were and what sort of personalities they possessed as individuals. Then along comes an order and be ready to leave at such and such an hour."

In mid-December, Newhall managed to finagle a pass for a visit to Paris—and found the city to be like "an old friend." He rented a room at the Hotel Continental, which contained the amazing luxury of "a bathroom and a bath-tub.

"Living out in the mud as we have been doing the prospect of a little vacation with a return to civilization seems to have an intoxicating effect which makes you determined to get as much concentrated enjoyment out of the few hours available to you as you possibly can."

For a few days, he took baths—hot at night, cold in the morning. He shopped and "spent a lot of money but I don't care." Among his purchases was a new tailor-made uniform, and on one afternoon he visited the Saints Chapel, built in the thirteenth century, where for a moment the war was forgotten and his passion for medieval history was reignited.

Its stained-glass windows were beautiful—"reds, blues, and purples, hundreds of Biblical scenes looking like kaleidoscopic designs. The walls themselves . . . were painted red and gold and decorated with fleur de lis and castles . . . The colors were subdued by the rather dim light which came thru the windows giving an effect of great richness."

That evening, Newhall took in the production of *Faust,* which he found "rather amusing." All in all, the trip reinvigorated Newhall. "My morale is very much improved," he wrote. "I feel more full of 'pep' than ever before."

Newhall headed back to Gondrecourt by train, his two days in Paris already becoming a pleasant and distant memory. On the way he read H. G. Wells's *Mr. Britling Sees It Through,* a bestselling 1916 novel about

English society. In it, Mr. Britling loses his son, Hugh, in battle in France early in the war but somehow manages to retain his faith in God.

In mourning, he decides that only a radical reshaping of the world can prevent such tragedies from occurring again.

"We have got to set this world on a different footing," Mr. Britling declares. "We have got to set up the world at last—on justice and reason . . . We have to put an end to the folly and vanity of kings, and to any people ruling any people but themselves . . . Kings and empires die; great ideas, once they are born, can never die again. In the end this world-republic, this sane government of the world, is as certain as the sunset."

Newhall, for obvious reasons, was "much stimulated" by Wells's book and elated to see his own vision of a new world order—the one for which he, at least, was fighting—presented in it.

"It said a lot of things that I have been thinking about. Its tone of liberal optimism I found most sympathetic," Newhall wrote. "That helped my morale too, for there is very little 'liberal optimism' in the army. I think I will write H. G. Wells and tell him so."

On Christmas Day, while still at Gondrecourt, Newhall and several other officers attended midnight mass at the local church. Ever the philosopher, he found it impossible to reconcile the celebration of the birth of Christ with the hate and savagery of the war.

"I failed completely to get into the idea that I was celebrating the birth of the Prince of Peace," he would write. "The idea was too incongruous, especially when I knew that there were gatherings like this through-out the enemy countries. Some how Christianity and the war refuse to mix."

Foremost in his mind was "Christ's intense pity for mankind. It was impossible to see the evidence of the longings and strivings of humanity, blind and aimless but still hopeful, which the service and the congregation showed, without being strongly moved. But it was tragically pathetic, and ever more much so when you considered this gathering as typical of the whole world."

Otherwise, he wrote, "the music was good, the church was cold," and at least for Newhall it was a reprieve from the barracks—where Christmas eve was being celebrated "with drinking and gambling."

Newhall was also lonely, thinking of his adopted family in Trevary. "For my part I wish that I could have been back in my billet with the French peasant family of whom I have written you," he wrote in a Christmas letter to his mother.

"There are two little girls with whom I have become very friendly, and to whom I have always brought something whenever I went away. When I left the last time the mother told me that the youngest, age 8, I think, had declared that when Christmas came she was going to hang her stocking not in front of the fire-place, but up in my room. Had I been there last night I know I would have been very welcome at their family celebration."

In late December, Newhall returned to Company L. Back among the ranks once more, he again was faced with the "impersonalness" of the army and chafed at his role of being a small cog in a giant machine. He tried to rid the folks at home of any grandiose notions about his mission—and that of the AEF, for that matter.

"The idea that the whole A.E.F. is absorbed in the issues of the war is quite erroneous," he would write. "Indeed it was rather a shock to me to discover so little comprehension of what I considered the main points.

"True, you can start almost anybody vituperating the Kaiser, who I suppose may be regarded as embodying the whole German system, but intelligent, detached thinking there seems to be none to speak of. Signs of heroic idealism, self-sacrifice, crusading idealism, etc. etc. are confined to the newspapers, and I must confess that there they appear exceedingly mawkish."

Upon his return to the company, Newhall would finally find something of a friend in one old-time sergeant who had been commissioned as a first lieutenant—Charles Stromberg, the same man who had helped save George Haydock's bacon as he struggled with his first duties.

Newhall and Stromberg billeted together during the division's maneuvers around Abainville in early January 1918, and Newhall would write of him: "I remember that often I have inveighed against the boorishness of so many American officers. Here is something much more like the true gentleman—though often wanting in the superficialities of table etiquette and the like.

"But he has the real kindliness of mind, the desire to be fair to all men, the willingness to give the devil his due, to do his share of whatever must be done, and to be fair spoken and friendly to whomever he is with."

He found Stromberg to be "an interesting type, of which I imagine there are a good many examples. I can't say that I would want to be in his company constantly, but there are no officers of our company or battalion of whom I would say that."

The maneuvers themselves only reinforced his distaste for the army's impersonal and perfunctory don't-think, don't-ask nature.

"Yesterday occurred an incident which I regard as typical of the army," he wrote upon the company's return to St. Amand on January 8, 1918. "We were standing or marching in the rain from 7 A.M. until 3:30 P.M. and continually got wet. Our overcoats and sacks protected us sufficiently except as to the feet, but every officer and man changed his foot gear as soon as he got in.

"At supper comes an orderly summoning the captain to the Major's office. A colonel and probably a general is coming to inspect! Every platoon chief will at once get his platoon to work drying clothes. So off we lieutenants hasten.

"Rout the men out of their billets. Make them tie their poncho ropes together and stretch ropes through the company kitchen and hang their coats on them. Fire-pails are started—though the supply of wood is very low and the available coal practically unburnable. A half squad is detailed to keep the fires burning all night. After which great show of energy, feeling safe before the inspection of even a major general, we go to bed."

However, no general arrived. "None at all," he complained. "This morning I asked one man, 'Did your coat get dry?' 'Oh, no Sir,' he replied. 'It is just as wet as it ever was.' The fear of generals is truly the beginning of military wisdom for young lieutenants!"

He would add: "Probably these remarks are violating some article of war. If I am court-martialed, however, I may be sent back to America so there would be compensating features."

The coldest French winter in memory added to the travails of the

AEF. "Isn't the cold a cruel thing?" Newhall would write. "It certainly is malignant. I never appreciated what a hideous thing it could be, and yet I have no doubt there are many places there where it is felt as badly as by the men over here.

"Poor boys, it seems impossible to make them comfortable. Indeed it is impossible to be comfortable. They are certainly a very plucky lot. Truly it is not the rushing into a cannon's mouth that is heroic, it is the enduring of the hardships of living—and millions of civilians are doing that along with the soldiers."

The intense cold forced the regiment to train indoors in mid-January—and Newhall found himself being called upon to lecture his platoon, just as he had done to classrooms filled with doe-eyed freshmen back at Harvard.

"We have been having 'indoor instruction' which means that platoon leaders like myself have had to gather our men about us in some barn and talk until we are about empty of ideas," he would write. "We even got to such straits that the whole company was assembled to hear me talk on how the German Empire came into existence.

"As a History lecture it was not much of a success. My vocabulary suffers from being too bookish and academic and I find it hard to talk modern history in words of one syllable, going on the assumption that most of the hearers have never before thought about it and know nothing of the common names and places.

"This evening," he added, "I am scheduled to talk at the Y.M.C.A. a mile or so from here on Joan of Arc. I am skeptical if many men of the 28th Infantry care a button who Joan was."

Still, Newhall's predilection for teaching was put to use in mid-January, when because of his stint at the 1st Corps school he was made the 3rd Battalion's "bombing officer," teaching others the functions—and dangers—of the French grenade. He found some intellectual stimulation in planning his lessons, just as he had back in Cambridge.

"It gives me a chance to think out little tactical problems and to make experiments," he wrote. "It has been good fun thinking up how to illustrate graphically the way to defend a trench with grenades.

"The men get very stale merely doing set drills and exercises and throwing at marks, and it seems to revive their interest and mine too if you can set them at something which looks more like the real thing."

He added: "The lecturing has been almost like getting back to college work. To have something about which I feel that I really know something and to sit down before a group which wants to know and to tell them about it seems to be the occupation for which I am best suited.

"Sometimes I fear that I tend to lecture my platoon, to explain the why's and wherefore's rather than bawl the men out for failing to do correctly something which they only half understood. The latter seems to be the more truly military method."

As much as Newhall found his classical education going by the boards, Alexander McKinlock was putting his Harvard connection—and gridiron fame—to good use. While picking up his mail at 1st Corps headquarters one day in late November, he was buttonholed by a young captain who asked his name and then "asked if I played at Harvard."

In the ensuing conversation, it came up that the captain was just then looking for an officer to serve as an aide to Gen. Beaumont Buck, commander of the 1st Division's 2nd Brigade. "I was then shown in and answered a few general questions as to my education and previous experience," McKinlock would tell his mother in a November 25 letter. It was a plum job, but McKinlock was uncertain whether it would be best to leave the 1st Corps school and lose "that extra knowledge which might advance me later on."

Like many a young officer, he continued to hope a "good job" would drop in his lap, but as many of the 1st Division's junior officers wallowed in the fields around Gondrecourt and gained, it was hoped, some practical experience in handling platoons and an understanding of trench and open warfare, McKinlock's world turned on theory only.

In the meantime, his exact fate uncertain, he continued to attend school. Allowed to find his own billet in mid-November and move out of the "cold and damp and uncomfortable" barracks, he took a place in the home of an elderly widow named Madame Fringant, whom he would soon come to call "Mama." "Madame Fringant takes pretty good care of me," he would tell Marion McKinlock. "She cleans my boots and brushes off the mud from my clothes, mends, etc."

Hastening to head off any sense that the doting Mrs. McKinlock had been replaced by a French "peasant," he would add: "Of course I am lonely and miss you a lot. The only compensation is the knowledge that this is a wonderful experience and one it will be most pleasant to look back upon; it's also a pleasure to be taking part in a big game."

As the days passed, he found his interest in machine guns waning, and he turned his ambitions to a more powerful weapon. "Next term I hope to attend the artillery school and later on to be assigned or transferred to that branch of the service," he wrote on January 2. "Artillery is an interesting subject so I am making a try for it."

McKinlock spent Christmas and New Year's Day at Madame Fringant's, though new orders required him to sleep in the cold and drafty barracks. "Last night some of the married daughters and their children came here for dinner; after mess I came down and went into my room which is just off the kitchen," he wrote.

"The old girl and her daughter who were a little zig-zag came in and stood over me while I ate some of the chicken cooked en casserole and then they brought in three dirty, ragged grandchildren who sang Tipperary in the expectation of being rewarded with bon-bons.

"The old girl and I had lunch on the remains of New Year's dinner and she was so cheered up that she went out and bought a rabbit which we shall have tomorrow. The cooking is excellent; in a house corresponding to this in the states, one probably couldn't eat the food but here it is well flavoured and really delicious in comparison with the officer's mess."

Later that month, McKinlock finally got his assignment. He was named liaison and intelligence officer for the 2nd Brigade's 3rd Machine-Gun Battalion, under command of Maj. Chester Arthur Davis, thirty, who had begun his government service as a diplomat, serving as vice-consul to then-Ceylon from 1909 to 1911. In 1912, he gained a civilian commission in the army and quickly advanced through the ranks.

Davis was "a fine gentleman," McKinlock would write, adding: "WOP Morgan from Highland Park is a 2nd Lt. in 'C' Co."

McKinlock left Madame Fringant's and moved into the battalion's headquarters in the château at St. Joire, where he soon found himself wearing many hats. "I am Provost Marshall, Police and Prison Officer, Fire Marshall, Battalion Headquarters (Bn.H.Q.) Officer's Mess Officer and Survey Office," he would write his mother on February 8.

"We are in a little French village and acting under the various titles given above I look out for the place; for instance in every café there is posted an order signed by me, of the hours the enlisted men are allowed to frequent it."

As had Haydock, however, he found difficulty in asserting his authority with the hard cases under his command. "I am in charge of the guard house and the prisoners who police up the town; a couple of wagons go from billet to billet every morning and the prisoners load in the refuse," he wrote.

"My first experience with enlisted men has been in handling prisoners who are the outlaws of the different companies, and they together with the teamsters, the hard guys, have led me quite a dance.

"I have not yet learned how to bawl a man out, that's one way you failed me, my dear. All the stuff one reads in the papers, magazines, etc. about 'we are all men etc.' is rubbish. To be any good an officer has to rule with an iron hand, of course, justly, that goes without saying."

Unlike the rest of the infantry, which through that month slogged through the mud, rain, sleet, and snow on endless maneuvers, McKinlock spent many of his days riding horses, as he had as a child at the Onwentsia Club in Lake Forest.

"Particularly was he pleased with his fine saddle mount and good stable accomodations so convenient to our billets," Chester Davis would remember. "We frequently rode along the canal bank to Trevary, St. Amand, Naix-en-Forge, Menoucourt, Ligny."

"I have a big, lanky sorrel horse who is a rough old devil, but strong and sound which is a rarety over here," McKinlock wrote. "I have enjoyed riding immensely; this is a great country for riding, not a single fence; it is wooded and hilly and I often ride up out of the valley and look down on our little town 400 or 500 feet below on the banks of a small river which feeds a canal that winds in and out like a snake.

"It's most picturesque and makes one forget the war."

It wasn't Paris but the New Year that had energized Bill Morgan. In command of a platoon of the 3rd Machine-Gun Battalion, he was feeling his way in learning how to lead, and he found great camaraderie among Company C's officers.

"Everything here in the company seems too good to be true," he wrote. A new company commander, Charles Walter Yuill, had taken over—"a young West Pointer, one of the most likeable fellows in the world," Morgan wrote, adding: "You would do anything in the world for him. All the other officers are mostly men who came over with me in the fall and every one of them are exceptionally fine, and we have a very congenial time."

On New Year's Day, he also paid a visit to George Haydock, "and we had a New Year's dinner at his officer's mess, and what a meal it was! Most of the food was bought, for the men aren't issued many frills over here."

Where before joining the new company he had sulked and complained, he found now that he enjoyed the responsibility of handling a platoon. "Thank heavens this military life is becoming not only likeable but natural," he wrote. "I have gotten so now that I spring to attention unconsciously and salute with a bang. Once you get into the swing of it you really get wild about this army stuff.

"How I used to loathe it all in the U.S. I think all this came to me after I had gone to M.G. school. It gave me great confidence in myself, because I knew that very few Americans knew more about this machine gunnery than I, and very few knew half as much."

His confidence was sky-high: "You yell out your commands with a punch you never knew that you had. You call a man down with more force which you never thought existed. You dress as well as possible, because you know that the men look up to an officer who is well dressed and clean and who doesn't slouch, who is full of snap and force at all times, and who is as soldierly to his superiors as the men can hope to be."

He applied himself to the science of war, learning the intricacies of handling men and machines. "I worked my head off with the men, and I got to know them by name, and to have my ideas of them personally," he wrote. "I made a lot of mistakes in handling them at first, but I tried not to make the same mistakes twice."

While the infantry spent long days racing around on the snow-covered fields surrounding Gondrecourt performing their maneuvers, Morgan found life a little easier with the machine guns, where the miles trudged were not quite as bad.

"Each morning we got up at half past four and the company fell in by brilliant moon light," Morgan wrote of the brigade maneuvers. "At dawn we moved off and by ten we were in certain designated positions, and being machine guns we 'stayed put' while the poor old infantry dashed around and practiced attacks.

"Our work is to stay a thousand yards behind the front line emplacements, and lay barrages on the enemy line. I tried very hard to interest the men and get them to understand it. I showed them all about the guns etc., so that I felt sure that my data would be accurately carried out and there would be no error in firing over the heads of our troops."

The sheer weight of the weapons, however, added to the discomfort of the activity. "It was pretty hard work walking across country through the snow with packs, and the last half mile you have to take these heavy guns off the carts and lug them on your shoulders. Sometimes you felt so tired you couldn't eat."

Where Haydock and McKinlock struggled, Morgan was learning to assert his authority. "You can't ever be sympathetic with these men or you will make them think they are sick or else tired," he wrote. "You'd laugh to see me with my platoon. I was easy at first, but they certainly jump now.

"The other day after a hard hike we were going up a pretty steep hill. I was walking ahead and I heard a gun drop. I looked back and the squad had all stopped. They said they were too tired to go on. Of all excuses! I nearly exploded. I asked them what they thought war was and I said the time was drawing too near, and I wanted to know whether I had men behind me or not."

By the time he got through with them, "they came up that hill at double time, and then to make sure that they had understood I sent them all back again to bring up heavy boxes of ammunition which I really didn't need. Since then they have jumped around very spryly when they receive commands. I learned a good lesson in time."

Still, he sympathized with their plight. "How the men stand this exposure I don't see," he wrote. "They get in a steaming perspiration and then stand in the bitter wind and snow for three and four hours, and it is always cold too.

"In the mornings the men's shoes are frozen to the ground, and the dampness from the day before has frozen in the inside of the shoes. Yet the men keep at it with a remarkably good spirit. We can't stop along the way and grumble at the cobble stones. C'est la guerre."

During the maneuver, Morgan encountered some "marvelous good luck" when the battalion's commander, Chester Davis, happened by as he was setting up and working out the firing angles of his machine guns.

"When he came up I sprang to frigid attention, and remained at salute until he acknowledged it," he wrote. "Then he got off his horse and said, 'You are a barrage battery. Now where are you going to lay your fire?'

"I had been sent up there without any having seen the orders, and I knew nothing, but I decided that he didn't know much more about the lay of the land than I did, so I said, 'No sir, I am using direct fire on that slope' and then I showed him where it would be senseless to use an indirect barrage."

Davis concurred, and "it turned out later that I was practically the only officer in the battalion who had his guns placed for shrapnel fire, and who had his spare men and ammunition out of danger in a sheltered place.

"All this was really nothing for me but unheard of luck, for it just happened that that one day I hit on a more sensible position than I was really capable of planning out."

The backline work of commanding and instructing his platoon energized the formerly dour Morgan. "I have never felt better in all my life," he wrote in the third week of January. "I am so delighted with this machine gun work. This is the way I am working these days: Up at 6:45—Breakfast. Inspection of billets until 8 AM. Then drill till 11:30. Officers meeting till noon. Then drill and dinner till 3:30."

Afterward, he taught other officers how to use machine guns. "Supper at five, then all the evening I am in my room. I work out problems for my school the next afternoon, and I instruct the officers and non-coms of our company when they drop in to learn a bit of it. By putting all the energy you have into it you can see the men buck up and respond, as if you had started an electric current between you and them."

He would reflect rather grandiosely on February 5: "More and more I am beginning to like this military life. It is marvelous. You are awake every second. You must have a punch in every movement and word, and there are no excuses. It's strange what this life has done for me. It makes me want to battle through life, to grip all the despicable and unjust things by the throat and see them writhe and die.

"There will be no compromise with me now. Men must have the right principles or they will not do. All this could have been averted if more independent thinkers had *dared*."

Thinking back to the previous September, he would add: "Do you remember how terribly nervous I was when I first landed with the Americans? Well you ought to see me now. Of all times when I should want to hustle and worry because of so much detail on hand, every thing is as calm within me as can be.

"If I had kept on the way I started three months ago I never would have gotten anywhere. It's not a question of rushing, that old American curse of life, and for the first time in my life I am trying to overcome that old habit of headlong plunging, for it pays in the long run."

All in all, Morgan was beginning to believe in the American effort.

"Things are much better with us now and they are straightening out," he wrote on February 21. "I can truthfully say that when we go up the line the Germans will stop this damnable joking. The men won't be made fools of again.

"We are now well equipped as to clothing and everything necessary and we will give those Huns what they are looking for and more too. Leave that to these wonderful boys in the ranks. I honestly am wild about this life. The hardships make us revel in it all the more. The men are such real men, and it is all a man's job."

Still, in his off-hours Morgan gravitated toward Harvard men—among these the brothers Roosevelt, Teddy Jr. and Archie, who were serving as officers in the 1st Battalion of the 26th Regiment, of which Ted Jr. was the commander.

After being one of the prime movers and shakers behind the Plattsburg movement, and attending the camps in 1915 and 1916, Teddy, twenty-seven, had returned as a major in the officer reserve to his $150,000-per-year job as a partner with the Philadelphia investment banking firm of Montgomery, Clothier, and Tyler.

Archie, twenty-three, had graduated from Harvard in 1916 and left Plattsburg late that summer as a captain in the reserve. Upon the declaration of war, Theodore Roosevelt had vainly pleaded with President Wilson to be allowed to raise a volunteer division in Rough Rider style and personally lead it in France.

Denied the opportunity for further battlefield glory, the elder Roosevelt appealed to John Pershing for his sons to be sent to France posthaste as privates; the secretary of war, Newton Baker, saw to it that the Roosevelt boys went over with the 1st Division in June 1917 as officers—Ted Jr. as a major and Archie as a first lieutenant.

In France, the ex-president's sons were naturally treated as celebrities—although, as biographer Edward Renehan would note, "the division included a number of majors several years Ted's senior who not only sized him and Arch up for amateurs, but also had them figured for cowboys and adventurers . . . Given this dynamic, it was imperative that Ted, in particular, prove himself quickly as the master of his men."

Archie—of the same graduating class as Haydock and McKinlock but two years ahead of Morgan—was "one of the least popular men in his class," Renehan would write. "Even as a youth, Archie had a reputation for being inapproachable."

Nevertheless, it seems Bill Morgan found Archie and his brother affable enough. "We three spent a great afternoon, and they kept kidding me about being in the machine guns," Morgan wrote. "They claim that you aren't in the war unless you are in the infantry.

"Just as I was leaving Major Roosevelt said that he would see that I was transferred to his battalion if I would give my consent, or if at any time I wanted to leave my machine guns."

Bill Morgan demurred and headed back to his billet, to study more on the wonderful new science of modern warfare.

12

A Most Perfect Friendship

It was in that dimly lit and cold Cave in the back of a peasant's cottage that they strutted their hour on the stage, as it were, two twenty-somethings passing an evening waiting for their war to begin, performing *Macbeth* for each other's pleasure and humor, the booming of the guns along the Lorraine front their dramatic drumroll, the lilting and phrasing of Shakespeare their respite from morning reports and officious battalion orders.

"Life's but a walking shadow," one of them said, "a poor player, that struts and frets his upon the stage, and then is heard no more; it is a tale told by an idiot, full of sound and fury, signifying nothing."

They smiled at each other, and laughed.

It had been a matter of just a few weeks before Richard Ager Newhall, PhD Harvard '17, and George Guest Haydock, Harvard '16, found each other in early 1918. Though each commanded a platoon in Company L—George the 1st, Newhall the 2nd—Newhall's absence at school in Gondrecourt, and Haydock's being under the weather for some of that month, obscured each from the other.

In fact, it was another short illness of Haydock's that seems to have led them to one another, finally, and to what Newhall would for the rest of his life consider the "most perfect" friendship he would ever have, though they were opposites in some respects, Newhall being a full six years older, a "Westerner" by birth and orientation, and, certainly by virtue of his reading and travels, more worldly than Haydock.

Despite their different origins and life experiences, Newhall seems to have at once recognized Haydock as the attitudinal kin for which he had been searching amid the impersonal and business-oriented culture of the army. In Haydock, the professor found not only his student but a confidante and willing disciple who shared his opinions about the army, about their commanders, and about the manner in which the war was being prosecuted. In Newhall, the gentle and reserved Haydock perhaps found something of a wise older brother who looked out for him, instructed him, respected him, and, despite a sometimes cold and imperious exterior, expressed unconditional and unabashed love. Above all, each found in the other a respite from the folly and grimness of soldiering.

Newhall's first mention of Haydock would come on January 27: "This week I have taken to playing chess and find it a very satisfactory relaxation after supper. There is a Harvard chap in our company, a 1st Lieut., with whom I play and who usually beats me."

Newhall in his later years would struggle to remember just how he became friends with Haydock, writing that "the earliest phases of my friendship with George Haydock are not very clear. He must have joined L Company shortly before I was sent to the Gondrecourt schools in November. So it must have been on my return to the company in January that we began to get acquainted."

Newhall remembered being taken aback at Haydock's spare living quarters, "the out-house of a peasant cottage, a very unsuitable place much inferior to my quarters in the Thierry house. Here he had set up a canvas cot, another contrast with the very comfortable double bed which I enjoyed.

"I must have been accustomed to stopping at his billet to pick him up on the way from the Thierrys to our company mess. What I recall is an occasion when he was sick with a bad cold and a fever. I remember his lieing abed and my knowing no other way to test if he had a fever than the way I remembered my mother using the back of her hand on my forehead when I was young."

The game of chess provided the common ground over which the intellectual and the innocent came to know one another—and to quickly develop a devoted and inseparable bond, sharing quiet and understanding laughter over the absurdity of their situation and of the characters and methodology they found in the army.

"We discovered our mutual compatibility and the extent to which we found moral support in each other," Newhall wrote. "There was a quiet, natural, spontaneous quality about our friendship which was unlike any other relationship I have experienced. Strangely enough I can recall almost nothing about our conversation.

"Probably it was largely concerned with our reactions to the war and the army, although I am certain that there was very little, if any, griping. We were both occupied with the same activity to which we reacted in very similar fashion. This meant that we accepted the necessity for being in the situation in which we found ourselves and attempted to do as well as possible the job in hand."

Another bond was the lack of any ambition outside of getting the job done and getting on with their lives: "Neither of us, I am sure, had any sort of military ambition, nor any disposition to imitate 'the army way' of doing things, such as bawling-out soldiers or indulging in any of the other forms of professional bullying which we sometimes observed."

Their quiet conversations over knights and pawns stuck to their present situation. "I cannot recall that we said much to each other about ourselves, apart from our army experiences, but I may be merely forgetful as to this," Newhall would write years later. "It seems to me that George was, by habit, more reserved than I.

"It is now clear to me that it was particularly significant that there were no competing demands upon us, either of society or family or other friends, so our personal affections were directed upon each other, free from distractions, frictions, or unsatisfied demands."

Haydock would first make mention of Newhall in a letter written on February 4, referring to Newhall as "a 2nd lieutenant about 30, Ph.D., and an instructor in History at Harvard. I play around with him a good deal.

"Even though he is a real highbrow, it's such a relief after some of the others. He is a walking encyclopedia and most interesting and sensible. He is about my speed at chess and we sit in the 'cave,' as we call our billet, and shiver in unison while we play."

In short time, the two became inseparable, and Haydock became a fixture at Newhall's soirees in Madame Thierry's kitchen where Charles Stromberg already had a chair in place.

"On Friday we had another soiree around the waffle iron, more vivacious even than the earlier ones," Newhall wrote. "In a group of five American officers and four French soldiers, besides the Thierry family we had talking in French, Spanish, German, and English all at once. It gave me an idea of what the Tower of Babel must have been like. Needless to say the conversation was *not* general."

Haydock would jokingly refer to Madame Thierry as "Madam Cherry," writing: "We got a Frenchwoman by name of Madam Cherry to make waffles for us. We sat around in her kitchen and talked to her and her family, consisting of a dirty husband and two dirty but very cute little girls.

"The old man made the waffles and we ate them as fast as he could take them off the iron. They mixed us up some sort of a red wine concoction and heated it and made a kind of Swedish punch which was quite good.

"I think I must have eaten 30 waffles, they sure were good. It was an odd kind of a party but very pleasant. The madam was very talkative but her speed was a little too high for me to get more than about half of what she was saying."

The evening Newhall and Haydock read and acted out Shakespeare's *Macbeth* alone in Haydock's billet marked the growing bond and melding of the minds of two permanent "civilians" who found themselves beset and bemused by the military way.

"It was a strange setting, perhaps, for a Shakespearean play—a cold, barn-like room with a folding cot, a table, and a bench in it," Newhall wrote. "A little stove set in a big fire place providing a scant heat. Two candles furnishing the light. And two very civilian lieutenants being actors and audience. For me it was one of the pleasantest evenings I have had in this place."

Prior to their meeting, Haydock had continued to flounder and struggle, though he slowly was developing the upper hand when it came to leading his platoon. The month of January had been marked by loss—the first one of Company L's enlisted men, "a barber in our company who was a bum," Haydock would write on January 10.

"We think he killed himself drinking bay rum or something equally attractive. At any rate he died on the last maneuvers from too much drink."

Haydock was "elected" to bury the poor soldier. "I was given a large motor truck, a fatigue squad and a firing squad, told he was in one place or else another, and that I was to bury him in a rather indefinitely located cemetery," he remembered.

"I started out with what paraphernalia I could get together, and the first stop was to get the chaplain whom I finally hunted out of his lair much to my relief, for I fully expected to have to deliver a funeral oration myself. We then proceeded on our way and after some trouble got a casket only to find that he was already boxed."

At the cemetery, "the fun began," he wrote. "It was very cold and snowing hard, of course the ground was frozen and it was a deuce of a job to dig. To add to the troubles we had to dig through rock to gravel which caved in about as fast as it was dug out, but after about four hours we were all set, and pulled off a pretty good military funeral.

"The Chaplain read the service while we all nearly froze and the firing squad was so cold I was afraid they would shoot me by mistake, but we finally did get through it without any mishaps, but it took all day to do it."

Heavy snow continued to fall and make for miserable conditions outside, and so Haydock and the other platoon leaders once again took to lecturing their men. "Spent four hours in the morning and two in the afternoon lecturing to my platoon in a cold, dark billet, and believe me it was a strain, both for the men and for me," Haydock wrote.

"If I have to do it again tomorrow I think I shall have to read the Bible to them. Believe me it is some job to keep 60 men interested and at the same time teach them something when you do not even have a blackboard. When I get through neither W. J. Bryan or William Sunday will have anything on me as an orator."

On January 22, Haydock suffered another loss when it was decided by his French hosts that it was time to kill his bunkie—the pig.

"They pulled him through the house by his ears, and 6 Frenchmen and 4 women hogtied him on the doorstep and one man cut his throat while the other 5 men jumped up and down on him to make him bleed faster," Haydock wrote.

"The women caught the blood in a bucket and the pig did himself proud in the squealing line. Then they put him in a tub and cut his insides out and displayed them on a table in the house. An elegant sight.

"They always do this butchering hogs, cattle, ducks in the street with the result that the gutters are usually filled with blood, also a nice idea. I don't know how I shall get along without the ole hog. It was fine to wake up and hear him grunt at night, and he has been around so long we were quite clubby."

Richard Newhall, meanwhile, was excited to see his platoon melding into a quality outfit in the month since he had returned from school at Gondrecourt.

"I am beginning to find that my declining opinion of men in general derived from association with my 'brother' officers is being bolstered up, even at times revived, as I get better acquainted with my platoon," he wrote.

Among the platoon, he wrote, was "quite a little group of slavs"—a common happenstance in the AEF. America's turn-of-the-century melting pot was strongly reflected in the ranks, and immigrants and first-generation Poles, Russians, Swedes, Italians, Germans, Danes, Rumanians, and other ethnicities mingled in the trenches.

He would describe an "experiment" in which a message was passed between the members of his platoon. "By the time it had gone through Glasky, Shutovich, Walozak, Ybarzabal, and Byrzck my original statement was quite unintelligible," he would write.

Newhall was also discovering that while the army could take a soldier from the Old Country, it was difficult to take the Old Country out of the soldier; old nationalistic slights and grudges had not dissolved or been forgotten for many of the Eastern European immigrants in his platoon.

"My best corporal is a Russian Pole who is just itching to get at the Germans," he would write. "In one of our maneuvers we practiced a raid to get prisoners, but he opined that it would be much better to kill all the Germans when we encountered them."

Newhall quickly came to look past the strange-sounding names and see the men behind them. "On the muster roll some of these Slavic names look very formidable but once you learn the pronunciation you don't have to pay any attention to the spelling. They are a good lot. I like them and feel sure I can depend on them. They are here because they want to fight.

"I know all my men by name now and have some ideas of their individualities. True, some of them are hopelessly 'pas bon,' but they are few. We are beginning to get the feeling of a team, I think, and that is just what is wanted. In our 'first game' I certainly expect them to give a good account of themselves."

Happy to have found a real friend, Haydock continued to seek some familial connection, but try as he might, his plans to hook up with his sister Louisa all came to naught. On the eve of one planned visit to St. Amand, Haydock told Lou to stay in Paris, thinking the cold, rough conditions might be too much for her.

"It is something to look forward to, and I won't let them stop the war till we do it," he wrote. "She was planning to come to these parts but I told her not to, life here is too darn crude. You get wet and then never get dry.

"However," he joked, "I am thoroughly hardened so I have just as much fun if I am cold, wet or dirty. When in France live as the Frenchmen, it takes a genius to do it."

With the advent of warmer weather at the end of January, more time was spent outdoors. The men were kept hopping with two reviews—one for the 28th Regiment's brass, another for those leading the 2nd Brigade.

"In both cases we passed in review to 'Our Director,' which has been adopted as our divisional song," Haydock wrote. "The words being: 'Here's to Uncle Sammy, faithful and true, here's to our banner of red, white and blue. Here's to all good fellows on land and sea, singing the battle cry of liberty.'

"I think one of the men wrote the words. They sound so anyhow."

For the brigade review, "We had to get up at 5 after having been out on night maneuvers late the night before, then had to stand for three hours in a cold mist. One of the machine gun mules got loose and cavorted down between two companies as they were passing in review. The next day the order came around that 'during ceremonies all dogs and mules should be kept tied.'"

The display of the military mind-set during the same review only irritated Newhall. "We had a brigade review which struck me as one of those stupid, unnecessary, very military things," he wrote. "The men had to be roused an hour earlier than usual (5 A.M.). it must have been worse in the other organizations which had to march farther than we did.

"The regiment when marched to the reviewing field then stood idle for an hour—and the morning was cold and damp. And all this was for the purpose of marching in review before the general, a proceeding which, for us, took about ten minutes and for the last company in line couldn't have taken more than half an hour."

For a moment, "you get a sense of the pomp and panoply of war," he wrote. "But that moment wasn't worth the effort, and the reaction, with me, had been a little demoralizing because it had impressed me with the hollowness of much of the military.

"To me and others like me who want to fight, fight, fight and get this vile war over so we can return to our true lives, this ceremony business seems, sometimes, worse than futile."

In his off-hours, Newhall investigated the old Roman camp above St. Amand. He found few relics, but on one day a "venerable old fellow" chanced by and invited Newhall to his home to see some coins he had dug out of an orchard.

The coins impressed Newhall. "One of these was a coin of Vespasian, in good condition, and really a very nice specimen (when I got back the captain admired it so much that I gave it to him). The other silver coin interested me more because the poorer quality of silver was such an interesting illustration of the Roman Empire's decline. It is of the Empress Julia Maesia about 230 A.D."

He showed the coins to Charles Stromberg, who was "disposed to be very skeptical of the genuineness . . . Still he was rather nonplussed in his skepticism when I told him that the peasant in whose house I am staying, M. Thierry, when he saw my coins said he had a find too; he then produced [a] copper coin of Hadrian which he had found in his field and gave it to me."

Haydock tagged along on some of these historical adventures but found himself unable to leave the army behind, even for a few hours. "We go up there at night and I suppose it might be considered romantic, but there is damn little romance in the army now," he wrote.

All he could think of was "how steep the blinking hill is, and when you get up it you wonder how in thunder you are going to find your way to where you belong, and what disposition you will make of your automatic rifles when you do get there, and you grumble and cuss when things go wrong, as they always do. You don't give a damn even if Caesar did have a squad of rock breakers building a wall up there."

As January turned to February, the drilling intensified. By then, the 1st Division's 1st Brigade had moved to the trenches surrounding Seicheprey, and a sense of urgency was palpable. In the warmer weather, the 2nd Brigade spent long days out in the field, and Haydock found himself trying to keep a stiff upper lip for his men.

"We grouse and kick a good deal to be sure, but then, you are not considered as part of the army if you don't do that," he would write. "The other day after we had drilled hard all morning, been through a very tiresome review all afternoon, [we] were then called out for a four-hour night maneuver. As we were moving up the hill to the trenches I heard one of my men say that he was going to turn in his cot and draw a lantern.

"They then began to discuss the 'spirit of the troops,' and decided that we had left them up the hill in the morning and were going back up to get them again. And so it goes."

Haydock slowly was finding his way in handling his men—and being the company savings and loan, as Company E's Lt. Maurice Edwards had noted, didn't hurt. One man, Patrick Fox, used his civilian talents to help the platoon win the "brown derby" in camouflaging. Fox, Haydock wrote, "did most of the work and then borrowed 20 francs from me and got drunk on Sunday.

"They are a funny crowd. I have loaned out over 300 francs to the men in the company and none of them have more than 20. As soon as pay day comes around they pay it back, and then about a week later borrow some more."

Like Newhall, the more he became acquainted with the various characters in his platoon, the more he appreciated their worth—and though he may not have known it at the time, he was constructing a two-way street in that area.

"They are a good crowd on the whole, mostly from the middle west and south and quite different from the types I am used to," Haydock would write, adding: "I find the southerners somewhat trying on the nerves. There are a lot of them around here."

In the first week of February, Company L drew the assignment of trying out the village's decrepit fire engine. "The captain decided that we had better have a fire drill," Newhall wrote, "in case some inspector should come along and ask about fire drills or sound fire call to test our efficiency. (I assure you inspectors are much more dreaded than fires.)"

The company assembled in front of a barn marked POMPE ET INCENDIE. "Here it was discovered that there was no way of getting in by the main entrance and getting the 'pomp' except by breaking the door open," Newhall wrote.

"This done we found that the school ma'am was using the 'fire barn' as a place to raise rabbits. (She could get in by a little door in the rear.) So one soldier had to be detailed to watch the rabbits to see that none escaped while the street door was open. This was to protect the government from exorbitant claims for lost property."

The company raced the pump "up and down the main street. Inspection of the leather hose showed that any fire more than 50 yards from natural running water would have to be quenched with buckets. Later we found that the pump itself was unworkable—clogged or frozen. That didn't interfere with the drill, however."

While the men tried to unfreeze the pump, St. Amand's mayor—"a much moustached, red beaked person"—appeared. The dignitary, Newhall wrote, "was evidently much disturbed lest the town property be damaged. He wanted the pump put up at once, and insisted that they never had any fires in the winter time.

"Fortunately by that time we had practically finished our drill and were prepared for any inspector so we supplied the mayor with reassuring explanations and put the engine away. None of the rabbits had escaped!"

The sentinel, bayonet fully fixed, "was the cause of some priceless remarks by the men," Haydock would note.

On February 8, Haydock received a summons at his cave on the "Rue de Duck": He was wanted at the regimental adjutant's office, pronto. "I was taking a nap, and began to think over all my past sins," he wrote.

He raced to headquarters, only to find that the adjutant had gone to dinner, "so I was left in a good deal of a stew." Returning to his billet, he was told that two orderlies had been around looking for him with orders that he go to the YMCA hut.

There, he found his sister Louisa and her friend Penelope Parkman, on leave from their jobs with the Red Cross in Paris, "sitting there as though they owned the place. As soon as I got word to go to the Y, I had a hunch what was up, but it sure took me off my feet to find it so, after so many unsuccessful attempts.

"Gosh, it was great," he would add. "There was a band concert going on but we sat and talked our heads off. Then I took them around to see the sights of the town, including the cave in which I live. It was a pitch black night but I think they got some idea of the place, and it was such fun."

He located Captain Van Natter, and introductions were made. "They made a big hit apparently because he told me I could have Saturday off, which made it nice," he wrote.

The next morning, the trio headed out of St. Amand for a picnic, all thoughts of war ebbing on a beautiful springlike day. "We raided the town for oeufs and a bottle of vin blanc to make the party real devilish," Haydock wrote.

"After we had as much as we could carry we paraded down the main street and out of the town. I found it rather difficult to balance a dozen eggs while executing the hand salute smartly and in military manner, but everything was plain sailing after we got out of town."

They went to the top of a nearby hill and "cooked and ate a most enormous meal lasting from 11 to 2 and then lay around and had a good old fashioned gossip," Haydock wrote.

Heading back to town, they "crashed into a back kitchen and asked the madam to cook us dinner. Thanks to Pen's fluent French we were successful, Louisa and Pen standing on either side and exclaiming 'ah, oui' and 'mais non' with the greatest intelligence and always at the right moment."

The next day, an adventure ensued as Haydock sought to help the women find a train back to Paris. After walking and hitching rides on bread and cattle trucks all day to reach the nearest village with a station, they said their good-byes, George heading back to the war, and the women to Paris.

"We are agreed that now we have had a party the war may stop any time," he wrote, "although we have arranged a spree in Nice for the late spring if I can pull a seven-day leave then. At any rate we are all bucked up.

"Lou wanted me to make a report on her," he wrote Annie Haydock. "She is, as far as I can see, clothed and in her right mind. She ties her rubbers on with a string and has a very snappy trench coat.

"At present her plans are a little vague, but so are everybody else's and I am sure she has proved she can take care of herself. I gave her a severe lecture on everything blue and will continue the course in a correspondence school. She was in rare form at the party and it must have done her good."

All in all, he wrote, finally hooking up with Lou "has made a new woman of me."

For the first time since landing in France, Haydock had something to look forward to beyond mud and drill and the odd hours in his Cave, and he would fall asleep thinking of Lou and Pen and the Riviera, which glimmered in his mind like a picture postcard from the future.

At 3:00 A.M., he was awakened by his orderly, and as Lou and Penelope receded on the rails to Paris, George Haydock began another day of leading his platoon in drills and assaults on an imaginary enemy, and learning how to handle men in wartime.

13

At the Circus

And then here was something like hell on earth, he would write; although he had been in the trenches once before he had not encountered ground like this; not seen the battered and splintered and charred sticks that represented where a forest had once stood; not seen the bleached bones of those who had come, and died, before him; nor looked across a moonscape to the looming form of Mont Sec, bristling with German field glasses and artillery; nor felt the presence of the snipers in the other lines watching and waiting for their chance across a clear field, waiting for some fool in a careless moment to pop his head above the trench, above this drooling and drizzling mud.

"Truly a battlefield in these days is a scene of desolation such as even Dante never imagined," Richard Newhall would write from such a front line on March 20, 1918. "I had read about the shell torn ground and ghostlike remnants of woods without having a vivid idea of what it all means. It is bizarre and eerie in its ghastliness.

"These places where men once lived, even if they be only trenches and dugouts, pounded to a pulp with artillery fire, soaked with rain till they are masses of mud, strewn with equipment of all kinds—for me it was distinctly 'something new under the sun.' It wasn't repellant. It merely excited a profound amazement.

"The German legend on the town hall at Bapaume 'Don't be angry, be astonished' became more intelligible. It was a thing indeed to wonder at, but not without anger. Let those who have done this thing suffer the like."

The place was called Seicheprey, and it was here that the AEF took a large step toward war, the real war, the 1st Division's 1st Brigade entering the trenches in mid-January while the 26th and 28th Regiments continued in their maneuvers and war games.

Where the quiet Sommerviller front had been occupied by the division the previous fall to give its men some seasoning, Seicheprey—fifteen miles north of Gondrecourt—offered an adult portion of activity, an introduction to the lifestyle that had put that glassy stare into the eyes of the British, Germans, and French for the past three and a half years.

As well it was an introduction to gas, constant shelling, bitter nights spent on alert while every burned and splintered tree trunk in no man's-land seemed to take on an armed, human form and creep closer and closer to where you stood, knees knocking, eyes staining into the black night, and your mind blank with exhaustion.

To the left of the American front line, Mont Sec rose like a sore thumb above the salient named after the village at its apex—St. Mihiel. Encompassing 150 square miles, the salient had been created in 1914, when Bavarian troops had attacked south toward the French positions and driven a wedge into the stabilizing Western Front in an attempt to isolate the fortress of Verdun to the northwest.

Its southern face ran for twenty-three miles from Pont-a-Mousson west to St. Mihiel, its western face thirty-nine miles from St. Mihiel to a point just south of Verdun, roughly paralleling the course of the Meuse River and its rugged heights. From the apex at St. Mihiel to its heavily fortified base, named the Michel Line, the salient was thirteen miles deep.

The scene of great fighting in early 1915—the French alone lost 40,000 men in back-and-forth battles while trying to retake it—the salient had gone quiet after April of that year. Since then the Germans had fortified the area with an array of artillery positions among the steep hills of the Meuse heights on the west, and strung trenches and fixed machine-gun posts across its width running across the Woevre Plain.

Since arriving in France in June 1917 the Americans had regarded the salient as a natural venue for an all-American effort, and plans for its reduction had been produced as early as September of that year.

However, it wasn't until mid-January that the 1st Brigade of the 1st Division had taken over the sloppy, sodden trench system running through Seicheprey. When it arrived, "you could have stood on the parapet and hung up your laundry, and so could the Germans," one company commander in the 16th Regiment recalled.

Still, there was the eminence of Mont Sec to contend with. "From Mont Sec," the 28th's history notes, "the enemy had excellent observation of the whole American sector and there was not a man in the 28th who did not cherish the ambition that some day they would drive the Germans from that hill."

Rumor had it that Mont Sec "was one mass of artillery and machine guns," Richard Newhall would write. "Thousands of Frenchmen had been lost in a vain attempt to storm that place. Would we have to capture it?"

Prior to moving, the 28th Regiment's pace of training, like the pace of the war, had increased with the steadily rising temperatures, and in late February, George Haydock found himself with an additional and unwanted burden: running Company L in the absence of Capt. Francis Van Natter, who went on leave.

"It is a good deal more than I was ever looking for, especially at this time, but I will make a stab at it," he wrote. "This . . . sounds perhaps as though I was quite a power in the barnyard, but don't worry I know better, and so do a lot of other people, darn their hides.

"I have had to get up at 5 or earlier every day, and at that time in the morning one does not appreciate the beauties of France or the joy of war, especially as we have been having it cold enough to make it necessary to thaw out one's toothbrush before using it."

Haydock led the company in a brigade maneuver, after which "the officers were entertained by the Roosevelt brothers. It made a very pleasant tea party as well as being instructive in the so called art of war.

"I saw several fellows whom I have not been able to connect with, McKinlock, Henry Russell, Alan Clarke, and some others I had met either on the boat or at school, and we had a chance to talk things over a bit."

One bright spot for Haydock was his finally being able to find a new billet and say good-bye to "the cave."

"I am thinking of moving from Rue de Duck to Rue de Cochon, properly known as the Grand Rue among the higher class of French society," he wrote.

He and his billet mates found a room in a local house, whose owner, an "old lady," was "a lonely soul if ever I saw one. She is very tidy and thrifty. She has a hard life these days.

"She lives in a room between ours and the street. She goes to bed (after putting on a night cap and taking off her slippers) under two large feather beds, at about eight and from then on there is a continuous tramp back and forth until about 10, and starting again about 5:30—orderlies, strikers, and ourselves. It never seems to worry her in the slightest though she sleeps until about 9."

His own days at St. Amand running low, Newhall retuned to his billet at Madame Thierry's from one maneuver and was touched when his host presented him with a gift.

"It bore a Virgin and Child in low relief," he wrote. "She explained that it would protect me, so I tied it to the string around my neck which holds my identification tags. The Madame is truly a kindly, and motherly person."

The anticipation of coming battle grew with every day, he noted. "The communiqués show that things are starting again," he would note of the activity on the Western Front. "I hope they are. That will bring the end more quickly."

As the time passed, Newhall found that despite his best efforts to control them, his thoughts were orienting toward purely military concerns.

"It is strange the way your point of view changes in regard to men," he wrote. "It used to be that I was chagrined at finding so few kindred spirits; now I find myself sizing up men from a very different point of view.

"I no longer consider, 'Is this chap a congenial companion?' Rather the question is, 'Would I feel easy if he were in command of the platoon on my right?' "

In pointed reference to his new friends, Lts. Charles Stromberg and George Haydock, he would add: "Thank Heaven I can say 'yes' with vigor to the lieutenants of L Company who command the 1st and 3rd platoons.

"But there are a lot of platoons in the Battalion which I hope won't be sent in to support me. I have a lot more confidence in my own non-commissioned officers than in some of my 'brother officers.' "

His noncoms, he added, "are an interesting lot. Two of the sergeants are Irish, very Irish, and very reliable fellows whom I will be glad to have with me in a fight. Among the corporals I find an Irishman, a German, a Pole, a Russian and a Texan, and they are a good lot. Often they, and the men, amuse me a lot, and I have no doubt I amuse them.

"We get on together very well. In regard to the men—well, the other lieutenants are disposed to make fun of me on the ground that I seem to have drawn most of the lame ducks. But that 'most' does not mean more than six which isn't very many. The rest of them are fine."

That wasn't necessarily so for some of his fellow lieutenants. "All during this letter I have been listening to a little red-headed 2nd Lieut. from Tennessee tell how to make money after the war is over," he would write of Lt. Edward Morgan.

"The latest suggestion is to establish a chain of billiard halls which will pay 100-200% per month! I doubt if I could successfully carry out any of his suggestions so I am planning to return to my own profession, instead of trying to make money."

He found better company among Haydock, Stromberg, and several "brother officers"—a term Newhall otherwise would use derisively so often—among the neighboring companies in the 3rd Battalion of the 28th.

On February 23, Newhall invited two of these, Company K commander Capt. Henry Ephraim Mosher and another of Mosher's officers, to dinner at Madame Thierry's.

Mosher, just twenty-four years old that spring, had been born and raised in the village of Falconer, in upstate New York. Following high school "he took a course in the National Preparatory School at Highland Falls, with West Point, which he had always been ambitious to enter, as his objective," his local paper would report.

He received his appointment to the military academy in 1913 and entered the same year—but dropped out, "presumably for academic inadequacy but he was a good leader," Newhall would remember.

He went on to work for the Remington Arms Company in Bridgeport, Connecticut, and then for the New York State Highway Department. Though West Point was no longer in his plans, Mosher had still craved a commission in the army, and he took, and passed, an examination for a civilian commission in October 1916.

Mosher was at Fort Leavenworth's Army Service School when war was declared—and though his training was only half completed, "there came the call to report to the East to join the first forces to cross the seas."

He landed with the 1st Division in late June 1917, one of the first Americans to touch French soil; by the winter of 1918 he had realized his ambition, taking over the reins of Company K from the 1894 Yale University graduate and Philippines veteran Capt. George Arthur Hadsell.

Hadsell and Company K were the first Americans to land on June 26, and Hadsell had proudly led his men off their ship to much pomp. "I expect to see old Yale lead the way through the Boche center this summer just as Heffelfinger used to go through Harvard," he would write to friends.

By the time Company K went through the "Boche center," however, Hadsell was long gone, a promotion to lieutenant colonel taking some of the sting out of his being sent back to the United States "as an expert and instructor in transportation problems," the *Hartford* (Connecticut) *Courant* would report.

For Mosher, the orders to join the 1st Division on its voyage to France were the culmination of a lifelong dream. "He often stated in his letters that to have been chosen to go with this pioneer band of Americans was all he asked," the *Jamestown* (New York) *Morning Post* would report. "Often he said in his letters home that he would rather have one year of life in France with the men than a whole life time elsewhere."

Richard Ager Newhall. *(Courtesy Williams College Archives and Special Collections. Used with permission.)*

Richard Newhall at Plattsburg Training Camp, summer of 1916. *(Courtesy Williams College Archives and Special Collections. Used with permission.)*

1st Lt. George Guest Haydock in a photo taken in France ca. spring 1918. *(Courtesy Williams College Archives and Special Collections. Used with permission.)*

William Otho Potwin Morgan as a boy. *(Courtesy of Hilary Morgan)*

Christiana Councilman and Bill Morgan. *(Courtesy of Hilary Morgan)*

Bill Morgan and Christiana Councilman on the eve of his departure for France. *(Courtesy of Hilary Morgan)*

Bill Morgan. *(Courtesy of Hilary Morgan)*

Company G, 28th Regiment's 2nd Lt. Jim Quinn, the toast of Memphis. *(Courtesy of William M. Quinn)*

Company K, 28th Regiment Capt. Henry Mosher. *(Courtesy of Paul Densmore)*

Company G, 28th Regiment Capt. Clarence Ralph Huebner, ca. fall 1917. *(Courtesy William M. Quinn)*

Lt. Charles Mord Stromberg. *(Courtesy of Don Lowe)*

Charles Mord Stromberg *(farthest right in front row)* with the 19th Infantry Regiment on August 5, 1905 in the Philippines. *(Courtesy of Don Lowe)*

Saint Amand-sur-Ornain, in a photo sent home by Lt. William A. Cross of Company I, 28th Regiment. *(Courtesy of Frederick W. Ford)*

Alexander McKinlock *(book in hand, second from right)* at a society event, ca. 1905. *(Courtesy Lake Forest College Archives and Special Collections)*

Twelve-year-old Alexander McKinlock *(on horse)* at the Onwentsia Club Horse Show in Lake Forest in 1905. *(Photo DN-0003108, Chicago Daily News negatives collection, Chicago History Museum. Used with permission.)*

Marion Rappleye McKinlock *(left)* being saluted by Miss Ermina Carry at the National Service School Camp Number Three in Lake Geneva, Wisconsin, in 1916. *(Photo DN-0066962, Chicago Daily News negatives collection, Chicago History Museum. Used with permission.)*

George Alexander McKinlock Jr. *(Courtesy of the Lake Forest-Lake Bluff, Ill., Historical Society)*

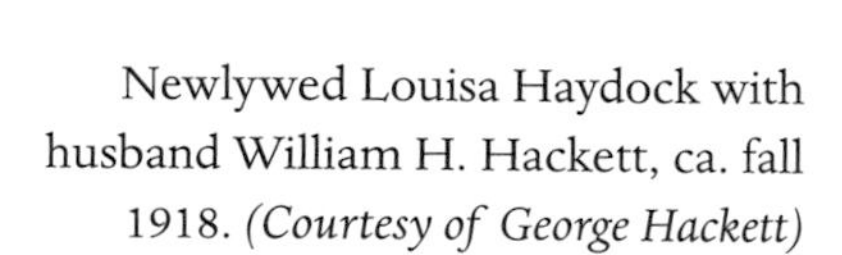

Newlywed Louisa Haydock with husband William H. Hackett, ca. fall 1918. *(Courtesy of George Hackett)*

George Buchanan Redwood. *(Courtesy of the Maryland Historical Society. Used with permission.)*

Officers of the 28th Regiment's 3rd Battalion, undated, but probably taken in February or March, 1918. *Front row, left to right:* Lt. George G. Haydock, unknown, Lt. George B. Redwood, Lt. Richard A. Newhall, Lt. John S. Morrison, unknown. *Back row, second from left:* Lt. Earle Carothers, Capt. Francis M. Van Natter, Lt. Charles McKnolly, Lt. Howard E. Hawkinson, Lt. Sam J. Ervin, Dr. Parker, Capt. Henry E. Mosher, Lt. John G. Mays, Lt. James T. Carroll, unknown. *(Courtesy Williams College Archives and Special Collections. Used with permission.)*

Company K's Capt. Henry Mosher *(front left)* with his men in the trenches at Seicheprey, France. *(Courtesy of Paul Densmore)*

A rare look at the trenches: Company K, 28th Regiment at Seicheprey in a photo taken by Capt. Henry Mosher. *(Courtesy of Paul Densmore)*

George Redwood *(left)* displays the four German prisoners captured March 29, 1918. *(Courtesy of the Maryland Historical Society. Used with permission.)*

The staff of the 1st Division's 3rd Machine Gun Battalion. *At center* is Major Chester Arthur Davis; Alexander McKinlock is at *far right*. *(Courtesy the Robert R. McCormick Research Center)*

Robert Roger Haydock *(right)*, George Haydock's brother Robert *(center)*, and his son Robert Jr. ca. 1918. *(Courtesy of Robert Haydock III)*

The officers of the 3rd Battalion, 28th Regiment, taken in Vollenes, France on April 24, 1918. Identification, according to postwar notes of Francis M. Van Natter and Herman Dacus, is as follows: 1. Lt. Earle Carothers. 2. Lt. James T. Carroll. 3. Lt. John W. Scott. 4. Co. L's Capt. Van Natter. 5. Lt. Lafayette I. Morris. 6. Lt. Daniel J. Birmingham. 7. Co. I's Capt. Willis James Tack. 8. Lt. Gerald R. Tyler. 9. Battalion commander Major Francis H. Burr. 10. Lt. John S. Morrison. 11. Lt. Charles McKnolly. 12. Lt. Paul C. Venable. 13. Co. M's Capt. Emmett W. Smith. 14. Lt. Jerome H. Brown. 15. Lt. John L. Dunn. 16. Lt. Carlos O. Cooley. 17. Co. K's Capt. Henry E. Mosher. 18. Lt. James W. Dye. 19. Lt. Howard E. Hawkinson. 20. Lt. George G. Haydock. 21. Lt. Richard A. Newhall. 22. Lt. George B. Redwood. *(U.S. National Archives)*

Elizabeth Howe Bliss, ca. 1917.
(Courtesy of Daniel Newhall)

Officers of the 2nd Battalion, 28th Infantry Regiment, U.S. 1st Division at Fontaine, France, on April 24, 1918. Battalion commander Axel Severin Rasmussen is seated *(fifth from left)*; 1st Lt. Irving William Wood of Company E is standing *(third from left)*. *(U.S. National Archives)*

Lt. Col. Jesse Marling Cullison *(fourth from left)* with 28th Infantry Regiment commander Hanson E. Ely *(fourth from right)*. *(Courtesy of the Colonel Robert R. McCormick Research Center)*

Supported by French tanks, the 3rd Battalion, 28th Infantry Regiment goes over the top at Cantigny on the morning of May 28, 1918. *(U.S. Army Signal Corps photo, courtesy of the Colonel Robert R. McCormick Research Center)*

Cantigny, view from the southeast of the village. *(American Battle Monuments Commission)*

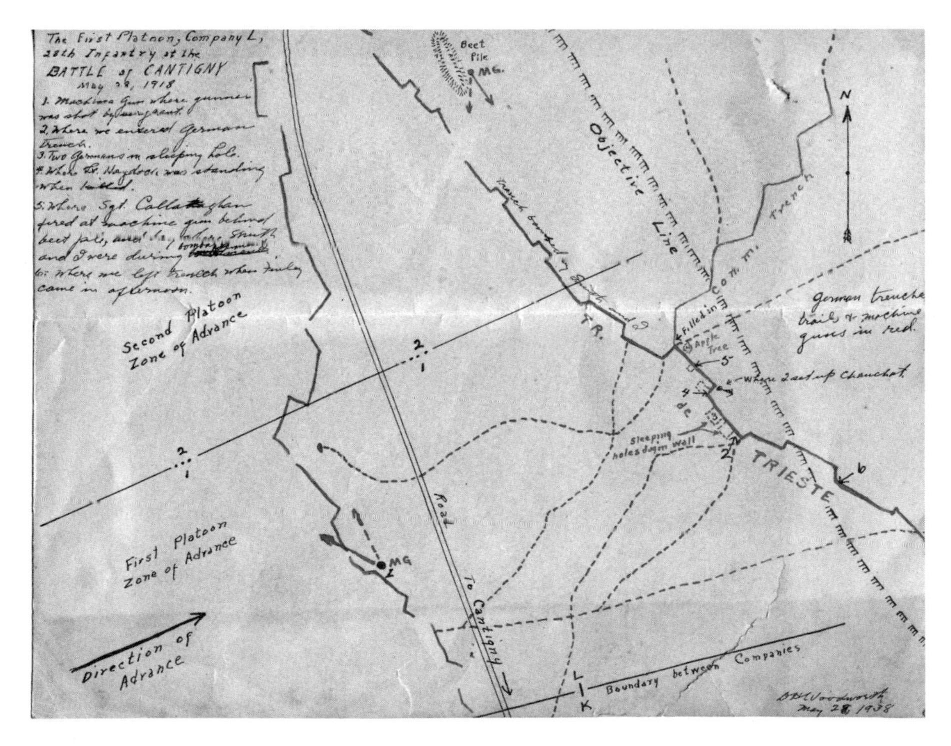

Map of Company L's advance at Cantigny, drawn by former Company L Pvt. Douglas Woodworth on May 28, 1938. The number 4 marks the spot where Lt. George Guest Haydock was killed by machine-gun fire. *(Courtesy of Robert Gould Shaw)*

Muriel McCormick in 1922. *(Courtesy of Todd Protzman-Davis, www.villaturicum.com)*

Richard Newhall *(center, back row)*, Elizabeth Newhall *(seated in front of him)*, and their family, ca. 1963. *(Courtesy of Daniel Newhall)*

Newhall would describe Mosher as "quite a crony of mine" and was happy to expand his soirees to a sister company. "It was pleasant to feel the necessity of being hospitable, for it made our rather dreary dining room seem quite festive for awhile," he wrote.

"It is hard not to talk military shop or local gossip in a crowd of very varied personalities but we even got away from that for a while—on to grand opera!"

Newhall did not look forward to leaving Madame Thierry's welcome home. "When the time comes I shall be sorry to leave old Madame Thierry," he wrote, "because she has been very kind and motherly to me.

"Yesterday she fixed me a belt for my oilskin, and the other day she made a cover for my helmet, and today it is a French pan-cake saved for me from supper, or a little glass of cognac from the French sergeant's mess, and tomorrow it is a glass of hot coffee brought up to my room before I go out in the morning.

"Sometimes I can't help feeling that we bourgeoisie have too much reserve in our relations with one another and that the franker, more readily assertive friendliness of the peasants is preferable."

Within days, the 28th Regiment left St. Amand, and Newhall bid good-bye to his host.

"I have had to say farewell to old Madame Thierry," he wrote. "It was a little incident, my stay with her, quite like a piece of a story book. She was truly very kind to me and I was truly sorry to say 'good bye'—in a way.

"She got up at 4 A.M. to see me off, having been very urgent indeed that I should not slip away without seeing her. At parting she was quite tearful, in a motherly way, and I was glad I knew enough French to be able to tell her how much I appreciated her kindness."

The "little old Madame," he would add, "certainly will be one of my pleasantly unique recollections of the war. Our parting stands out in the livid, melodramatic light of an early morning departure, bright fires, hurrying shadows, men and vehicles crowded together, bustle and commotion but no confusion, a final wait for the laggards or the words of command and then we are off for another place."

The regiment arrived at Mandres, behind Seicheprey, in early March.

Like many other villages near the front lines, it was but a pile of ruins—just another "desolate place, one of the most desolate imaginable if you have to walk through alone about 2 A.M. of a moon light night," Newhall wrote.

Its inhabitants gone, Mandres soon buzzed with military activity.

"If the civilian population is gone you really hardly think of the place as a town anymore," Newhall wrote. "The question of the moment is too much that of finding adequate shelter for the men in undestroyed buildings, and in locating the 'abris' to be used in case the enemy is impudent enough to shell the place.

"Perhaps we may sometimes recall that the battered quarters occupied by the company's officers were once part of some person's 'home,' but if we do, it is to be thankful that they can't see its present condition. For us it is a very comfortable accomodation of which we make grateful use. Its abandoned state has advantages.

"If the sleeping room, with its five occupants is stuffy and the window refuses to open, a shoe in a firm hand quickly knocks out a pane of glass, providing immediate ventilation. Out houses, no longer needed, can be used for fuel."

Military necessity overruled all other concerns—although on occasion a bill would come due for the army's renovations. "At one place where we had a company officers' mess the proprietor presented us with a bill of 286 francs for rent and damages," Newhall wrote. "We eventually settled for fifteen."

A big plus to moving into the lines was that "drill and maneuver are now things of the past," he added. "There may be fatigue parties instead, usually at night, expeditions to put up barbed wire or carry up material or dig. Often it is hard work and at a distance, but there is at least the feeling that it is important and necessary, and that it contributes directly to the desired end.

"Then too the proximity to the front gives a zest to any form of 'war work,' and there is always the excited anticipation of going into the line."

Though the sector was mainly used as a rest area by German troops, the front was active—much more so than that at Sommerviller.

"There was continual rifle and machine gun fire on the front and daily artillery fire," the anonymous authors of the 1st Division's history would remember. "Patrolling became very active and each side contended for the mastery of no-man's-land."

Soon after taking over the lines in mid-January, a patrol from the 16th Regiment had been cut to pieces in an ambush, the German fire killing five men and wounding several more. Hundreds of German shells tumbled out of the sky and into the American lines each day, and the Americans responded in kind.

Compared to the relative quiet at Sommerviller, the Seicheprey front—also known as Ansauville—had its dangers. Many of the men of the 1st Division who had still been in training camps or en route to France when the division first entered the trenches would receive what amounted to a crash course in trench warfare in the mud- and gas-infested ditch there at Seicheprey, where the threat of a full-bore German offensive was unlikely, but where the Germans' love of gas kept all on edge.

In addition to shells, canisters filled with chlorine and phosgene were tossed the Americans' way by the Germans, but the most feared chemical weapon was mustard gas, which was first used by the Germans in July 1917 and by the following October had caused more casualties on the Western Front than all of the other gases combined.

Hard to detect, mustard gas caused chemical burns that "were said to take from three to five weeks to heal and made a man 'practically useless for that length of time,'" Rexmond C. Cochrane of the U.S. Army Chemical Corps would write. "Its least effect on the eyes was a loss of vision for from three days to three weeks."

The 1st Division's soldiers were issued French and British gas masks, and while they were difficult to see through and breathe through, they afforded some protection from the gases, which were usually more debilitating than lethal.

Mustard gas, which pooled in the soil and in the bottom of dugouts, was the most insidious of all, even working its foul way into clothing and food. Because of its nature, Cochrane wrote, orders directed that "anyone passing through a gassed area was to beat and shake his clothes before entering a dugout, and to use soap suds as first aid treatment for liquid mustard on the skin."

The Americans returned the favor with gases developed by the French—mostly phosgene and cyanogen chloride—but their ability to return fire was at the mercy of the French, who supplied the ammunition and artillery. At Seicheprey, the 1st's guns were provided an allotment of fewer than one hundred gas rounds per day.

The 1st Brigade also endured several raids-in-force, the most severe coming on March 1 after three consecutive days of intense artillery pounding. The Germans went over at daybreak "in 6 columns under the protection of a rolling barrage," the 1st's history says.

The brunt of the raid fell on the 18th Regiment, most of which had been withdrawn from its frontline positions. At 5:30 A.M., the forward lines were engulfed in a "tornado of bursting shell and bullets," and the backline artillery positions were "deluged with high explosive shell and mustard gas . . . Trenches, parapets, shelters and emplacements were demolished . . . One platoon had returned to its front line position and was caught by the German box barrage.

"The raiding party, consisting of two hundred and twenty men, taken from shock troops and provided with light machine guns and flamethrowers, rushed over the little band of Americans, who suffered a loss of twenty killed and twelve prisoners, besides a number of wounded."

The Americans in the reserve trenches opened up with salvos of their own, quickly killing seventeen of the raiders. The Germans withdrew, leaving behind a trove of hand grenades, explosives, and four of their dead found with flamethrowers strapped to their backs. "Some of the American dead in the front line dug-outs had been burned to death by these cruel devices," the 1st's history says; the doughboys would turn these same "cruel devices" on their foes before long.

Shortly after the raid, Newhall and the other officers in the 28th Regiment prepared to take over the lines held by the 18th Regiment. The relief was carefully made on March 7, being preceded by "visits of personal reconnaissance by the officers to their sectors, consultation with the lieutenants in the position, exploration of the routes for coming and going, inspection of the dugouts and store rooms, questioning about the enemy's habits," Newhall wrote.

"There is something eminently practical and common-sense about it which is a wonderful relief to me, sick to nauseation of the simulated conditions of maneuver."

George Haydock also made ready for his first tour of the American trenches. "I think I shall see some of that part of the world that I got familiar with last fall, only under a little different circumstances this time," he wrote on the eve of moving up to the line. "They have gone and cancelled leaves, but that is to be expected. We will see the circus instead."

Soon enough, Haydock and Newhall found themselves slopping around in the trenches that cut through the heart of the ruined village of Seicheprey, where constant worries over gas attacks, shellings, and German raids indeed made life a "circus," though a deadly one.

"There's nothing you can conceive that can picture to your mind the conditions of No Man's Land," the 3rd Battalion's 1st Lt. Daniel J. Birmingham would write on March 19, 1918.

"It certainly was named correctly. Such a damn place must be a part of hell in some sections. Dead Germans. Equipment, legs, wire, stink, mud, water, holes and more holes and oh, my, the barbed wire.

"It's a strange sensation when the shrapnel starts to drop all around you, alarms of gas screaming all over the area, mud waist-high and not a dam dug out in sight, trench not four feet deep and a gap wide open between your parapet and Fritz's. It sure is not a glorious feeling."

"Our men were splendid and always kept keen and cheerful even under somewhat trying conditions," Haydock wrote upon his return from the lines on March 17. "It is pretty hard to ask a man to be on the alert for 14 hours standing in mud and then get him to do any work in the day time."

His own duties were more tiresome. "It is a good deal of a strain being on the job 24 hours out of the day but that is all made up for now where we can sleep to our hearts' content."

In the trenches, he wrote, "we had some bombardments which are indeed very noisy things and make you move around with a crook in your back or to hang on to the front of the trench as if you expected it to get away from you.

"One very nasty one lasted about two hours and then stopped very suddenly. There was a few minutes of silence that seemed worse than when the guns were going, and then just as the sun started to come up the birds began to sing as though nothing had happened and it made you feel that everything was all right."

On another night, "during a little excitement some M.G.s were on the job and for the first time I had the experience of hitting the dirt by reflex action," Haydock wrote. "The first thing I knew I was flat on my face in a mud puddle, which in itself is proof that I did not do it consciously for I was wet the rest of the night."

What he couldn't accomplish in the dreary drill of the previous winter, Haydock accomplished at Seicheprey. "It was at this place that he won the highest respect of every man in the platoon," one of Company L's regulars, Pvt. John D. A. Rader, would write.

"Lt. Haydock never asked a man to do a thing or take a chance that he wouldn't do or take himself. But when the machine guns were in action against us he would hold his hand above the parapet, and if they were not near enough to hit his hand he would rise up and look out into 'No Man's Land.' He never became excited and was always calm. He became popular throughout the entire company and from that time on was looked upon as a fearless man."

Gas attacks forced men to resort to their cumbersome masks—and a smaller enemy helped add to the misery of the long nights on alert. "There were lots of rats up where we were, and their moving around got a rise out of me," Haydock wrote.

One night, "there had been a rumor that someone was in our line and I had gone to investigate. My runner was right behind me and we were pussy footing down a C.T. [communication trench] when we heard a splash, which made us stop and listen.

"I had my gun cocked and started to snoop around a corner when I heard another splash and then a little one like a person putting his foot back to catch his balance. We crouched down and waited for about five minutes for another move. We both felt pretty sure it was a rat but were not taking chances.

"It turned out that the first noise was a rat and also the second. The third was made by my stepping on a long handled shovel which had made the noise several feet away."

By dawn's first light, the frazzled and exhausted troops, nerves shot, imagined the worst.

"We were on the edge of what had once been a wood but shell fire had left nothing but stumps," Haydock wrote. "In the early hours of morning these said stumps had a habit of walking around and forming up in line in a most astonishing way. In fact we even had to go so far as to shoot a couple of them."

Familiarity with the terrain and where each German outpost was located could mean the difference between life and death.

"I got to know almost every trench and the older shells holes," Company K's Henry Mosher would write. "If a bombardment started I knew right where to go and about what to expect."

The Germans' habit of repositioning their guns during the night added to the peril. "Usually we can tell where Fritz has his machine guns, but last night he moved in a new one," Company K's twenty-five-year-old 2nd Lt. Lafayette Irwin Morris wrote on March 25.

Returning from a nighttime patrol one morning in the predawn, "I stumbled against a stake and he at once opened up and *put, put, put* and I dived into the first hole. Said hole was ninety-nine-ninety-ninths filled with mud and water, but I could stand that better than those little leaden messages that were zip-zipping over me. Boy, I was close to Mother Nature for once.

"Tomorrow night I am going to take a handful of lemons (grenades) and try to bring in a Boche gun. We usually find the machine gunners wearing Red Cross arm bands. Can you beat that."

He would close: "Somebody has sent up a red rocket and the artillery is sending over some steel beer kegs to the Hun. Guess I'd better get on the firestep at once."

Richard Newhall found his life at the front to be one of "absolute quiet alternating with pandemonium, with little intervals of minor excitement. I got plenty of time to ponder things during the long nights when it was necessary to be on the alert but when nothing happened."

Seemingly unperturbed by the reality of his situation, he instead reveled in his deadly and grotesque surroundings. "Really it was the most picturesque sitting out under a clear sky watching and listening," he would write.

"The outline of the gas sentry's head and shoulders was the only thing to keep me company. At intervals, off to the left and right, the Germans would shoot up flares which would light up the landscape and make big shadows for a moment.

"Occasionally a machine gun would rip off a short burst of fire. By and by over head came the angry burr of a squadrilla flying over into Boche-land. Not long after came the sound of distant bomb-dropping.

" 'Hear that sonny?' says I to the sentry. 'They're dropping bombs on the German dumps.'

" 'I hope to Christ one of 'em hits the Kaiser right on the noodle,' came back the answer from the most boyish member of the platoon who happened to be on post. I guess we should all say 'Amen' to such a prayer.

"A rat splashing along the trench arouses my suspicion that some one is approaching and my hand goes to my pistol, but it doesn't take long to be able to detect ratish sounds and I ignore them. Over on the right one of our big batteries starts bracketing (i.e. firing a long and a short shot at the same point), trying to find a German machine gun."

In return, "the Hun machine gun would come back with a laughing burst of fire as much to say, 'Never touched me,' and by and by our guns give it up. Not so my platoon for whenever the German shot off his rat-tat-tat I would hear an answering pump-pump-pump from my right automatic rifle and would know that Corporal Stetz was right on the job."

He would add: "The cheerfulness with which the men adapted themselves to living in such surroundings delighted me."

As to whether they were in any real peril of being attacked, Newhall was dubious.

"I doubt if there were many (if any) Germans in the enemy front line," he wrote. "They usually went back quite a ways to sleep during the day. There are those in our battalion who advanced the theory that even at night the Germans held their first line with a wooden-legged flare shooter.

"The theory was that he marched up and down all night shooting flares at frequent intervals to make it seem to us as if there were quite a number of soldiers opposite us. The choice of a wooden-legged man was because the trenches were so wet. An unmaimed soldier would have to have rubber boots and rubber, you know, is scarce in Germany.

"Efficiency again!"

Although Haydock was several hundred yards away with the 1st Platoon, Newhall managed to find some needed human companionship in his runner, Pvt. Robert Powell, who remained at his side at all times.

"You can't help getting a friendly feeling towards the man who always goes with you into the unknown and possible danger," Newhall wrote. "And he is always willing to go without question, either with me or carrying messages by himself. In addition he looks after me, rolls my pack, washes my mess tin, runs my errands. I like to think he is fond of me.

"Certainly I would feel a personal loss if anything happened to him. He lived with me in the same dug-out and ate the same food and led the same kind of existence as I did, and naturally a pleasant relation develops under such conditions if there is not some good reason for the contrary."

Almost nightly, Newhall and the loyal Private Powell were called to action. Newhall would describe a typical incident:

" 'Lieutenant,' calls the sentry. 'Barrage rocket on our left.' He might have saved himself the trouble for he had scarcely reported when BINGO the whole horizon behind us flashes. Boom-boom-boom-whing-whing-whing-bang-bang-bang—just as fast as you can say it.

"Some one in the extreme front line had signaled for artillery protection and in less than a minute had got a curtain of explosions along our whole position. Everyone with me moved to his battle station and waited, listening to the sound of our own shells singing over our heads."

All the excitement was confusing.

"We didn't know what it meant. It might be the Germans were trying to put on a raid. It might be the beginning of the 'big offensive.' It might be merely the presence of a nervous lieutenant in the forward trench. The last theory was the one to which I held—correctly I believe.

"Three times in one night this happened, which must have amused Mr. Boche immensely if he was not trying to start anything. Another time, however, the barrage came when our side was starting something and then there was answering fire from the Germans. That was the real thing.

"We just hugged the enemy side of the trench and waited. There was nothing else to do. The trench was the best protection there could be. There might be a counter attack on us after the bombardment. Anything might come. Nothing did come, but the eagerness and coolness of the men under bombardment delighted me. I hope I have at least one chance to lead that 2nd platoon 'over the top.'"

Richard Newhall would get his chance to do just that, and before too long.

14

Orders Is Orders

Sometimes when he was out there the night would explode, and he would drop quickly and press his nose deep into the musky chalky earth of France and lie still, detecting no sound but his own heartbeat and the slow hissing from above, as the torn-up ground around him turned as vacant and white and forbidding as the surface of the moon and shone, almost as if lit by the sun; and it was at times like those that he waited, and he waited, and he waited.

This was one of those nights that found George Buchanan Redwood prone and waiting in the sticky mud, vainly watching at the edge of a German trench until the dawn brought just enough light for him to espy the silhouetted shape of the sentry.

Then, with no sound, Redwood and four Americans leaped over the parapet and in a wild, muffled melee made some history, securing four of the Boche and dragging them back through the perilous light of dawn to the American lines, where newspaper reporters and a bucketful of medals awaited the five doughboys who had become the first to secure live German prisoners in a trench raid.

Redwood's notorious exploit would put him on the front pages of the newspapers back home and crown the 28th Regiment's experience at Seicheprey, which until that point of March 29, 1918, had consisted of the usual—the usual hail of gas, sometimes as many as five hundred canisters per day; the usual shelling, hundreds of rounds blanketing the American lines on an average day; and the usual patrols, which until now had secured some information but no real, live prisoners to show off to the Allies, and to the folks back home, and to the German Army itself, which had been the source of many a black eye dating back to the deaths of Gresham, Enright, and Hay almost five months before.

The 26th Regiment had launched a daring raid on the Germans on March 10 and gotten nothing for its effort; in retaliation, the Germans on March 19 sent a large raiding party toward the lines held by Capt. Edward Johnston's Company E in the Bois de Remieres on the right of the American line.

"All was still along the front except for an occasional rifle shot and the ever present display of star shells," the 28th Regiment's history says. "Suddenly, about 3 A.M., the whole of the German line seemed to burst into a blinding flame, and the roar and crash of trench mortar bombs and high explosive shells shook the earth."

The German attackers were cut down by the division's artillery, and the survivors hied back to their lines. Disaster had been averted by the quick action of the 5th, 6th, and 7th artillery regiments, but the regiment lost its first junior officer, 2nd Lt. John B. Graham—a "wealthy Irish-American from New York, a brainy, likeable fellow," Company E's 1st Lt. Irving W. Wood would remember.

Graham, twenty-six, and a squad of men had been sent forward into no-man's-land by Johnston to establish a forward post, only to be "caught in the midst of the enemy fire. Three men were killed outright." Graham and two others were wounded, Pvt. Robert West dying two days later, and Graham on April 1.

The commotion led to the expectation that an assault would follow all along the line. "We had every reason to believe they were about to follow their barrage with one on us," Henry Mosher would write.

Just prior to the raid, Mosher had loaned his Colt .45 to a machine-gun officer who was setting out to inspect his lines. Needing to do the same in the face of the German barrage, Mosher realized he had only his cane and a Filipino machete known as a bolo.

"Of course I could have borrowed my man's rifle yet I have never had more confidence for a scrap than I had with that bolo that morning," he would write. "My plan was to fire a Very flare into a Boche's face and then go after him with the bolo."

The German raid having fizzled, Mosher would not get a chance to use his bolo that day, but he was prepared in other ways than physical should the Germans start coming over.

"I have never called for a barrage, and none in the company has ever done so, for I have always felt that our infantry was as good as the Boche without the assistance of our artillery and I have never been wrong yet," he wrote.

"Instead of staying in a dugout and immediately calling for a counter-barrage whenever Fritz put one down (as I must admit more than one has) I have waited for the [operation posts] to send word that the Boche were coming across.

"Personally when I fight I don't want a barrage over my head (with its inevitable 'shorts') if I can help it. One can hear nothing and with the trenches so close together he can seldom tell his own bursts from those of the enemy unless they are in his immediate vicinity."

Something of a race ensued in the attempt to be the first regiment to secure one or more German prisoners. Company G's 2nd Lt. Jim Quinn would claim that he made a bet with Teddy Roosevelt over who would be the first to bring back a "Fritz," the prize a bottle of cognac.

Being discovered by the Germans was only part of the risk, Henry Mosher would write: "I was sniped at by the Boche a number of times . . . yet my narrowest escapes from bullets have thus far been from my own men. One night about the middle of March about 2:30 in the morning I was inspecting our outposts. Sgt. Mcginley who had posted the men was with me and told me he knew the exact shell hole it was in."

Also with Mosher was his orderly, a seventeen-year-old private named Jack Lipschitz. "It was pitch dark," Mosher wrote. "The Boche had shot up our wire so bad that we hardly realized that we had left it until we ran into the Boche entanglements.

"We then started back across toward our own line when without a challenge or warning of any kind a rifle shot was fired point blank at me from a hole less than ten feet away and an automatic opened up with a full clip (almost 18 shots)."

The bullet "could not have missed my neck by a half inch and the Chauchaut bullets went on both sides of me and the sergeant and orderly declare they went on both sides of them. We instantly fell into a shell hole and I yelled the name of the corporal who was in charge of the post for I recognized our Chauchaut rifle and knew it was the post we had been looking for. When we reached it the men were almost trembling, thinking they must have at least wounded all of us."

Pvt. John H. Tritt, he added, "had followed me ever since we left the Boche wire and thought as he fired that he had me point-blank. And how the automatic could have missed the three of us is the greatest miracle I know of but on the whole it has given me more confidence than anything else that has happened."

The military career of George Redwood's friend and fellow lieutenant Sam J. Ervin would fall victim to just such a case of mistaken identity that March, and the incident proved a cautionary tale for the young officers manning the line.

The twenty-one-year-old Ervin, a graduate of the University of North Carolina, joined Company I in November 1917 after receiving his commission as a 2nd lieutenant at Fort Oglethorpe near Chatanooga.

Destined for a long career in the U.S. Senate—which culminated in a belated rise to national fame as chair of the committee investigating Watergate in 1973—Ervin in 1918 was just another wet-behind-the-ears junior officer struggling to lead a platoon in the mire at Seicheprey.

"I was solicitous concerning the men of my platoon, but disdainful of my own well-being," Ervin would write years later. Company I's position in the lines was in the "deepest depression in the immediate area," which was "filled with icy rainwater and could not be drained," and so Ervin sought some place where his men could rotate for rest and sleep.

On his left, the company's Lt. Frank Naibert occupied a portion of trench with a "dry and somewhat commodious dug-out," and by arrangement with Naibert, Ervin was able to give some of the men in his platoon a respite from the ice and muck and rainwater. Ervin himself stayed awake for several nights in his sloppy sector seven hundred yards away. One night, however, one of his men wandered outside the sector and, returning, was challenged by the sentry.

The errant doughboy—"a native of a European country"—became excited, "lapsed into his native language," and was shot and killed by the sentry, who believed he was a German trying to infiltrate the lines.

A rumor that the Germans were coming over followed the single shot, and Ervin fired a rocket to signal a request for a defensive barrage. Quickly realizing no raid was imminent, and that he was unable to make good judgments in his present condition, the exhausted and ill Ervin left his platoon in charge of a couple of noncoms and made his way to Naibert's dugout, where he fell asleep.

The next morning he returned to his platoon and found all well; later in the afternoon, however, he was relieved from command. His absence from his own sector had been discovered during the night, and because he had left for Naibert's dugout, "and I had gone to it without the authority of any superior officer," Ervin realized that "a case could be made for the proposition that I had technically abandoned my post in the face of the enemy, and was subject to court martial if my act in so doing was willfully committed."

Though such courts-martial were rare, they were not unknown; in 1918, 250 lieutenants were tried on various infractions. In 1919, another 1,461 junior officers were tried. In fact, the performance of every officer in and out of the lines continued to be scrutinized that spring, and those found wanting were weeded out—a luxury that would end with the heavy turnover in dead and wounded among officers when the 1st Division entered battle in May and July.

Another of Company I's junior officers, Robert Obadiah Purdy Jr.—a 1914 graduate of the University of South Carolina School of Law and the son of a prominent judge in Sumter, South Carolina—faced his own troubles that March when company commander Willis J. Tack recommended that a board of officers be appointed to determine whether or not Purdy's commission should be "terminated."

The son of a small-town Wisconsin businessman, Tack, a 1914 graduate of West Point, had risen to the command of Company I at the age of just twenty-three, taking command after Charles Senay fell ill with dysentery.

He quickly found that Purdy, twenty-six, exasperated him, and he wrote the 28th Regiment's commander, Col. Hanson Ely, on March 19 to say that Purdy was "not capable of properly performing the duties of a platoon leader. In every case where I give orders to him I find it necessary to repeat them several times and unless he is given minute instructions as to the smallest details, he seems helpless . . .

"A typical example of his inefficiency is: During the alert drill on the night 18–19 March, 1918 it required 40 minutes for Lieut. Purdy to move his platoon about 500 yards and place them in position, after he had previously reconnoitered his position twice. The platoon became lost in moving to their position."

A board of officers was indeed convened to determine the fate of Bob Purdy; in the end, "the recommendation made thereby was not adverse to that officer," a War Department report says, but Purdy soon found himself being transferred out of Company I and into Company M.

(Any questions regarding his leadership abilities became moot when he took a machine-gun bullet in the heart while advancing at the Paris-Soissons Road on the morning of July 19.)

Ervin faced accusations that went beyond mere ineptness. Distraught, he brought his "warm-hearted friend" and billet mate George Redwood to a meeting with the Baltimore attorney Col. Redmond C. Stewart, the judge advocate for the 1st Division, who was investigating the incident.

Stewart would remember Redwood making a case for the "raw, young officer . . . George gave me his thoughts about the fellow, and having absolute faith in George's opinion, the man was not tried, but given another chance and made good; very, very good."

Stewart subsequently informed Ervin that as far as he was concerned, the incident was the result of his "inexperience, over-exertion, and illness and not by willfulness," and that he would recommend that any charges be dropped.

Ervin, however, found it tougher to make his case before the 28th Regiment's commander. Ervin wrote that he "begged" Ely to reassign him to the front line but was refused; desperate, Ervin sent a letter "through military channels" to the AEF's headquarters asking that he be allowed to be discharged as a second lieutenant and reenlist as a private.

In the end, "I was honorably discharged as a Second Lieutenant for inefficiency, enlisted as a private, and assigned to duty with my old outfit," he would write. The now-Private Ervin would redeem himself in battle soon after his reenlistment.

On March 11, German artillery nearly killed one of the most famous of all doughboys—Lt. Archie Roosevelt. "The Huns were strafing heavily and an attack by them was expected," his older brother and commanding officer, Ted, would recall. "He was redisposing his men when he was hit by a shell and badly wounded."

A fragment from the first shell caught Archie just above the left elbow, wrote Alexander McKinlock, who subsequently visited his Harvard classmate in the hospital, where Roosevelt was laid up for four months. "He said it didn't pain much so he stayed up until another went off and a fragment pierced through between the kneecap and knee and then he was down and out."

Because of the heavy shelling, Archie could not be removed from the lines that day. "The next day when they (the Red Cross) started to take him out the trenches were narrow so they tried going over the top," McKinlock wrote, "but the Boche immediately opened up on them with shrapnel and the Red Cross jumped into the trenches and left him lying on top (he had quite a few people to thank for a pleasant ride) and came out afterward and took him in without further mishap."

The wires hummed with news of the former president's son's injuries, and within days the French pinned a Croix de Guerre on his pillow—"merely for being wounded," Richard Newhall would note sourly.

The elder Roosevelt, meanwhile, took the news in ho-hum style. "I'm glad he wasn't killed," Teddy harrumphed. "I guess that he will get over it all right and be ready to go on the firing line again."

Though not slopping in the trenches with the mud-spattered infantry, McKinlock managed to get his first taste of war. Reconnoitering the 3rd Machine-Gun Battalion's approach to the sector, "we arrived at the cross roads at Baumont and while waiting there for our horses in order that we might get back to the troops since we were to supervise the guiding of them to their positions in the line, the Boche dropped a salvo on the cross roads and but for good fortune in having walked across the road from where we had been standing, we would probably both have been killed, or at least seriously wounded," Maj. Chester Davis would tell Marion McKinlock.

"I was amused that this experience enthused your son. I was rather disturbed because of his expressed desire at that time to actually see a shell burst. Personally I cherished no such wish."

McKinlock "enthused" over being in another tight spot with Davis while attempting to make contact with a French regiment on the 1st Division's left. "It was not a dark and stormy night, it was just a plain night, not dark nor was it light when the Major and I embarked in the General's car," he wrote on April 3.

Heading for the French command post, McKinlock and Davis chose the shortest route on one of the main east-west roads that paralleled the Seicheprey front, about three kilometers behind the lines. Though shells fell on the lines to the north, "it took the form of ordinary counter battery work and did not appear to be worth any thought," McKinlock wrote.

Approaching a small village, however, they found the ruins aflame from German high-explosive shells. "We decided to go through and as we went ahead a couple of 77s [3 inch] dropped in the ruins on either side of us.

"I was pretty darned scared because we were in one of those enclosed [automobiles] which are all glass windows just like a fish tank and I could just see a big one landing near and the concussion shattering the glass."

On the edge of the village, "we had to pass in front of one of our batteries against which the Boche were doing some counter battery work, when I was really scared green.

"For just at the place where we ought to have put on full steam ahead, we were held up by a ration cart with a four mule team which was directly across the road with one mule, the off wheeler down, and no driver (the driver and mule I afterward learned had been killed by fragments)."

McKinlock jumped out of the car "like a shot out of a gun (it was a relief to be out of that plate glass car palace which may be as good as the pictures show in the *Saturday Evening Post* to protect the family from dust and rain but which ain't much when 'Fragments From France' are flying around) and ran after that mule stick in hand and heart in mouth."

Unable to corral the three animals, McKinlock managed to run them far enough away to let the car go through. "It isn't very thrilling to read about," McKinlock acknowledged, "but there are thrills in the doing."

A greater thrill awaited George Redwood, who in early February had been selected to serve as intelligence officer for the 28th's 3rd Battalion.

At Seicheprey, Redwood quickly became busy fulfilling his duties, spending long nights on patrol in no-man's-land, listening at the edge of a German trench or wire, mapping the enemy's position in the dark.

He had collected some trophies, odd bits of German memorabilia, which he sent home to Baltimore for the edification of his younger brother, Francis, and other relatives.

"I am enclosing Francis a German shoulder strap of the 259 Reserve Infantry Regt and a piece of collar," he wrote to Mom-Mom on March 7. "The silver lace is the mark of an huteroffizier [unteroffizer] or corporal and the Piping signifies infantry. I wish I could send him a Boche helmet I have, but fear it would be stolen."

To a "Miss U.L.H.," he sent another shoulder strap. "It is an Infantry shoulder strap of the 259th Reserve regiment which comes from Hanover whence also flows some of the blood royal in British veins today," he wrote on March 20.

"Thus, for all we know, the erstwhile wearer may be a sixteenth cousin many times removed from George V, by the Strafing of Gott, king of Great Britain and Ireland, Emperor of India and all the rest of it. But I doubt it."

"I am not in the habit of toting a bayonet about, but am armed only with an automatic pistol for self defense," he would tell one "bloodthirsty" cousin who had sent her wishes that he push "a bayonet through a Boche."

"I have never yet had an occasion to shoot even that in earnest, and for all I know, I never may."

Still, he was happy to provide some of the fruits of his nighttime labors: "Well, since you have such feelings here is a scrap of German uniform on which I think by careful scrutiny I have detected GERMAN BLOOD! (but sh! suppose it were only vin rouge or red ink!)

"You had best spill on more to get proper effect and possibly a little white enamel judiciously worked in might be palmed off on the unsuspecting as GERMAN BRAINS!!!"

Redwood got his opportunity to collect more than memorabilia when on the morning of March 29 information was passed to the 28th's headquarters that six Germans had been observed entering and leaving an observation post in the German front line.

At 3:00 A.M., Hanson Ely issued orders for a patrol to be sent out to capture them. "Lieutenant Redwood was awakened immediately and ordered to 'go get em,'" the Associated Press would report. Redwood asked for volunteers from the 3rd Battalion's intelligence unit, comprised of noncoms and enlisted men from each of the four companies.

Although the late hour gave the patrol little chance of returning before daylight, two corporals (Carson L. Shumate of Company I and Henry J. Mongeau of Company L) and two privates (Edward V. Armstrong of Company L and Bernard H. Bolt of Company K) quickly volunteered. Five others joined in as a "covering detachment" posted in no-man's-land.

"Of course we all wanted to go with him," Armstrong would recall. "Well, he picked four of us to go, and then prayed that we might be successful." As well, Redwood promised the men "that if we took prisoners . . . he would read us the Gospel on Easter Sunday."

The prepatrol prayer was true to form for Redwood. "Men who went on patrols with him have told me that after leaving the trench and entering No Man's Land, he always knelt in a shell-hole and prayed," Sam Ervin would recall. Redwood, he added, was to him the true incarnation of the "Christian soldier."

However, Ervin would note, Redwood didn't expect whatever beseechings he may have made for his own success and safety to be returned by the Almighty as blanket insurance for the men in his patrol. "He always regarded his men," Ervin wrote. "As to himself, he sought the place of greatest danger and fear was a word with which he had no acquaintance."

Prior to leaving the trenches, Redwood and his party removed anything that might identify them and their units and blackened their faces with burnt cork. By 4:00 A.M. on March 29, the Christian soldier and his men were deep into no-man's-land. "It was very dark and raining, we had a very hard time finding our way around," Armstrong would write.

It was so dark, in fact, that Redwood lost his way and reentered the American lines. "By the time he discovered his mistake only a short period of darkness was left, and most officers, I think, would have considered it unwise to make a second attempt," the 1st Division's chief of staff, Maj. William C. Sherman, would write. "George, however, with the determination which characterized his entire service, pushed on again into the German lines."

Armstrong would remember: "During the day we had spotted a pill box that we thought had some guests, so we started after it, but we couldn't have found the cords on our leggings that night. It was so black and wet and we floundered around in the mud until nearly six o'clock."

Redwood painstakingly led the patrol through the mud and detritus of no-man's-land and then through the German wire. Crawling to the edge of the German trench, they could just make out their target: a "little concrete cupola"—a pillbox—from which the American lines could be observed and raked with machine-gun fire.

As Redwood and his men huddled silently, two Germans made their way toward them through the trench. Redwood motioned to let the Germans pass—and then the five men slithered into the trench and followed their prey to the observation post, from which emanated the smell of coffee and fresh bread.

At the door was a sentry. He was quickly subdued, and then Redwood peered into the dugout and saw six Germans inside, their backs turned. He "motioned his men to come nearer and when the muzzles of four rifles and one automatic pistol were pointed in the Germans' direction the lieutenant, in German, demanded their surrender," the Associated Press would breathlessly report (in fact, all the men carried automatic pistols).

"Ergebet euch!" Redwood shouted in his "best High German," the *Stars and Stripes* would say. Four threw up their hands and yelled, *"Kamerad!"* The other two "started to comply, then changed their minds.

"They leaped to the ground at the side of the observation post. 'Halt!' shouted the five Americans. The Boches paid no heed. The Americans did not call again. They fired, and the two refractory Boches dropped in their tracks."

Redwood then sent Armstrong to block any Germans that might be headed their way from farther down the trench. "One of the Heinies, a member of a working party, came down the trench," Armstrong said, "and I was waiting round the corner to drop a revolver butt on his skull, but in some way he could see over the earth-line of the trench into the pill box where his comrades were standing with their hands at half-mast.

"He let out a yell for help and started back. I closed in on him and caught him in the head with a revolver bullet. I caught another one that was coming up and succeeded in wounding him. There were about forty Germans in their working party, and thinking we were a raiding party they held off for a few moments."

Redwood, meanwhile, took identifying insignia and shoulder straps from the dead Germans, then called for Armstrong. "Well, the sun's coming up and here we are, back of a German observation post," Redwood said. "The only thing I can see to do is go on home. Come on boys, let's go."

They crawled from the trench and raced for the American line, pushing their captives before them. No shots were fired by the Germans. "Either the Germans failed to see them because of the rain that was falling or held their fire because they did not desire to kill the prisoners," the AP would say.

One of the five Germans lagged behind, "trying to attract attention, and he was immediately killed," one of the men recalled. Halfway across no-man's-land, "not knowing when the Germans might start to fire on them," the group was surprised by "three or four heads covered with *pickelhaube* helmets," the *Stars and Stripes* would claim.

Redwood "saw but one thing to do. Right at the helmeted figures he charged, firing his automatic point blank. Like a covey of partridges raised by a shot, 30 life-sized Germans rose from that spot. By the time he had exhausted his magazine, the 30 were in full flight in the direction of the Rhine."

The Americans brought in the four prisoners. The one noncommissioned officer and three privates from the 259th Reserve Infantry Regiment were the first captured in a raid by the Americans after numerous attempts; any Americans that expected them to look like the crown prince were sorely disappointed. "Outwardly they were well clad but underneath they wore the thinnest and dirtiest underwear their captors had ever seen," one paper would report.

Escorted to the rear, they were handed "platefuls of steaming food and white bread with coffee," the AP said. "They stuffed themselves full, remarking afterward that it was the best meal they had had for many months. The youngest was the first to say that he was glad he was captured and then begged permission to go to a certain listening post to get his brother, who he thought might be there."

The same lad, it was claimed, was effusive in his detest for soldiering for the kaiser: "If I had known I would be treated like this, I would have deserted long ago. Everybody back there is being killed. We have all had enough of this war. I never wanted to get into it and tried to escape to Holland, but was forced into the ranks, where I had nothing to eat and had death staring me in the face every second."

Redwood's accomplishment was noted up the chain of command to General Pershing and made Redwood one of the AEF's first stars. The exploit also won each member of the raiding party a Croix de Guerre, a Distinguished Service Cross, and a ten-day leave from an army eager to show that its boys were accomplishing *something*.

Redwood's cool also won him the lasting respect of the men.

"I have been in nearly every corner of the globe and have mixed with all kinds of people," Edward Armstrong would write. "Have been in places where a man's courage was tested to the utmost, and I have seen many brave men, but I firmly believe that George Redwood had more 'sand' than any man I ever saw."

Correspondents were summoned by the 1st Division for interviews and photographs—which when they ran in U.S. newspapers showed Redwood and his four acolytes "with clubs in their hands and their faces blackened like negro minstrels," Redwood would write.

Redwood characteristically downplayed the effort, correcting the AP's high-minded identification of him as a "Regimental Intelligence Officer" and instead insisting on calling himself a mere "Battalion Scout Officer."

As for the raid, Redwood referred to it merely as "our little adventure, which in several ways was one of the quaintest bits of comic opera (considering that it was really supposed to be war) that I have run into . . . Do not imagine for a moment that I was one bit anxious to do it or anything of the kind. 'Orders is orders,' that is all."

He would add that the newspapers' dramatic versions of his exploit "varied from facts at sundry points, but here and there hit points quite correctly. The part about the fellow wishing his brother had been captured was true. The 'four rifle muzzles' was not; 'pistols and shillalehs' would have been the proper description."

Responding to an excited inquiry from a cousin, who had read of his deed in the next day's *Baltimore Sun,* Redwood would write to Mom-Mom: "She surely is bloodthirsty. *No!* I did *not* shoot two Boches with my own hand. Neither did I—newspaper reports to the contrary notwithstanding—remain inside an enemy's line to search the bodies of dead Germans while their excited comrades were only a few yards away!"

Redwood, ever the Christian soldier, dwelled more on the humanity of his captives than on the heroism he had displayed in taking them prisoner.

"One of them asked one of our men in an awestruck whisper, 'When are they going to shoot us?' (*Wann werden Sie uns shiessen?*), and was relieved when told that we were not in the habit of shooting our prisoners," he would write.

"Another, after they had been safely brought behind the rear of our line, asked permission to smoke; when it was granted he jauntily pulled forth a well-filled cigarette case and offered it courteously to me before helping himself."

He adhered to his Christian upbringing. "Honestly, I don't believe in this business of hating your enemy," he would write. "It is pitiful when a Boche prisoner, clean cut and apparently a good, intelligent little fellow, asks one of his captors in an awestruck whisper, 'When are they going to shoot us?' and after being reassured says, 'They told me, 'Woe to you if the Americans ever take you,' and then adds, 'We thought you were all going to be Indians!'

"It's pleasant to see them, too, if scared, regain confidence when they find that they are going to be well treated. Some are frankly glad to have been captured, and all that I have seen ploughing the fields of France appeared quite contented with their lot.

"*En masse,* of course, they are formidable, but individually they don't seem to be so eager for a scrap from all that I have heard and seen."

The Germans were in fact proving themselves plenty eager for a "scrap"; just a week before Redwood's bit of "comic opera," the other shoe dropped on the Western Front when on March 21 Germany launched its expected spring offensive in an attempt to bring the war to a close before enough Americans could arrive in France to tip the balance in the Allies' favor.

With the withdrawal of Russia from the war the previous December, Germany had been free to turn its attention—and fifty divisions—to the Western Front, and planning for the offensive had begun in late January.

Dubbed Operation Michael, the massive assault sent seventy-six first-class German divisions smashing into the Somme sector held by the British 5th Army.

Advancing after a surprise artillery bombardment, and storming eerily from a mist of gas, the Germans quickly overran Gough's forward positions and took 21,000 prisoners while leaving 7,000 English dead. Within weeks, they had retaken Albert and Bapaume, at which Haydock and Morgan had first seen the results of modern warfare.

Even as they manned the slick and slimy trenches at Seicheprey, the Americans wondered when and if the coming advance would fall on them.

"We are all wondering about the German offensive," Bill Morgan would write on March 16. "We are ready and prepared for what to do if they come. We are expecting them all the time, and there is a good deal of tension now and then of course."

Instead, as the German divisions rolled up the desperate British, the Americans were left in the last week of March to man the relatively quiet lines at Seicheprey, where Bill Morgan found himself on March 24.

"I am certainly in one hell of a place at present, but the daily expectancy of an attack is wearing off," he would write his fiancée amid the usual desultory shelling.

"I don't think that there will be one here for various reasons, mostly topographical. The place ought not to get on my nerves, but you should have seen me jump about five seconds ago. About the third week it is apt to be rather trying on the nerves. However this last jump was only due to concussion."

Morgan found that any ideas he had had about machine-gun duty proving safer than infantry duty soon dissipated. Just a few nights before he took position behind the American trenches, a single German shell killed and wounded fourteen men of the 2nd Machine-Gun Battalion; harassing German fire in the back lines, meanwhile, continued to destroy batteries, kill and maim artillerymen, and plough into the division's kitchens.

Not quite in the front lines, Morgan wondered at the bravado and fearlessness of the infantry while traipsing the lines.

"George Haydock took me considerably too far toward Germany the other day when he took me over some ground that he had been in," Morgan wrote on March 24. "How he ever lived through the shelling I know not. He has gotten very nonchalant about No Man's Land, being in the infantry."

Morgan found the back lines held their own danger. "I was eating on a box beside our kitchen, and the cook with much sense of humor came out and began scraping some stuff off the tar paper just above my head, and asked me if I knew what it was," he wrote.

"He told me that two men had been blown to bits sitting on that same box I was sitting on two weeks ago. I laughed and told him that one of them must have been the man that they discovered they were burying with two right legs."

Pausing, he turned serious: "I am telling you all this," he would write Christiana Councilman, "to show you how we look on this life of ours over here. It is unbelievable when you stop to think about it, but we don't stop." Still, he added, "it does make you wonder about the whys and wherefores of man under conditions like these."

On March 30, he would write: "The other night, as the shells dropped nearer and nearer, another lieutenant was here and tried to decide which end of the dugout was the strongest, but the only conclusion I ever reached was that it wasn't a case of how strong the roof was or the steel helmet, it was a question of how strong our necks were.

"My P.C. (dugout) is in a quieter end of town than the Captain's and I certainly had to laugh when I went up there for supper to hear him cuss those Germans who had gotten a direct hit on his roof—fortunately it was a dud. I told him he was never going to see the sunrise, and he told me to go to hell.

"I've never laughed more."

Like many of the other doughboys in France that spring, Morgan often lost track of the time, his duties, the sameness of the days, and the changing French weather conspiring to leave him unsure if it was Monday or Sunday.

"This morning my runner came in and announced the news that there was turkey for dinner," he wrote on March 31. "I asked what occasion this was and he told me that it was Easter. What a strange Easter!

"A cold, dark, drizzling day, and we were laughing last night about fixing up our helmets for Easter Sunday! I thought what a picture I would make strolling down Fifth Avenue with hip boots, heavy cane, gas mask, pistol, helmet, and black rubber poncho hanging around my shoulders, and mud from head to foot."

On the same day, he would write of receiving a "new rush order"—and went into a tizzy over its implications.

"The combination of today being Easter and the prospect of what lies ahead of us has affected me strangely," he wrote. "By the time you get this, much will be behind me—would that I could know now what you will by then. God only knows what is ahead. We have not heard exactly how the battle is going but we will beat them back—we *must*!

"Personal sacrifice is easy in this great effort, no matter what it may mean. There is no need of worrying. I don't know yet just what they are going to do with us. I will write you whenever I get a chance, though that may not be for some time. Of course there will be no leaves now. We are four days behind with the news of the battle. How I hope we will not be too late to help out.

"I have only a short time to prepare everything for our departure. We leave within a couple of hours. 'Cheery-o'!"

15

A Very Present Existence

It was a cold day in April when he gathered them around him and told all those fresh-faced young men—among them Richard Newhall and George Haydock and George Redwood and Bill Morgan and Alec McKinlock—something to the effect that their playtime was over, their childhood had come to its end.

Newhall would paraphrase John Pershing's remarks to his officers: "The period of training was over. They were about to go into a fighting sector, and eventually into battle, the first American division to do so. The eyes of America and the Allies would be on them to see what the Americans could do.

"They were to set the pace for the expeditionary forces . . . Nobody knew just what this meant, whether an immediate offensive or merely a readiness for any eventuality, but everyone took it to heart."

By the time the American supreme commander had finished his short speech to the officers of the 1st Division on April 16, 1918, "every officer was inspired to do his best out of loyalty to the chief, even if for no other reason," the 16th Regiment's Gen. John Hines would remember.

The "new rush order" that had agitated Bill Morgan so had been notification that the 1st Division was pulling out of the Ansauville sector and heading to new ground—and to battle. The massive German offensive that had nearly swallowed and destroyed the British 5th Army had in two weeks run out of steam, as British resolve stiffened and French soldiers had been rushed in to fill the breach.

The Germans' gain of twenty miles on a fifty-mile front had pushed a bulge through and past the British lines to a line running from just east of Arras in the north to Noyon in the south.

Although the situation by early April had temporarily stabilized, the Germans remained "menacingly near the English Channel and threateningly placed for any push to break through the Allied line and reach that Channel, separating the British and French armies—a manouevre that would have ended it for the French at least, and probably also for the British," 1st Division commander Gen. Robert Lee Bullard wrote.

On March 28, understanding the peril, John Pershing finally swallowed his pride—and temporarily put aside his long insistence on maintaining a homogenous American Army.

For months, he had resisted the entreaties of the French and British to place American units piecemeal at their disposal to fill holes in the line; in the face of the enormous German gains and the crisis enveloping the front, Pershing finally gave in and told Marshal Foch: "I have come to tell you that the American people would consider it a great honor for our troops to be engaged in the present battle. I ask you for this in their name and my own. At this moment there are no questions but of fighting. Infantry, artillery, aviation, all that we have is yours; use them as you wish. More will come."

The question remained: "Where would we be put?" Bullard asked rhetorically. "The enemy was at Montdidier and Amiens, in a very advantageous position to push his advance west toward the English Channel along the south bank of the Somme River.

"Attempting this, he would be greatly favoured by the river's making difficult any cooperation between the French on the south and British on the north of the Somme . . . The Allies knew the danger; everybody was looking for the next move to be here."

On April 1, the day after Morgan and the 3rd Machine-Gun Battalion had been issued its rush order, the 1st Division was relieved by the less-experienced 26th Division and began pulling back toward Paris, near which it would engage in further open-warfare maneuvers before embarking, finally, for battle.

The relief of Company L would remain etched in Richard Newhall's mind. "As we got to our new position," he would write, "where the men were to sleep in one big dugout, a sort of dormitory with a long, low wooden platform on which they lay, my sergeant came to me and said, 'Sir, so-and-so and so-and-so aren't here. They were on a special outpost in the trench going to the Bois de Rehame.' They had been forgotten and I felt responsible."

Perhaps with thoughts of Sam Ervin's misfortune racing in his mind, Newhall prepared to look for the men. "As soon as the men were bunked for the night I turned to go back to the front line," he wrote.

"Just then the missing men appeared. They had been relieved by the in-coming outfit. The profound sense of relief that I felt at that moment is still very clear to me. It is almost surprising that I didn't embrace them."

The next morning, the 28th Regiment was put on the move with the rest of the 1st Division. "This thing is coming to be like a big human kaleidoscope," Newhall wrote, "shifting all the time. Sometimes I wonder if it isn't a sort of a dream."

He saw "something very poetic and dramatic in a night full of moving troops—long files of shadowy figures stumbling across a field, columns passing each other on the road, mule trains and artillery lined up waiting to move, the rattle of wagons, the occasional salvos of artillery, the heavens lit up with illuminating rockets, the continuous tramp and splash of marching feet, the drizzle of rain, very little talking other than commands.

"It all goes to make a most picturesque scheme, dreamlike and theatrical yet very human and pathetic. The out-going troops are glad to be leaving and are wondering where they are going next. The in-coming ones have before them an adventurous prospect. For both there is a possibility of shelling while on the road."

The philosopher in Newhall was pushed aside by the need to live only in the moment.

"For me it was another novelty, a series of new sensations, impressions, memories," he wrote. "It is all a very present existence. The past is gone, the future too indefinite for contemplation. The getting of enough to eat and a place to sleep absorbs most of one's attention.

"News is scant. Newspapers reach us only occasionally. We have tried to follow the big battle as best we could, which is not very good. It is the climax of the war certainly and I hope we are to have a part in it."

Despite Pershing's talk, the division's movement, and the anticipation of coming battle, Newhall would write that he had "not yet got over the feeling that we are still on a big maneuver. There is so much that is plainly ridiculous. Our life has come to be a cross between an unsuccessful camping trip and an amateur vaudeville show. It is touched up at times with pathos and heroism and in the background (for me still very much in the background) there is the element of tragedy.

"I begin to get an idea of the welter of emotions which a Beethoven would try to put into a symphony. The more I think of it the more it seems that that is the only way it can be expressed. Words are too trivial and inadequate. Pictures make too superficial an appeal . . . They all lack that human touch which can't be expressed."

He had one consolation—his friendship with George Haydock. "When one does come upon the possibility of close companionship under such conditions as present, I find they can become very close," he would write in early April. "Lieut. Haydock and I find each other a very considerable comfort and I am hoping we may sometime find the chance to have a little pleasure together."

Haydock and Newhall reveled in finding some sleep, and some fine dining, in the city of Toul once out of the mud and slime of the Seicheprey trenches.

"I had one grand dinner at a *hotel* the other night, and it sure seemed fine," Haydock wrote on April 4. When he walked into the restaurant still begrimed by the filth of the trenches, "they thought I was a prank because I came in looking like a tramp, no insignia of rank.

"Two lieutenants covered with mud of a month's collection, no belt and in need of a haircut. We came into town after an all day hike having had no food but a breakfast of Campbell's soup and coffee.

"The first thing we saw was two staff 2nd lieutenants all shined up within an inch of their lives. They thought we had the plague (as a matter of fact we were only unclean) in a way that made me smile.

"It is a funny war."

On April 11, George Redwood and the men of his patrol were decorated while the 1st Division bivouacked near Toul. "We marched about two miles from our camp to a high hill," wrote Company I's Cpl. Newell B. "Paddy" Davis.

There, the entire 28th Regiment was lined into a "three-quarter hollow square. Lieut. Redwood and the four men were in the center with three officers at one end, a lot of French soldiers, women and children were watching from outside our lines."

A French officer "marched up to where Lieut. Redwood and the men were, [and] made a fine speech about the valuable work these men had performed in getting the German prisoners. Then the medals were pinned on and I was watching to see what they would do next. I believe they shook hands. Then the band played some piece (The French National Air I guess) and Lieut. Redwood snapped up to a salute.

"We came to present arms, after which we marched in review to the music of the band. That means all the companies marched past Lieut. Redwood and the four men and came to 'Eyes Right.' "

"It pleased me mightily that the officer who received the Croix de Guerre was the least military officer in the battalion," Richard Newhall would write of his friend Redwood.

"Truly it is not the fire-eaters who have the real back-bone. It is the men with moral courage, and usually they are the thoughtful, modest men. Too often they lack the ability to advertise themselves and so don't get credit for what they do."

In contrast, Newhall seethed over the commendation won by 2nd Lt. Edward Morgan—the same who had loudly expounded upon his postwar plans to make his fortune in billiard parlors.

Morgan would get a head start on his stateside career, too—his commendation came with a trip back to the United States, where he was to serve as an instructor in the training camps. The citation claimed that he "exposed himself in a most courageous manner while placing and encouraging his men during a heavy bombardment" at Seicheprey.

Newhall doubted the bombardment—and Morgan's courage.

"In our company I have just seen an example of what self advertisement can do," he would write. "Merely by a little systematic boasting one lieutenant has gained the reputation of being a hero, and has been rewarded by being detailed to return as an instructor to America, and has been cited in orders.

"He repelled a German attack which I am convinced was imaginary (and I am not alone in my conviction, being sustained by the two other lieutenants whose commands were in the vicinity. I was, myself, within two or three hundred yards.)"

Morgan's story "grew with the telling, and didn't seem to me to endure cross examination," Newhall added. "By the time the colonel came to write a letter describing the incident I couldn't recognize it from his account. Truly the work of the historian of finding out just exactly what happened is well nigh impossible."

As for Redwood, "he pulled off quickly and on the spur of the moment a little raiding stunt which produced results," Newhall wrote. "I had seen thousands of dollars of shells used and lives lost in trying to get the same results without success.

"Had this lieutenant been a Roosevelt think what a fuss would have been made over him. Archie Roosevelt has been decorated merely for being wounded under the most ordinary circumstances."

It was all too absurd for Newhall. "It is a great thing to be well advertised!" he wrote. "If his older brother had been able to do what my friend has done I'll bet he would be commanding a regiment or perhaps a brigade. I have heard some of my companions telling about 'our experiences' and what they had to say sounded like so much rot when put into the form of reminiscence that I am more than ever disposed to keep my mouth shut.

"It only takes a few adjectives and the proper tone of voice, an imagination and a slight regard for Truth to make trivial incidents appear as adventures with the story teller in the heroic role. So far everything I've seen has been either ordinary, ridiculous, or irritating."

He allowed that he was becoming a "crabber," but in truth Newhall found it harder and harder to accept the pettiness and self-aggrandizement that ran rampant in the army.

Gently admonished by his father in one letter to put aside his grouching and strive for "excellence as an officer instead of regarding the military profession as merely a temporary occupation," Newhall let fly, taking a swipe at his company commander, Francis Van Natter, who (he would write years later) "worked hard at his job but gave the impression of feeling inadequate (which I thought he was). He certainly was excitable, not to say jittery."

"The truth is that my idea of 'excellence' is not at all in accord with the 'customs of service,'" Newhall would add that spring. "I am keen for the things that seem to me to have some bearing on fighting Germans, and it plagues me that there seem to be so many other things which take precedence.

"The over-emphasis on the non-essentials and the absence of that moral devotion to a cause (which I had expected to find) makes me sometimes angry, and sometimes cynically amused."

Of Van Natter, he would write that he had learned to pay "the required, outward, respect, and to obey the orders even to endure respectfully the censures, of a man with very little more military training than I"—even though he considered Van Natter to be less experienced in handling men than he and complained that his captain had "a flighty excitable temperament which I regard as dangerous."

Van Natter was, in short, "a man whose judgment I hold in small esteem, and whose personal courage I am disposed to question. In addition, he is some years my junior. However, when I look at Lieut. Stromberg, who is an old soldier with service medals won in campaign, and note that he has to undergo the same, I feel that I have not cause to complain.

"And I don't complain—I laugh, to myself. Still it is a bit hard, indeed impossible, to allow such men to set me my standards of excellence. I prefer my own."

In his better moments he saw an upside to his predicament.

"Perhaps it is a valuable experience for me to be placed where I must work cheerfully and smoothly in a system which irritates me, and under men who too often excite my contempt," he wrote. "It pleases me to find that the men towards whom I am attracted as friends have the same difficulties as I to adjust themselves."

Newhall realized a change in himself; where before he had enjoyed reading and attending musicals while at rest, he now craved action, activity—anything that could help him not dwell on his current predicament.

"I am getting to prefer the active if more dangerous tours," he would write. At rest, "I get moody and irritable. The unpleasant features of the army stand out. The want of congenial occupation and companionship becomes oppressive.

"At the front, however, or on the move I am thoroughly occupied and I like it. It seems then as if I was really working on the job in hand instead of futilely marking time and enduring petty inconveniences. At the front too I am more by myself with my platoon, which satisfies my craving for independence."

He worried he would go too far in his criticisms one day and pay the consequences. "If we don't have too many or long 'rests' I will be able to sit on the lid, otherwise I fear that I shall explode some day and get court martialled," he wrote.

"The summer promises to be sufficiently 'restless' I think to keep me safe from the crime of insubordination. Perhaps in a month I will have my leave and by that time I think I will be ready for it, even if I have to go off by myself."

Having offered the 1st Division for use in battle, Pershing set it to work in "a great test manoeuvre in open warfare" outside Paris under the watchful eye of the French, Bullard wrote. The division was deemed "quite proficient"—and "it was decided to send us on toward the enemy."

First by rail, then by trucks, and finally by foot, the division headed north toward Picardy, and to a point where the German offensive had ground to a halt in the face of furious resistance from French and French colonial troops. Their destination was a tiny village called Cantigny, fifty miles north of Paris, where French and Germans faced each other across a one-mile sea of dead and slowly rotting bodies.

"We are now in the most beautiful part of the country," Bill Morgan wrote from a point twenty-five kilometers north of Paris. "You would never really know that the filthy horrible place that we have just left was in this same country. All the fruit trees are in bloom, and the country is very fertile and green."

Morgan did not share Newhall's growing contempt for the army; he had bought in heart and soul. He found himself becoming tougher, harder, and more resourceful and enjoyed the change within him. He was learning to lead and inspire men by example, by displaying bravery and fearlessness; and he was learning to discipline his hard cases with his fists, if necessary.

His confidence bubbling over, he envisioned someday using his experience to lead the great unwashed masses with whom he had had little contact while growing up overprotected in Highland Park and later while ensconced behind the ivied walls at Harvard.

"I have been thinking a great deal how interesting it is—this coming in contact with people whom I should otherwise never know or understand," the supposed heir to the Chicago Varnish Company would write his fiancée.

"We are surrounded by such varied types and classes in the army. I feel that I am fitting myself in many ways to help these people who are so little able to be heard among those who rule the laboring classes. I shall try in the great reconstruction to aid and steer the types of men that I am coming to know.

"You have noticed, haven't you, that these people distrust anyone with education. They are afraid of cleverness. I can see it among these men—these men who do not count on you until they have seen you laugh at shells.

"It is that way we must gain their confidence, for it is no use putting on overalls and going through what they go through. They only laugh at you and say you can quit and ride around in automobiles whenever you wish."

Enduring without complaining, putting in longer hours than others, and bearing all with a smile—that was the key to leadership for the young Morgan.

"I love the expression of 'Heads up!' " he would write. "I use it all the time with the men. If you let them see that you are still smiling, and these long hours of drill and wet are forgotten, they come with their shoulders thrown back and their chins up.

"I asked them the other day if they had noticed the latest German prisoners, and there was no spark in their eyes, and I ended by saying, 'There is just one thing about Americans. You can not kill their spirit.' The men have bucked up and are going finely."

He would admit, "I have doubted my ability to handle men, especially some of the hard ones. I didn't think that I had the kind of discipline that these older regular army officers want."

Finally, he had realized that "reserve officers with hardly any exception handle their men too easily. If they get sick they sympathize with them, and baby them. Whereas if you are going to make a man a good fearless soldier, you have got to be strict with him.

"We have been here long enough for some Reserve Officers to get a little careless, but they will lose out. Any number of them have already. I don't see how they can ever hold up their heads. To have failed in this great test would be worse than anything I could think of. I feel that I have changed much in these last seven months. I have found my strength and measured it against the most awful odds that anyone can meet."

He would add: "I have never felt before the satisfaction of feeling behind me a *real* day's work done, with nothing shirked and nothing left undone. It makes you feel like clenching your fists and looking the whole world straight in the eyes and daring it to come at you."

As the 1st Division was relieved, Morgan was ordered to stay behind at Seicheprey and go over the ground, and the ropes, with the incoming 26th Division. The New Englanders shocked Morgan, who now considered himself as hardened and adept as any regular.

"It is a disgrace the lack of discipline they have," he wrote. On the morning after the relief, "I got up and found them wandering about without steel helmets or leggings and their gas masks not in the alert position.

"They knew nothing about S.O.S. barrage data, their gas sentries did not know which dugouts they were to wake up. The night they came in to relieve us, I had them all under cover, and a sergeant came in with his flash light still going.

"I then lustily cursed the whole outfit, and said my men had been given absolute orders to shoot at any light they saw, whereupon their jaws dropped, and they sort of wondered what kind of a crowd we were."

Returning to the 1st Division on its march to Picardy, Morgan was deeply affected by the plight of the French refugees who streamed south before the German onslaught. "It is pitiful to see them plodding along beside their clumsy wagons, heaped with chairs, bedding, and everything else. They are cheerful but sort of bewildered and dazed as though in a dream."

The refugees, he would add, "go from house to house looking for a place to sleep, but most of the houses are full already. In the small city where I went a few days ago there was a whole column of inquiries of refugees as to where their daughters and little sons were.

"One man and woman, two little girls and a bright manly little boy came by the road the other day. They had left from in front of Montdidier with only four cents. I gave them my last 50 francs and told them it was from you. The woman was pathetically grateful and said that she would write you."

The plight of the refugees only increased Morgan's ardor for battle—and his pride in being in the vanguard of the American effort.

"We have moved out each day so early that it is still dark, and we have it down to quite a system," he wrote while on the march. "Now we are ready at all times to pack up in few moments. This is where the regulars prove so efficient.

"Our division is moving up here at the greatest crisis of the war, and there should be thousands of others behind us but they can't depend on them," he wrote presciently on April 14.

"I have seen some of the National Guard in the line . . . In a crowd they are all yelling, and unless an officer yells loudest he is unnoticed. The fools are going to lose a lot of lives through carelessness."

Just six days later, as the 1st Division neared its destination, its old haunts at Seicheprey were raided by a German contingent known as Hindenburg's Traveling Circus. An early-morning barrage cut down the 26th Division men in the front line; the inexperienced doughboys left the shelter of their second- and third-line trenches for open ground, and they also died in rows.

The Germans took what was left of Seicheprey and inflicted 669 casualties—including 81 dead and another 187 captured or missing—before retreating as planned on April 21.

"The Germans actually came over and sat around in my dugout," Morgan wrote ruefully on April 22.

He couldn't know it, but the 1st Division would soon be employed to erase the "stain of Seicheprey."

Newhall and Haydock found time for "a little pleasure together" as the 1st Division approached its destination, and the duo took in the sights of Beauvais one afternoon.

"I had a chance not long ago to get into a fairly good sized town and of course took advantage of it," Haydock wrote on April 24. "I went with my intellectual friend, and he really is doing a good bit to educate me. History is his specialty, and he has been to many of these places before. He knows all about them and what has happened there as well as the date.

"It has made all the difference to me to have some one to play around with. We saw all the sights and then decided to go in quest of tea."

They stopped in at the local Red Cross headquarters, and "on inquiring we were informed that the 'Smith College Unit' would not only feed us, but that we would be entertained by charming American girls."

Newhall and Haydock soon found themselves being "talked at a mile a minute," Haydock would write. "They gave us a lot of news we were glad to get, and we even went so far as to take two of them out for dinner."

The two women, Elizabeth Howe Bliss, thirty-one, of Worcester, Massachusetts, and Ruth D. Joslin, twenty-seven, of Chicago, had sailed to France the previous July with the Smith College Relief Unit. Bliss had graduated from Smith in 1908, and her specialty was social work; Joslin was a 1912 graduate of the school and in France mainly worked as a chauffeur.

The unit, organized by Smith alumnus Harriett Boyd Hawes, performed "practical work for the suffering French people"—providing food and shelter, medical treatment, and hope to a populace whose homes and livelihoods had been destroyed by the German Army during its occupation and subsequent strategic retreat in 1917.

On March 21, the Smith unit was stationed in the village of Grécourt, just ten miles from the German breakthrough on the Somme. Its members joined the long lines of refugees moving west just ahead of the German storm.

"Never can I forget that sight," Bliss would write home. "Old women with their possessions on wheelbarrows trudging along the road, little children dragged by their terrified mothers, everybody with their live stock, dogs, rabbits and chickens, driving their cows and goats before them, all rushing madly away from the flood of terrible destruction pouring down upon them."

The two women, ironically, had been under fire as much as or more than had Haydock and Newhall. "They had a real hot story to tell," Haydock would write. "They have seen the elephant sure enough."

He and Newhall escorted the two women to a nearby hotel for dinner. "None of the other officers found the place so we had it all to ourselves," Newhall wrote. "It certainly was fine to get a little wholesome American, feminine companionship for a little while. They were good talkers and had had lots more exciting experiences than we had.

"We all had lots of opinions about the war and the French and the English—and the Americans, which need comparing. Truly it was one of the most refreshing Sunday afternoons I have known in a long time."

If Newhall was particularly struck by Miss Bliss, he didn't mention it. He would write later that he and Haydock, in their haste to return to their company, made "a very unceremonious departure leaving Elizabeth on the curb in front of the hotel."

He would meet Miss Bliss again, though under very different circumstances.

The April 21 dinner with real, live American females lifted both men's spirits. "You can say what you like about this being no place for women, perhaps in many ways it is not, but I know one thing for sure and that is that all of us are darn glad to see them, and seldom pass up a chance to talk to them even if it is only to say hello," Haydock wrote.

"There is a very likeable camaraderie among all the people in this country who can speak English, it goes all the way from a British Tommy to a Red Cross nurse and is one of the things I should like to see survive the war, but of course it won't. When you are continually surrounded by 'frogs' as we call the French anyone who can *parler* so you can understand them is a long lost friend."

On April 24, the division's 1st Brigade entered the lines just west of the hilltop village of Cantigny. The azure sky and brilliant spring sunshine contrasted sharply with the grim surroundings before the village, where no-man's-land was carpeted with the bodies of French colonial troops and Germans who had fallen in vicious fighting in the early days of April, as Operation Michael ran out of steam just west of the Cantigny plateau, which the Germans continued to hold.

In the meantime, the American and German artillery dueled twenty-four hours a day, the Germans flinging shells "at anything that moved," Company E's Edward S. Johnston would write. "They concentrated on the smallest group moving within their range in daylight, and pursued single ambulances down the road with malevolence and fury.

"As to communication trenches, there were none at all until the veriest essential trenches were hurriedly constructed," Johnston remembered. "Over great areas, movement had still to be on the surface."

The men spent long nights digging—"work, work, work and shelling all the time. The ground was usually a-tremble. Men were little burrowing creatures that scampered through the herbage, scuttled along walls and hedges. Even at night they must be always on the dodge, or be dumped unceremoniously like limp brown rats beside their pathways."

Half a mile away, the splintered and battered village of Cantigny hovered like the ruins of the Acropolis. "Look that place over. You may have to capture that town some day," the 1st Division's officers were told.

While the 1st Brigade inhabited a string of grimy and cootie-infested shell holes and began combining them into trenches, the 2nd Brigade found billets in surrounding villages. Company L was assigned billets in Maisoncelle-Tuilerie, about eight miles southwest of the front lines.

"The army is a funny animal," Haydock would write. "We breeze along the road, come to a perfectly innocent little town where we are to stay, and then a mighty interesting metamorphosis takes place.

"I locate my non com who has gone ahead, he shows me where my platoon is to be billeted. It is a typical farm yard in the town. That is you go in from the street through a large door, and find yourself in a quadrangle which is the barnyard. The front side is the house, the back the barn and to the right and left chicken houses, rabbit pens, hay sheds, etc. In the center is a charming pool of green slime, next to this the mill!"

His platoon waited while he looked the place over. "On the door is written '40 men.' I find a pile of straw in the barn so all is jake. The men come in with a rush and settle to the four winds to get the best bunk. Ten minutes later they are all settled and looking the place over as if they owned it.

"They have to chase the ducks and chickens out of their billets and sometimes said poultry gets in the way and there is a casualty. Result: claim, interpreter, much talking with the hands and loud cries ending up by my having to get 20,000 francs from the platoon to pay for one old hen."

New uniforms preceded the company's arrival at Maisoncelle, and Newhall found himself deciding "who was to have what" in his platoon.

"This was a rather ticklish job," he would recall. "It was necessary to line the men up and look them over to decide whose pants were in the most dilapidated state, who simply *must* have a cap and whose blouse wouldn't stand much more wearing.

"When it came to underwear I had to group the men by threes. Then under my supervision each group threw dice to determine who should have shirts and who drawers. This made the thing a sporting proposition which quite appealed to the men. Certainly there was considerable amusement. I never expected to see the day when I should be running a crap game!"

Newhall and Haydock, meanwhile, set up camp in an abandoned cottage. Newhall would many years later remember their days there fondly, writing that it was during that time that he and George "became most intimate.

"We were together a great deal. At night, each rolled up in his own blanket, we could talk as long as we chose without fear of interruption. Probably this period from the middle of April was the happiest of the year."

Newhall wrote at the time: "We have made ourselves most comfortable for there is a bed which will accommodate us both, and a bed and sufficient water is all that is necessary for house-keeping.

"In addition, however, we have three chairs, a little table, a box, and such part of an old ward-robe as is not occupied by the property of the proprietor, whoever and wherever he may be."

Years later, Newhall added: "I shall always think of that place with George sitting on the bed reading aloud by candlelight Sir Douglas Haig's report of the British campaign of 1917—and very thrilling reading it was. In themselves, those days were really very happy."

Appropriating one of Haydock's pet phrases, Newhall would conclude in one letter that spring: "There come times when we are willing to admit that it is a 'bonne' war. When the days are bright tramping about over the hills or along the roads is quite a pleasant occupation.

"And when the weather is bad there is always that favorite in-door sport 'Knocking Your Superiors' at which we are all adept . . . Thanks to Haydock's companionship I keep in good humor for the most part."

His billet mate agreed: "It is more fun to laugh at the army than almost anything I have ever done, and is the greatest past time of all."

16

A Cold Business

William Otho Potwin Morgan had been sure he was ready for this, pretty sure the trenches he labored to dig in the summer heat and the nighttime battles at Fort Sheridan had prepared him for what he might encounter Over There.

However, there had been no way to fake the way a man's insides turned black and maggoty after laying in the sun for weeks on end, and no way to simulate the staccato of the hours-on-end bombardments, and the way the plumes of earth seemed to steadily walk toward him as if tracing the footsteps of some invisible giant, clumping and kicking up dirt and chalk in brown and white puffs and seemingly intent on burying W. O. P. Morgan with all the others that already lay moldering and rotting under his own feet.

"You would have laughed at me just now," he would write Christiana Councilman from the lines at Cantigny on May 19. "I was sitting here talking with some of the men when some of those nasty 'three-inchers' came so fast I didn't hear them until they exploded. I made the quickest dive for my helmet that ever mortal made.

"When I looked up my man was tearing down the path. Then he suddenly stopped and tore back again thinking I was hit. Then we both squatted down under our tin lids while the pieces rained around, hoping that if anything landed on us it would glance off.

"It was the most ridiculous performance you ever saw, and pretty soon my corporal's head came up out of our dugout like a turtle, and with a delighted grin he said, 'Pretty warm out there, isn't it?' "

The 1st Division had begun its trench experiences in a "very quiet sector," the 28th Regiment's history would note. "Next they had gone into one that was moderately lively, and now they were in a sector where there was always something doing, where the whine and crash of shells could be heard at all times."

Thousands of shells crossed the lines between the Germans, who held Cantigny and had placed their artillery on high ground in the woods to the east of the village, and the Americans, whose batteries were several miles to the west.

One German bombardment that May lasted twenty-seven hours and sent eight thousand gas shells toward the American lines, where the infantry huddled and slept by day and stood ready for attack under the glow of Very lights and the pounding of incessant shellfire by night.

It was in those lines before Cantigny, just a few kilometers northwest of Montdidier, that Bill Morgan found himself manning a machine gun for days and nights on end through May of 1918, and there he tried to reconcile himself to his membership in the "Suicide Club."

"The reason we are called the 'Suicide Club' is that if we are not smashed before an attack we will cause terrible losses, and therefore they use every means to knock us out just as the show is about to start.

"M.G.s very seldom have orders to retire, they just stay where they are, for their greatest effectiveness is at close range, and they keep on firing until they are finally rushed and overrun by the infantry."

Morgan had matter-of-factly anticipated the role of the 3rd Machine-Gun Battalion days before being sent forward to establish his position just to the rear of the front line.

"We will set our gun up at night in a shell-hole and try to hide it in the daytime," he wrote. "We have to be terribly careful about camouflage and not giving ourselves away. Of course the big thing is to keep your head and outmanouvre the barrage, moving into shellholes, and knowing just when to dash through it or go around it, to save casualties and smashing of guns.

"We shall have no trenches, no dugouts and only one meal every twenty-four hours cooked way back and carried up at night. I don't think it will be too comfortable lying around in the mud, especially as we do not get relieved like the infantry every four or five days."

The duty "is simply a question of sitting at the gun all night, just waiting for them to come over," he wrote. "It's a bit of a strain, but after all they either come or they don't, and if they come it is a question of how many you can mow down before they swarm over you."

Still, the anticipation of mowing down wave after wave of oncoming Germans before succumbing himself caused some nausea in young Bill Morgan.

"At times I wish I were in the infantry," he would admit. "They claim it is better to fight man to man and hack and slash than to sit cold-bloodily by a gun and wipe out a battalion by pumping 250 shots a minute into men, with the pressure of one finger.

"We kill them more cleanly, our bullets are such nice smooth clean-cut affairs. It's like our scientific slaughter houses as compared to these Frenchmen who butcher their cattle out in the gutter of the streets."

He and his men quickly learned the lessons of their new position.

"Our other sectors were more or less rest sectors, and we didn't have to pay an awful lot of attention to staying out of sight of aeroplanes, balloons, etc. but this is business here, and they are after every single man and shell most anything," he wrote.

When he needed to move, it was at night and, despite the dangers, aboveground. "It is too hard to get anywhere in trenches if you are going any distance. They are narrow and every ten feet there is a traverse and four corners to get around, and so we usually go along on top.

"It isn't dangerous because the Boche can't shell a whole area, only cross-roads where paths and trenches join. That is the reason there is less danger after you are in a place for some time. You know where the Boche shells will fall and about what time."

On one quiet afternoon George Haydock came through "intermittent shelling" to visit Morgan. "I walked on with him up to the front line, and then out to a small wood which the Germans had bombarded about a week previously," he wrote on May 7.

"What a mess those trenches were in, the dugouts smashed, tremendous shell holes, equipment lying all around . . . Haydock had been down the day before collecting rubber boots for his men.

"I think I told you of the one he tried to pull out of a fallen dugout and found there was a leg in it. He worked three hours trying to dig the body out to identify it, but finally had to pile dirt up and put up a rude cross."

At that point, Morgan claimed with bravado to be unrattled by either the sights of the dead Americans or the constant booming of the artillery, which sent many a man burrowing further into the ground.

"The Capt. hasn't been around to see me yet, he drives me wild he is so nervous," he would write a few days after being in the lines. "I am sorry to say I am beginning to think he is plain scared that he will be 'Bumped off.' One of the men came up laughing last night and said that the Capt. was having his dugout dug ten feet deeper, the Major's still deeper, and the Colonel's is down in some bottomless chalk mine."

One night, "the Capt. took a couple of us out reconnoitering . . . thinking we were going to relieve my old company which I was first with. It is about 1500 yards further forward, almost in the front line.

"He was so nervous he ducked his head every time one of our own guns cracked, and I ran right into him several times when he dropped flat."

Morgan and another lieutenant were merely amused. "The lieutenant behind me kept jabbing me in the ribs with his cane, and we couldn't stop ourselves from laughing. Then we began singing and it nearly drove the Capt. mad because he couldn't hear the shells whine.

"Finally I got exasperated and thoroughly ashamed when he gave a great jump, and landed flat in a deep trench beside the road. We just walked on past him and I think he must have felt pretty cheap, but even after that he couldn't control himself. It will mean an end for him if more officers of the battalion see him. No one will follow a man like that."

Yet as the days passed that May of 1918, Morgan's bravado began to ebb; each plume of exploding earth seemed to put a chink in his psychological armor, and the constant artillery duels opened a crack in his soul. Gone in a matter of weeks was his boyish wonder at the "science" and mysteries of the war; gone, too, was any appreciation for the supposed romance of the war, and its purpose.

He would complain of the "infernal racket going on all the time" and write: "There is one thing which no human being can picture, who has not known it, and that is shell-fire. It is that which takes every bit of romance out of this war. You can't possibly imagine it and I can't possibly describe it.

"It's so damnably cold-blooded and calculated and mercilessly figured out. It's so impersonal. I find it mighty hard now to see the side of this war which once submerged me to the chin and threatened to call forth tears and sobs whenever I heard a band play. Now it's a cold fighting, a business."

He would laugh off the images seen on recruiting posters—"a man about to charge forward, waving his arms and shouting, with hoards of exulting men pressing along behind him.

"What the man was probably actually doing is lying out in a shell-hole while the Boche artillery reduced trenches and everything else to a level. And after the fire if he is still alive, he rushes out to meet the Huns who are nearly as insane as he, having come through a French counter-barrage."

Presciently he would write: "I can well see how a man . . . could lose hold of himself after a few sleepless nights of wandering up and down, looking out into a pitch black no-man's-land, especially if he had imagination. You've got to kill your imagination and on top of that swing into a certain savoir-faire, 'To hell with it' mood, coupled with the idea that the Boche haven't a piece of lead in Germany that can kill you."

Sleep deprived, under almost constant bombardment, Morgan began to realize that there were in fact thousands of shards of German lead seeking his warm body, and despite his best efforts to kill his imagination, it ran wild with all the thoughts of what could—and probably would—happen.

"It is these little things, the little strains, which stretch your nerves to the breaking point, that make a fight out of this war," he would write achingly, "the little things you never read about, the things you can't see."

He recognized his state of mind. "It is all covered by that vague malady called shell-shock."

At Maisoncelle, the 28th Regiment invented activities to keep rust from building in its men as they waited to enter the trenches.

"Time: 11:30 P.M.," Richard Newhall would write on May 9. "Haydock has just crawled into bed, and I am in the process of undressing. What is that bugle blowing off in the distance at this time of night? Perhaps there's a fire. Anyhow it isn't our town. Still it didn't sound quite like 'Fire Call.' Righto. It was not."

A bugle sounded—the "Call to Arms." "Haydock jumps out of bed cursing because the thing didn't come ten minutes sooner and starts to dress," Newhall wrote.

"I pull on my shoes, slip into my overcoat; throw on my haversack; buckle on my belt; swing my glasses and gas masks over one shoulder and my musette bag over the other; grab my helmet with one hand and my flash-light with the other; and get out into the street."

"We were to have late breakfast today and Newhall and I on going to bed decided that they would surely pull 'alert' or something else on us just to get us out," Haydock added.

"Sure enough soon after we were in bed we heard a scurry in the street, the call to arms and the usual rustle to get things right quickly. It is a form of drill that always amuses me and is something like what my old idea of war was . . . It adds to the interest not to know whether it is [a] drill or not."

In the dark street, they found Company L already assembling. Orders were given to draw ammunition and roll packs. Each man was given four boxes of hardtack as emergency rations.

"A frightened old French woman on the edge of the crowd inquires 'Quelles nouvelles, quelles nouvelles?'" Newhall wrote. "Then 'Recall' sounded. It was only a drill. Still it was one of the most realistic drills I have ever seen, with all the touch of excitement which an actual call would have had. Personally I expected to be loaded on a truck and hurried off to the front."

Their time for rushing to the front would come, but for the first few weeks of that May, the men of the 28th Regiment had it easier than ever.

"Don't think of me as always lieing in a wet shell hole in no man's land, because the chances are I am lying in a comfortable bunk with a large meal inside of me and not a care in the world except that they won't let me sleep more than 12 hours," Haydock wrote his mother.

"We have seen enough of the show to know about what to expect and we just say let her come. Of course, we are all fatalists if that is what you call it, because you can't dodge a whiz bang no matter how fast you are on your feet, and if there is one with your name painted on it why it's just up to you to stop it, and I would much rather stop one now and be in my present frame of mind than stick around 50 years more and be worrying all the time."

In a pointed reference to Van Natter, Haydock would add: "We have a captain who takes himself seriously and he has shown us the light on that subject."

Newhall's influence on Haydock that spring is unmistakable, and their letters home reveal the subjects of conversation that occupied their hours. Both would inveigh against the overly dramatic picture of their war and activities provided by the newspaper correspondents.

Both wrote to say they refused to wear the gold stripes they'd received for their first year's service. ("I . . . will not wear one until I have done a little more than chase Indians," Haydock would write.) Both ridiculed the pettiness of the army—and were united in their lack of respect for Van Natter.

Both, it seems, had learned something of leadership as well. As the 1st Division's commander, Robert Bullard, would write: "'Waal, now,' said an old soldier once to a young lieutenant, 'soldiers is queer bein's. Yer have to get so yer understand 'em.' Getting so you can understand 'em may, of course, come to an officer by the gift of God, without the necessity of having to live with soldiers; but generally it does not."

Haydock, who had struggled to understand 'em the previous winter, had come to know the men in his platoon individually and had earned his men's respect—in part by not taking things as seriously as the army demanded.

"We haven't yet gotten over the idea that because we are at war we must always be just as uncomfortable as we can, do things in the least sensible way, and never act naturally," he would write.

"I have spent so many hours doing things of no value with my platoon that now when I get that sort of an order I use a little camouflage, march them out in the fields or woods sometimes well out of sight, sit them down, and if I have anything to say talk to them. Otherwise I let them do the talking. I find they pay more attention then when I have something worthwhile to do."

The formerly reserved Haydock also seemed more assertive and less the passive victim of his circumstances, and also seemed to be emerging from the shell of humor and self-deprecation behind which he had hid.

In short, Haydock that May seemed to have found his perfect equilibrium between performing the straight-faced serious duties the army required of him, then blowing off steam by laughing at the absurdity of it all in the understanding presence of Newhall.

His spirits seemed to soar, and his sense of humor was in full bloom, even as—and he must have had an inkling—the most deadly serious part of his service was fast approaching.

"I am sorry they have stopped shipping packages because I should like very much to have *Alice in Wonderland,* it is the best description of the army and the war that has ever been written, read over the mad tea-party and thee will have it in a nutshell," Haydock wrote to his mother on May 10.

That Mother's Day letter, too, was oddly filled with kvetching—another Newhall trait, or perhaps just the idle rantings of one who had now been in the army for a year and had had enough of living on that side of the Looking-Glass.

Haydock and Newhall continued to take solace in each other's company, going on long walks after evening mess, lounging under apple trees on odd afternoons, all the while awaiting their turn in the front lines before Cantigny, just a few miles off, from which the roll and echo of the artillery's thunder echoed, and from which when the spring breeze was right the smell of rotting and decaying flesh could spoil a man's dinner.

"If you try to picture me in my normal surroundings you want to imagine an obscure and dirty country village in which I share a billet with some other officer," Newhall would write from Maisoncelle. "With this as a base of operations we go out drilling every day, doing as many futile and needless things as headquarters can devise, including a prescribed schedule of games."

In the evenings, "I like to go out after supper to stroll over the hills in the long twilight, either alone or with Haydock," Newhall would write. "There is a charming wood nearby which is a beautiful place for conversation or restful meditation. Yesterday I heard my first cuckoo there."

Still, amid the pleasant surroundings, Newhall's thoughts drifted to the certainty that the regiment would be going over the top.

It was an experience to which he looked forward.

"I have a most intense curiosity to see what a battle is like," he wrote on April 30, "what my platoon will do, what I will do. I have the uneasy feeling that, like everything else, it won't come up to expectations, but will merely be hideous, terrifying, and fatal to some of my best men.

"I won't pretend that I don't expect it to be all of the three above, but in addition I do expect an excitement of unprecedented intensity."

Where Haydock and Morgan had struggled to command, and earn the respect of, their men, Newhall—older by six years and more worldly and authoritative—had few complaints or concerns about leading his platoon, other than being interfered with by higher-ups.

He did allow that he still had much to learn about leadership—and found a case study when a new commander replaced the 3rd Battalion's Maj. Francis H. Burr, who had been gassed at Seicheprey and subsequently assigned to a training school.

After the war, Company M's Cpl. Floyd Weeks would call Burr "the dugout king" and add: "His favorite words were, 'Where they hittin', sentry?'" Newhall also considered Burr "a light weight" and added: "I am sure it wasn't accidental that he was sent off to a school on the eve of our first battle."

But Lt. Col. Jesse Marling Cullison, an old regular who had enlisted in May 1897, immediately drew Newhall's admiration.

"I hasten to tell you of our new battalion commander, whom Haydock describes as a 'bearcat,'" Newhall wrote his mother on May 12. "He is magnificent. I imagine he is a type of the old army at its best."

Years later Newhall would describe Cullison as "a big bruiser type who talked like an Oxford man without an English accent, mild spoken and a gentleman, no nonsense and no bullying, obviously self-confident, a thing which inspires confidence. I had the impression that he recognized boot-licking and despised it."

That May, Newhall wrote: "He knows exactly what he wants and can tell his subordinates what he expects of them briefly and clearly, without scolding, lecturing, or threatening them. This is also very rare . . . He is the first of my superiors who has really excited my admiration."

Newhall would add that he wanted to, in effect, study the "suberb, vigorous, confident, poised" Cullison.

"It interests me hugely to see what qualities it is which make for true leadership such as this man has," he fairly gushed. "In the last year I have learned a lot of things *not* to do, and observed a lot of things which met with my hearty disapproval but which seemed to work, why I have not determined.

"I hope he remains with our battalion but I am afraid he won't because he is the Lt. Col. of the regiment. Still he may be with us long enough to lead us into battle. I hope so. He would lead, too, right up in front—which theoretically is not the place for the high ranking officers."

Musing over the officers he had encountered in the army—good and bad—Newhall would allow that "the rapid expansion of the army has necessarily entailed the rapid promotion of young, inexperienced men who too often have to cover up their uncertainty by mere exercise of their authority.

"They are *not* sure of themselves at all and try to conceal that fact by excessive positiveness to their subordinates who can't answer back, and similar submissiveness to their superiors who have the power to make and break . . . Power is a most insidious thing and I begin to appreciate better than ever before why the 'lust for dominion' is one of the most hellish lusts."

He didn't say the name, but it's clear that Van Natter was at the forefront of Newhall's mind.

On the night of May 14, the 28th Regiment relieved the 18th Regiment in the lines before Cantigny. Where some casualties were suffered in the 1st Battalion as the men entered the support trenches, the perilous relief went without a hitch in the 3rd Battalion.

Company L took position in the unfinished, waist-high support trenches, where the intense shelling in the sector forced the men underground in the day. "I never before lived quite so much like an animal in its burrow," Newhall would write from the lines.

"There are other 'animals' occupying this particular hole, to my regret, some of whom I fear will accompany me when I leave. A visit to the 'disinfector' will be in order. It is a lazy way to be waging a war."

With spring in full bloom, "the hours of daylight in a northern latitude like this are pretty long now and during them we remain under cover, sleeping and being very lazy and quiet. Then when it gets dark, out we come like a lot of mice to frisk about in the open and do whatever it is do be done.

"The men get their three meals all in one issue and eat when they like, heating things with cans of solidified alcohol. In my pocket I have Haydock's copy of 'Macbeth,' and have occasionally tried to memorize parts of it. But lolling in the sun is not very stimulating to intellectual endeavor so I have not got very far."

The existence, he would write, was "unheroic," and he would describe a typical nighttime event:

"'Lieutenant, they're shooting up red and green signals in M company ahead of us.' This from the sentry. It is now dark. I crawl out in a hurry.

"'It is those g –d – d 37's. They're shooting up our own front line!' Poor M company is using up its stock of fire-works trying vainly to signal the artillery to cease firing, and I use up mine trying to re-lay the signal back.

"Then there is nothing to do but to double time back myself towards Battalion Headquarters to try to get the word back. By the time I got there the firing had stopped. If no one in M company was hurt the incident is amusing and will lead to much banter and cursing of the artillery officers."

On May 18, Newhall's platoon suffered its first combat fatality when

Pvt. Robert Woods was killed. Newhall found himself surprised at how easily he took Woods's death in stride.

"I have been wondering whether it is merely another sign of the heart-hardening process which I have mentioned before, that I should consider the matter very tearlessly and perhaps in a rather calculating mood," he would write on May 20.

"Probably had there been any suffering connected with the incident I would have felt differently. There was none. Even had a very close friend been involved I think I would have felt the same."

His bedrock philosophy—that some good comes out of every experience, even death—remained intact.

"The idea of death isn't terrible or even one associated with regrets except as it may be connected with sorrow or pain which latter always seems very unnecessary in a divinely ordered scheme of things."

He would add, fairly coldly: "My chief concern in regard to casualties is lest they should occur before the victim has done his 'bit' by getting a German. They can't afford to trade even with us."

Newhall on one dark night was able to put his thoughts on life and death into more stark relief. "Once when moving alone in the open I heard the approach of a really near shell and dropped flat," he would remember. "The shell was a dud and did not explode so I jumped up and proceeded, whereupon the same thing happened again.

"This proved to be really unnerving because the momentary tension which comes with flopping is immediately relieved by the explosion, but when there is no explosion it continues and builds up while you wait and decide when it is safe to move. What I recall is being jittery for a notable period after this episode."

He, like all other men in the trenches, had learned to distinguish the shells that might have his name written on them. "A shell that is not going to hit near you can be heard a long ways off because you are at an angle to catch the sound waves produced while it passes through the air," he wrote.

"Those that are dangerous are not audible until just the instant before they strike. Consequently there is nothing to do but flop on your belly and hug the ground. If you get down quickly you are safe 99 times out of 100. You don't have time to be scared—which is fortunate."

The worst experience, he would add, "is to sit in the bottom of a trench and listen to the shells come . . . When you can't see where they are falling and have your ear close to the ground they seem to be right on top of you when in reality they are several hundred yards away. There isn't anything to do but sit tight and wonder where the next one is going to land. It is reassuring to know that it takes about 10,000 shells to kill a man."

Though unscathed, Newhall would find himself dealing with the "pathetic and painful" consequences of his being falsely reported wounded—reports that, because of rigid army procedure, he could not correct.

"The basis for the rumor lies in the following incident: A soldier in a carrying party was wounded about fifty yards in rear of our trench," he wrote on May 22. "The medical corps man and I ran out to him. A shell burst near us throwing up a clod of earth which hit me in the side.

"For a moment I thought I was hurt and so did the other but I immediately felt to see if my blouse was torn. Found it wasn't and that I was only slightly bruised. So we picked up our man to carry him in. Getting winded I called one of my men from the trench to come and relieve me for the last twenty yards."

The "rumor" of Newhall's supposed wounding made its way quickly to Van Natter, who, instead of confirming it, simply—and perhaps quite happily—listed Newhall as a casualty.

Newhall remembered George Haydock hastening to his position in the trenches that same evening. "I must have learned that I had been reported wounded by a visit at dusk from George Haydock who evidently came over from his position, quite a ways from mine, to find out what had happened to me," Newhall remembered.

"The vivid memory which I retain is of his sitting on the back edge of the shallow trench and inquiring with obvious anxiety if I was hurt. Since George was a reserved person this is one of the marks of his friendship with me which I treasure."

Even as Jesse Cullison took over the 3rd Battalion that May, the 2nd Battalion was saying good-bye to an old friend, Maj. Axel Rasmussen, whose leadership abilities and common sense in handling men had led Company E's Edward Johnston to wax rhapsodic.

There wasn't an officer or enlisted man who didn't hear of, and mourn, the loss of Rasmussen, and his death was noted widely in the newspapers in the United States.

At Seicheprey in mid-March, Rasmussen had received a bad dose of dreaded mustard gas. "My eyes were so bad that I had to have poultices over them for four nights and days," he would write his brother on April 1.

"They have improved greatly, although I have to wear smoked glasses yet. I never realized how terrible this mustard gas was until then. My eyes felt as though they were coming out of my head. Particularly was the pain severe under the eyebrows—only another score I have to settle with the 'Bosch.'"

In early May, the Germans upped the ante on Rasmussen, who had made his headquarters several kilometers west of Cantigny in the village of Villers-Tournelle in "a stone French house with a courtyard behind," Company C's Charles Senay remembered.

On May 4, as Rasmussen was eating dinner in his headquarters with his adjutant and a French liaison officer, the Germans began bombarding Villers-Tournelle. One shell exploded in the courtyard; another demolished a stable beyond.

As the trio raced for the safety of the cellar, Rasmussen suddenly turned and said, "You fellows stay here. I left my cigars and a couple of letters from home upstairs in the kitchen. I'll go up and get them and be back again with you in a minute," Irvin S. Cobb would write in the *Saturday Evening Post*.

"Thirty seconds later, to the accompaniment of a great rending crash, the building caved in. Wreckage cascaded down the cellar stairs but the floor rafters above their heads stood the jar and the two who were below got off with bruises and scratches."

Making their way upstairs, the two officers found Rasmussen lying "helpless and crushed." They called for the regimental surgeon, who found that Rasmussen's spine had been severed.

"You've got it pretty badly," he told Rasmussen, "but I guess we'll pull you through."

Rasmussen looked up with a "whimsical grin."

"Doc, your intentions are good," Rasmussen told him, "but there comes a time when you mustn't try to fool a pal. And you can't fool me—I know. I know I've got mine and I know I can't last much longer. I'm dead from the hips down already."

As he struggled with his last breaths, the thirty-eight-year-old Rasmussen would say (according to Cobb's reconstruction of the scene):

"I'm passing out with the uniform of an American soldier on my back and that's the way I always hoped 'twould be with me, but I'm sorry I didn't get mine as I went over the top.

"Boys," he would add, "take a tip from me who knows: this thing of dying is nothing to worry about. There's no pain and there's no fear. Why, dying is the easiest thing I've ever done in all my life . . . So cheer up and don't look so glum because I just happen to be the one that's leaving first."

He died five minutes later—"like a true fighter," 2nd Lt. Vinton A. Dearing, of the battalion's Company G, would write, "and almost his last words were, 'It has been a great fight, boys. Give them hell for me.' "

They buried Rasmussen on May 6. "The Generals came to do him honor," Johnston would write, as did "the Major's old comrades who had also come with him from the British armies to serve their old flag again." Among the honorary pallbearers was Rasmussen's best pal, Capt. John "Jock" Manning.

Lt. James Leo Hartney, of the regiment's Company A, was put in charge of the funeral escort. "The major's death caused quite a little depression," Hartney wrote. "He was a fine likeable man himself and a mighty good soldier."

The funeral, he added, was "impressive . . . The battalion standing at 'present arms' as the coffin draped with the flag borne by six splendid big sergeants, preceded by the band and our company and followed by the honorary pallbearers is carried to the grave.

"Marching is in slow time to Chopin's funeral march. The coffin is placed over the grave, the battalion stands at 'parade rest' while the chaplain reads the funeral service.

"Afterwards the band plays 'Nearer My God to Thee,' we come to attention, three volleys are then fired over the grave, a bugler sounds 'Taps' and all is over . . . It is a service I would like to have for myself only I do not want it for quite some time."

Charles Senay would remember that the weather, like the occasion, was "gloomy. Within the graveyard were yew trees garrisoned by a colony of rooks or ravens," he wrote. "Leaning on the wall within was an old Frenchman, perhaps the sexton. He was greatly interested.

"Finally came the three volleys of the firing squad. These were a startling surprise to the old Frenchman and the ravens. The Frenchman ducked each time and, like a Jack-in-the-box, bobbed up again. The ravens rose in croaking disordered flight but circled overhead."

Jock Manning lingered at his friend's grave for some time afterward. "His dearest pal, another 'Canadian,' mourned in silent dry-eyed anguish at his grave," Johnston wrote, "and lived—a man alone and shaken—till the light Maxims set him free" the following July at Soissons.

"Yes, like the kings of old, the Major even took with him a human sacrifice—a willing sacrifice—to Valhalla."

17

The Day Before

He awoke with a start, as the first dim, gray light of morning eased into the cottage, and sat up straight, collecting his thoughts, trying to shake the dregs of a nightmare. Looking around the room, he saw Haydock already up and dressing, and in an urgent tone called him over.

"Whatever happens," Richard Newhall told George that morning, "always remember me as a friend who loved you."

Talk of a battle to come had dominated their lives by mid-May and became a constant presence even in the back lines. The possibility of going, finally, into battle, and thoughts of what might happen to one or the other or both of them, grew with each day and made their time together more precious.

Though "neither of us were morbid or pre-occupied with this," Newhall would write years later, they made arrangements that if either should be wounded or killed, the other would write with details to his family.

The 28th Regiment was, at that point, preoccupied with a single plan: the taking of the hilltop village looming less than a mile from where the Americans lived like moles in their pitiful but expanding trenches.

The assault on Cantigny "was to be a demonstration of what the Americans could do," Newhall would write. "It would be staged with all the frills of modern warfare. The artillery concentration for the preliminary bombardment would be greater than that which opened the battle of the Somme.

"There were to be tanks and flame-throwers, and, if the wind was favorable, a smoke screen. Every precaution was being taken to assure easy victory so that all the infantry need do was to walk over, occupy Cantigny, and send back batches of terrified prisoners."

The 18th Regiment had originally been pegged for the assault, with the date set for May 25. However, a gas attack on May 3 had disabled about a third of the regiment's men—the equivalent of an infantry battalion—and forced both a postponement of the attack and a change in the regiment that would perform it.

The 28th Regiment would take the 18th's place in what was now a May 28 assault. After nine days in the trenches, the regiment was pulled out of the front and support lines on May 23 and trucked twenty miles to the west for four days of practice on ground similar to that at Cantigny.

"Our 'training' for the attack as far as my experience and observation noted was no more than lining up in an open field outline of take-off trenches and waiting," Newhall would remember. "Perhaps there was a simulated advance eventually, but I do not recall one.

"Chiefly I remember standing idle with my men long enough to run through in my mind all the music of *Aida*. Perhaps the field officers were working out details for the attack. There was a group of them within my field of vision, but they did not seem to be up to much."

The plan of battle was simple enough. At 4:45 A.M., the artillery would open a crushing barrage on the German-held front lines and on the village. Two hours later, at exactly 6:45 A.M., the three battalions of the 28th Regiment would leave the trenches and advance a kilometer or less toward the town, where in every bombed-out cellar the enemy lurked with machine guns, rifles, and potato mashers.

Once the town was consolidated, the battalions were to push east across five hundred yards of exposed, flat ground and dig in. The 3rd Battalion was to take the sector north of the village, the second the northern half of the village, and the first the southern half of Cantigny.

Teddy Roosevelt Jr.'s battalion of the 26th Regiment was also to take position on the far southern end of the field in the Cantigny woods on the right of the 1st Battalion, and several companies of the 18th Regiment were to be held in reserve.

Three rehearsals were performed before the 1st Division was satisfied its plan was sound and the troops were ready. After the last, Company I's 2nd Lt. Herman Dacus would write, a French general gave his opinion of the effort—in fluid French.

The 1st Division's commander, Gen. Robert Bullard, then turned to his officers. "Gentlemen, you have heard the General's comments and suggestions, please give them careful consideration!" he said.

"We were all sure he had not understood any more of the French General's remarks than we had," Dacus wrote.

On May 26, Haydock and Newhall returned to their billet with the full knowledge that in fewer than forty-eight hours they would go over the top. Haydock reflected on his time in the lines.

"Everything jake and back for a bit of a rest away from the everlasting racket," Haydock would write. "These long days and short nights make a big difference in the war. We had wonderful clear days but very, very hot about noon. The nights were cool and also very bright which I may say added considerable interest.

"All the time it was light we would crawl in our holes, sleep and try not to be bored. (I was reduced to reading Shakespeare and racing beetles for amusement.) At night we were of course very busy, so many things to be done and so few hours to do them in, also Fritz got very rude at times and would interrupt us."

One of the many things to do was bringing the food to the line nightly in "chow parties." Haydock found the duty among the most hazardous of all he faced at Cantigny. "The first night I was shown a spot on the map and told to take the carrying party there. I had never been over the route but took a compass bearing and went to it," he wrote.

The countryside, he noted, "was much the same as that around Middlesex and we had to go about as far as from the school to Concord, cross country and avoiding certain shelled areas such as corners of woods, little valleys, etc. We got through O.K. and got the chow in every time although the returning party was on several occasions shelled.

"We would be going along perfectly peacefully listening to the nightengales when all of a sudden there would be a whiz and a bang (we were usually on our tummies by the time the bang came) and we would see flashes all along a certain place.

"We then decide that was an unhealthy spot and carefully avoid it. It's a great game trying to outguess him. You get out of the shelled areas and then you have the M.G.s to dodge. They are nasty, for you have no warning."

Because the perpendicular communication trenches were still being dug at night, Haydock and his carrying parties had to go "over the top all the way. You break up into small parties and use all the cover you can find." He had "no trouble about making the men keep quiet or do what you tell them. You get down, come back, a little check up on your party and heave a sigh of relief."

The quiet and reserved young man from Milton had matured by leaps and bounds since the previous November; partially from his experience leading men in the front line, and partly no doubt because of the influence of the older and assured Richard Newhall, he had become more secure in his own abilities and less intimidated by his "higher ups," whom he now regarded with some derision.

"When we are 'in' they don't bother us much, and when they do come around we tell them what is what, stuff them to the eye-balls, scare them out of hanging around and they are just as meek as can be," he would write.

He found it "great fun to pay back a grudge. We hear from the boss that such and such a thing is done, we say, 'Yes, sir, come and see it.' The boss comes (in a great hurry) we take him along said communication trench and come on a stretch that is only two feet deep for a 100 yards or so.

"We slow down going across it and casually remark that it is likely to be swept by M.G. fire at any moment and say to our runner, 'This is where so and so got it in the arm last night, isn't it?'

"The runner being well trained says, 'Yes sir.' The party which has been pretty well strung out becomes noticeably crowded from the rear. We remark that it is well not to get bunched up (but do not move away any faster). An M.G. way off on the right (probably one of ours) opens up. We hear a thud and turn around to see the impossible taking place, a fat man getting out of sight in a shallow and narrow trench that is 'finished.'"

He would add: "It is astonishing how quickly one can discover and get into a small hole or ditch when occasion demands. I have seen my entire platoon self included disappear off the face of the Earth in a plowed field in less time than it takes to tell. As divers, all my platoon goes in Class A."

He would conclude cheerily: "This is an awful lot of talk, but never mind, I had a good time writing it. Don't take it seriously."

Haydock, ever cheerful in his letters home, showed a darker side just prior to the regiment's move to the front lines in preparation for the attack on Cantigny. He and Newhall quarreled on the eve of Newhall's departure for the jump-off trenches; Newhall would never forget the spat.

"I had had the only clash with George of our whole period of friendship and I was very unhappy about it," Newhall would write exactly forty-three years later, on May 26, 1961. "It was because he refused to let me share with him a modest supply of chocolate which I had.

"Our preparations for the approaching battle included carrying, each of us, a limited amount of emergency ration. How I happened to have chocolate I do not remember. It wasn't an issue. That I should have this and George have none, for me was intolerable, and his refusal to take any seemed to me unfriendly. There was no bickering, but the idea that he could be unfriendly distressed me, which, as I recall, is why I went off by myself to write a letter."

That letter to his mother reads, in part: "This isn't the eve of battle but it is so close to it that if I don't write now I won't get another chance. Of course this will reach you long after the newspaper accounts have appeared. If the regiments engaged are mentioned, as probably they will be, you will have learned that I was in it.

"Really, I must confess to a certain feeling of embarrassment in writing this letter. The traditional 'just-before-the-battle-Mother' line evidently doesn't come natural to me, so that I am disposed to write a very ordinary letter."

Because of the spat with Haydock, he added: "To be frank I have on an awful grouch, just at this moment, combined with a case of the dumps, neither of them in any way connected with coming events."

He would admit to a certain excitement at the thought of going over the top. "Indeed the prospects of the next three days are intensely interesting. Again, I am going to see something new under the sun, at least new to me, and such a prospect is always alluring. It all still seems like a big, sporting proposition.

"Indeed it is so very business-like, carefully calculated, and the costs and results of various sorts worked out so far, that I am losing touch with the pathetic features."

There was another element to his gloomy frame of mind—the knowledge that he and Haydock would soon go over the top and "my realization that some gesture and expression of farewell with George was appropriate, and my refusal to accept this fact with its inherent implications."

Instead, it was the temporarily petulant Haydock who tacitly and touchingly bid au revoir to Newhall, who left on the evening of May 26 to make final arrangements for Company L's occupation of the forward trenches.

"When we marched down the street to the place where the trucks were waiting, perhaps a quarter of a mile, in the twilight, George came and walked beside me," Newhall wrote. "I do not recall anything we said to each other, if we did speak."

Newhall and his platoon climbed into the trucks, and as the motors revved and lurched into gear, he looked back through the gloom of twilight and saw his good friend George Haydock, waving good-bye.

He was going out again but had to wait for the last tentacles of light on that long spring evening to recede, leaving the jumbled ruins of the village just a dim and ghostly whitish outline against the deepening cobalt sky.

As he waited, George Buchanan Redwood found time for a little philosophy, some consideration of all the what-ifs he and the regiment faced on the cusp of battle, the brink of America's first assault of the war.

"My platoon was occupying a sector in the front line and your son was taking a patrol out in No-Man's Land from my sector," Company K's 2nd Lt. John G. Mays, a twenty-nine-year-old graduate of the University of Georgia, would write Mary Redwood.

"While he was awaiting the appointed hour to go out, we sat there in the moonlight on the fire step of the trench talking for an hour or more along spiritual lines. Although not in the same Company, we were in the same battalion and in the last few months I was thrown rather intimately with George Redwood and we grew to be close friends."

Sitting on the firestep, Mays brought up an article he had read in that month's *Atlantic Monthly* entitled "The New Death," by Winifred Kirkland of Asheville, North Carolina. "He had not read the article but was much interested as he had known the author," Mays wrote.

"The view of death in battle as developed by Miss Kirkland was so helpful and inspiring that I sketched it roughly to George, which turned our talking into the channel of speculation as to the nature of the life to come."

Writing with the backdrop of almost four years of slaughter, and the certainty of heavy casualties with the impending entry of the United States into full-fledged combat, Kirkland in her article attempted to offer some spiritual solace and guidance—not only to the combatants but to their loved ones.

Her concept of a "new death" was not so much about a new reality as it was about a new way to salve the enduring pain of the past and coming losses—and a perhaps new manner in which to accept the physical death of a loved one.

"The old death, like many other things remade by the war, was too often self-absorbed, self-pitying," she would write. "In terms of immediate living, the New Death is the constant influence upon us of the boys who have passed."

She would note of the young lives that had been, and would continue to be, cut short: "There is something strangely persistent about any unfulfilled life: it always leaves a curious sense of abnormality and waste, and a deep blind impulse somehow to give the aspirant young soul the earthly gifts it lacked . . . There is always this psychological continuing of an arrested life, and it is inevitably the more powerful, the more personality the dead youth had attained."

She would seek to detect evidence of another, upward existence after death in the simple fact that men willingly faced death in battle, as if they sensed that physical death was somehow not final.

"That multitudes of soldiers have met their end, not only with serenity, but with a high-hearted gayety, is a fact of overwhelming evidence," she wrote. "This hilarity of heroism is the highest proof a man can give of his certainty that soul is more enduring than body; and exhibited so often at the very instant of passing, may be, to the open-minded, argument for some strange reassurance from that other side."

Certainly the Christian soldier George Redwood would need little convincing of his own soul's immortality; as for the "hilarity of heroism," he had already proven himself something of a comic master in that vein. Judging from subsequent events there's a strong suggestion that he found Kirkland's idea of achieving immortality through death alluring: What better way to fully realize his being as a soldier? What better way to give one's all, show the others they need not fear death?

What better expression of true leadership was there?

Perhaps as a reward for his exploit at Seicheprey, Redwood had been relieved for a time from his intelligence duties, and found a billet in the home of a local curé with Lt. Daniel Birmingham, the 3rd Battalion's gas officer.

"So far we have been making out very well together indeed," Redwood wrote on May 1. "Our principal fear was, at first, that some higher officer might find how good our lodging was and rank us out of it. This made us rather chary about entertaining guests among the other officers and caused us to slip a word of warning to all that called."

He was at that point serving, somewhat reluctantly, as the 3rd Battalion's acting adjutant, a position "which is not my rightful one and which I hope—fervently—soon to be rid of. It was through an unfortunate combination of circumstances that I had this 'greatness thrust upon me.'

"I should say 'pettiness' for it seems to be nothing but the remembering of countless details involving an extensive knowledge of the battalion itself, of Army regulations, Military etiquette, Customs of the Service,

Manual of Court Martial, etc. etc. etc. all of which my C.O. amiably presumes I have—and I haven't!"

In mid-May, Redwood was set free from the desk job and happily returned to his position of battalion scout officer, this time with a new sense of urgency, as the 28th Regiment prepared to take the battered village that loomed before the Americans.

Already a legend, Redwood burnished his reputation for derring-do. Night after night, leading small parties, Redwood hauled himself from the trenches and slithered into no-man's-land looking for intelligence, anything that might reveal the Germans' movements, their strength, the identification of units, the location of artillery and machine-gun posts hidden in the wheat.

He put his fluency in German to good use.

"Lieut. Redwood used to go over into the town at nights to get information and he used to bring back wines and things to eat back with him," Cpl. Newell Davis of Company I would remember. "The joke of it was that he captured them from under the Germans' noses and if any of them spoke to him he would reply in German and they would not know but that he was one of them."

On twelve successive nights Redwood "made his way into the enemy lines, and into the town which was in the enemy's hands," another soldier would remember. After locating and sketching machine-gun and artillery emplacements, Redwood "would come in about daylight, covered with mud from crawling around in the trenches and under the barbed wire, and looking like anything but an officer." Redwood would then "change his clothes, get a bite and turn in for some sleep, and do the same thing the following evening."

In one "particularly bold stunt," Redwood performed "a very difficult piece of reconnoitering work against a long stretch of the enemy's opposing line and was even more daring" than the capture of four Germans in March, yet another soldier would recall.

Late on the night of May 17, he led six men into the night and headed for the road linking Cantigny with the village of Villers-Tournelle to the southwest. "Several shell holes were found near the northwest edge of this road and reconnoitered from flank and rear but discovered to be untenanted and unimproved for machine guns," Redwood would report.

"About 1–1:30 AM sounds were heard from Cantigny resembling the rattlings of wagons mingling with the dumping or packing of broken stone. One German was heard to call another, among the buildings or near them, but words were indistinguishable."

The next night, Redwood again went out with six men. Working in conjunction with a patrol from the 1st Battalion "for the purpose of jointly trapping a hostile patrol, outpost, or covering party," the patrols split, the 1st Battalion's moving stealthily to a position on the Cantigny–to–Villers-Tournelles road, Redwood's group to within 150 yards of Cantigny itself.

The patrols linked at 3:30 A.M. Redwood and the 1st Battalion's men "pushed on up to between 50 and 75 meters of the edge of Cantigny," the after-patrol report would state.

"Here a hollowed out place for an outpost group was found, with four potato masher grenades. Two of these were taken."

Redwood's reports of his activities "were often given in with a touch of humor and not infrequently with some quotation in verse," 1st Lt. Joseph E. Torrence remembered. "What was nobody's work he volunteered to do. He was 'the willing horse' and he was overworked."

Redwood's humor extended to an elaborate code he devised for transmitting information over wires the Germans might have tapped. An American raid was an "entertainment"; "sandwiches" were machine guns; "fruit" meant grenades; "coming out parties" meant a group was beyond the wire. "Wines" meant gas; "soup" was a 37 mm gun and "salad" a 150 mm.

On this night, after spending an hour pondering the nature of the afterlife with John Mays, Redwood gathered his small band and left the trenches once more to prowl out there in the blackness of no-man's-land, beyond which loomed the ruined village that held the key to his own hilarious heroism.

By that morning it had become easier to not even notice the shelling, its frequency and constancy and cadence and roar becoming part of the surroundings, reduced to the subtlety, almost, of the far-off rumbling of a thunderstorm on a hot and muggy day.

The early morning of May 27, 1918, was different, somehow. There was a barely detectable increase in the number and rate of the shells, just enough to create a sense that something was wrong, something brewing, although through the haze of half-sleep in his dugout it was hard for him to put a finger on just what that was.

Sent forward to the front line on May 26 with Company E to relieve a company of the 18th Regiment in anticipation of the assault on Cantigny, Capt. Edward S. Johnston tried to ignore the rumbling; it was just as he felt the tentacles of deep sleep pulling him back that his number two crashed into the dugout and startled him awake.

"Captain," 1st Lt. Irving W. Wood told him, "I don't want to wake you up about a mere bombardment, but this has been getting steadily louder, and I don't like it."

Hardly had the words left Wood's mouth when "the trench was enveloped in a cascading roar of explosives," Johnston would write. "Viciously, uninterruptedly, malevolently, the thunder-clapping shell ripped into that shallow ditch in the loamy earth. Gusts of machine-gun fire also swept the parapet from moment to moment. Here and there someone cried out; all along the trench men were falling . . .

"The platoon sergeant, moving along toward the center, was suddenly wrapped in smoke and fire; when the scattered mist of high-explosive fog and the uprush of earth had cleared away, the sergeant lay dead in two pieces, his trunk severed below the shoulders."*

All along the front, the intense German shelling forced men to seek cover in the chalky earth. "A shell exploded quite near, and then another and another," Company M's 2nd Lt. Gerald R. Tyler, a native of Aiken, South Carolina, and twenty-three-year-old graduate of Clemson University, recalled.

"Then they began hitting everywhere. No such thing as a dugout in

---

* Johnston's account of the raid on Company E's lines comes from his chapter "The Day Before Cantigny" in *Americans vs. Germans: The First A.E.F. in Action*. New York: Penguin Books; Washington: Infantry Journal, 1942.

the sector, so we lay like lizards in the bottom of the trenches. The awful explosions would come, the ground would rock, then dirt would fall in on us. Things were getting embarrassing."

Crawling through the intense shelling to another of the company's lieutenants, Blanford Daniel, Tyler told him, "This is no place for us."

They went skittering through the trenches.

"Hardly had we done so when a 105 hit the place we had just left and blew it off the map," Tyler wrote. "Shells were falling thick and fast. Our faces were blackened with smoke and we were getting quite enough of this strafing."

Unable to go back because of the shelling, Tyler and Daniel decided to follow a communication trench and make for a forward position 150 yards away. "I do not know on earth how we got there," Tyler wrote, "falling down over picks and shovels, knocking off corners of traverses . . . Part of the time I was turning over and over.

"When we reached the front line we found that things were in much the same shape. Two privates attached themselves to me and we buddied ourselves up in the bottom of the trench. Finally a message came down that Germans were coming across just to our left."

Soon enough, gray figures cautiously approached out of the dawn—fifty handpicked Jagdkommandos, members of a permanent raiding party, heading for the front line held by Company E.

There was a "certain discord" in the "symphony of the attack," Johnston would remember. "The proper thing would have been to issue early from the trench, crawl forward under cover of fire, and then, when that fire lifted, throw grenades and rush."

Instead, the Germans had waited for their artillery's preparation fire to lift. The raiders then stumbled and paused briefly at a "little strip of straggling wire" across the front.

"The first effort of the defending machine gun was not too successful," Johnston remembered, "but the second took the rear wave in enfilade at the wire, and cut down more than wheat."

Five Germans approached Company E's lines, and to his amazement, one of the unit's young officers saw "one of his own men run out from the trench, hands above his head, and dash forward to meet the attack," Johnston wrote.

"Five gray-clad figures at once appeared around him; he spoke to them with animation, and they manifested a quite evident pleasure—in fact . . . they jumped up and down in excited joy. One of them then raised a hand to his mouth; the raid commander was about to give the signal for withdrawal."

Before they could turn, the six men, including the erstwhile American, were cut down. "Gray and olive drab alike, they fell in a huddle in the wheat, and lay still."

Quiet ensued, and the company collected its dead, sent its wounded to the rear, and went in search of the missing. Particularly disturbing to the close-knit group of officers was the disappearance of 2nd Lt. Charles Avery, a twenty-four-year-old former newspaperman from Emporia, Kansas.

"I think of the relationship enjoyed by the officers of Co. E as that of a family for we were closer than friends, and we were brothers in thought, action and feeling," the twenty-six-year-old Wood would write.

Avery's best friend in the company, 2nd Lt. John Curry—a twenty-two-year-old former clerk at the Scranton, Pennsylvania, city hall—scrambled across the caved-in trench, frantically seeking Avery amid the ragged arms and legs jutting from the tortured earth.

"I was pinned under four feet of dirt and as soon as the fire slackened a bit, John came to look for me," Avery recalled. "He walked all over the sector which had been devastated by shell fire calling my name. When he was immediately over me, I answered, and he and some of my men dug me out.

"Ten minutes more and I know I would have suffocated. I shall never forget his calls of encouragement while they were digging me out nor the tender way he lifted me on to the stretcher when I had been unearthed."

Happily reunited and gulping in fresh air at last, "I think we both cried a bit," Avery would remember.

Avery had been buried for three hours. "His whole right side was paralyzed," Wood remembered. "I saw him on a stretcher on the way to the ambulance, smoking a cigarette and smiling with the side of his face that he could yet control."

Between the German barrage, an American counterbarrage that had mistakenly fallen on Company E's position, and small-arms fire, twenty-four of the company's men had been killed and thirty-nine wounded. Only three or four of the raiders, however, made it back to their lines.

As the dust settled, Johnston would find George Redwood hovering over the bodies of the five Jagdkommandos and the lone (supposed) doughboy that had been cut down at the end of the melee.

"He appeared, now, suddenly, in No Man's Land, sitting in the wheat, industriously working at something," Johnston wrote. "He was noted for roaming about the area, searching out this and that."

After pawing through the effects of the dead doughboy, Redwood looked over to Johnston. The man, a recent replacement to Company E, was a spy, he told him.

Richard Newhall had just attempted to turn in when the shells began flying. After leaving Haydock at Maisoncelle, he and twenty men made a final reconnaissance of the company's approach to the jumping-off trenches.

"This consisted of following out in the dark the route by which every platoon was to march from the detrucking point to the position in the front line. The distance was about four kilometers, mostly cross country, because the roads were shelled," Newhall remembered.

"The positions themselves were especially dug trenches, in these it was necessary to measure off the space to be occupied by the platoons in order to prevent crowding or overlapping on the morning of the assault. This took quite the whole night. Being completed, I curled myself up in a corner of a communication trench, with a view to getting a little sleep."

Before he could doze off, "for an hour and three quarters I had more shell fire than I ever had before," he wrote. "It seems that they tried to pull a little raid on a small sector of the front line in my neighborhood. It was a failure. As I did not belong to the Company that was occupying the line, I had no duties in connection with the situation. Indeed I did not believe at the time that the enemy was really coming over."

By 7:00 A.M., he wrote, "everything was quiet, but the day was spoiled for much sleep, such opportunity as I had to move about in the open I spent in locating the burrows and dumps, the aid station, and the different headquarters.

"Inasmuch as the troops then in that sector were to be relieved that night it was exceedingly difficult to find anybody who had any information and nobody seemed to care, which I may assure you is a normal state of affairs."

After lying low through the day while Company E picked up its pieces, Newhall toward midnight placed his men in the jump-off trench assigned to his platoon. He then sent off guides to lead the rest of Company L forward.

"At midnight with two runners, I posted myself at the last stage of the march to lead the way through the French positions to the trenches which L Company was to occupy," Newhall wrote.

"Then came a wait of perhaps an hour before the first platoon, with Haydock leading, appeared out of the dark. It did not take long then to get the whole Company into position although there was a time when we had to march with our gas masks on, which was a nuisance."

Company L, on the extreme left of the American line, relieved a French unit. "All I can recall is the dug-out which served as their headquarters company," Newhall wrote. "And the personnel whose response to my appearance as representing the American relief was one of impatience to get out—not panic but no delay."

Finding that the 2nd Platoon "was in its assigned place at the extreme left of the American assault line it occurred to me that I should make contact with whatever out-fit was on my left, French of course.

"This was a 'duty' peculiar to the position at the end of the American line. Since all that the men in my platoon had to do was to stay in position until zero hour, which was all of four hours away, I thought it safe to go in person to make contact with the French."

He found to his dismay that the French unit on his left was expecting to be relieved as well. "Nothing had ever been said about it to me, no arrangement had been made, the position assigned to us in the line of assault made it impossible for us to extend our front to the left three hundred yards in order to occupy their trenches," he wrote.

"Nevertheless out they pulled. This meant that I had to go in person to the officers of the next French Company and arrange for covering this gap."

Newhall, less than fluent in French, tried to apprise the French of the dangerous gap that existed. "Presumably I made this explanation to some sort of officer but whether commissioned or non-commissioned I did not know," he remembered.

"What I recall is a small group in the dark, not particularly young seemingly, who accepted my statements imperturbably and seemed unconcerned at the extent of empty trenches on their right.

"We didn't make much of an arrangement, we couldn't, the attack was imminent, neither of us could move, so the best we could do was assume that the vacant space was well covered with machine gun fire. This took up the greater part of what remained of the night. They probably wished me 'bon chance' and I returned to wait in my position for zero hour."

Newhall then sought out Haydock, whose 1st Platoon would jump off to Newhall's right; together, their platoons would comprise the first wave of the company's advance, their job to reach the German trenches, overwhelm the occupants, and then push forward with the rest of Company L and dig in on a new forward line.

At 4:45 A.M., American artillery unleashed a terrific bombardment on the village of Cantigny and the German front lines. Newhall would recall that his men "were excited at the near approach of an event long anticipated, and seriously subdued that at last they would be under fire in the open. There was nothing, however, which looked like fear, only eagerness to get into the big game.

"In such a frame of mind the time passed quickly, and indeed after 4:45 A.M. there was plenty to occupy one's attention . . . If the men felt confident before, they were doubly so as they watched the 'big ones' dropping on the enemy position."

At 6:30 A.M., Newhall again made his way through the crowded jump-off trenches, found Haydock, and talked to his friend for a few minutes about "trivial things . . . Neither of us seemed to have any feelings of parting, any realization of imminent danger." To Newhall, it seemed "so impossible that we were now to go into battle instead of a mere maneuver, that we only discussed the details of what we planned to do, and picked out the landmarks by which we could direct our movements."

He then returned to the 2nd Platoon and confidently awaited the order to advance. "I had always supposed that the last few hours before going into battle were full of tense excitement," he would write. "They're not. We had practiced it until each man knew just what he was going to do. Our artillery was pounding the German lines in such a way as to make it probable that we would merely walk over and occupy them."

Soon enough, word came down the line: "In five minutes we go over. Get a foothold in the trench wall so as to be able to get over quickly."

"Each lieutenant," Newhall wrote, "gets out his whistle and figures how he is going to jump to be sure he is the first man of the platoon to get onto the parapet. His eyes clutch his wrist watch. The moving barrage has started.

"Whistles pipe shrilly along the line. A succession of single figures seventy-five yards apart line the parapet for an instant, the platoon chiefs—'Come on—platoon!' "

Into the bright rising sun stepped Richard Newhall, leading the 2nd Platoon, just a small figure, just one of some 3,500 men plodding east toward an imaginary line beyond the first German trenches, the Harvard PhD finally finding his chance to make some history, finally taking part in a grand crusade of his own, finally and eagerly about to discover what a battle was like.

As he stepped forward amid the smoke, amid the din, amid the chunks of earth peppering the sky from the rolling barrage, Newhall chanced a look to his right, where George Haydock and his men trod slowly east.

"I caught a glimpse of George walking at the head of his platoon," he would write, "and that is the last I saw of him."

18

Don't Tell Him

It didn't take long for them to find him, tall as he was and walking steadily at the head of his platoon as if he were simply off on a Sunday stroll and not leading men into battle. The first bullet hit him in the right armpit; the stinging blow stunned him and put him on his back on the ground, but he managed to pick himself up and move on.

Before he'd taken ten steps the second bullet hit him, in the left arm, and that put him to ground for good. For good measure, as he lay helpless and in pain a third bullet crashed into his upper left arm, smashing through the bone and leaving an exit wound seven inches long and two wide in the rear of his shoulder.

"That dazed me and I lay still," Richard Newhall would remember, one of the few details he would have to relate about the Battle of Cantigny, his own experience of it being reduced to forty hours of sleepless agony, of longing vainly for unconsciousness, of feeling that his lifeblood was slowly draining from him as he sat propped against the wall of a small hole while the bulk of the 28th Regiment stormed and took the village, then moved east five hundred yards to dig in under murderous machine-gun and artillery fire.

While the regiment suffered but held, Newhall would sit helpless, all of the long months of training, of seemingly pointless maneuvers, of enduring the pettiness of the army coming down to this, the image of a small, half-alive, and helpless second lieutenant from Minnesota gritting his teeth and longing for unconsciousness or to be found by friend or foe—he cared not which—and rescued from the absurd situation in which he now found himself.

So this is a battle . . .

Company L had jumped off just moments before, moving steadily and in line with the rest of the 28th Regiment across the slightly undulating fields toward the first line of German trenches to the east of the road leading north to Grivesnes; all along the line the men were singing, some even "laughing hysterically," Bill Morgan would say, as they advanced on that Tuesday morning.

After several hundred yards, and before he reached the German first line, Newhall went down. "I think there was a sniper in front of us picking off the officers," he would write. Pvt. Roy A. Hall, of Columbia, South Dakota, stopped to tend to him, but Newhall told him to continue on with the 2nd Platoon, which "rushed the German trench where they met with no resistance.

"Then half of them fell back to dig the trench which was to connect our old line with the new one, and the other half established out-posts to cover the digging."

Newhall, meanwhile, lay stunned and dazed. "I never lost consciousness but it was some time before I began to take an interest in things, I then discovered that one of these outposts was right beside me and [the men] had dug a little trench ten feet long and three feet deep," he would write. "We may have exchanged remarks but, if so, I don't recall them."

The trench at that point might as well have been a mile away; Newhall, in shock and his left arm in pieces, could only lie helpless as his men stepped over him and into the rising din of battle that morning.

Moving with relative ease, the 1st and 2nd battalions to the south routed the Germans from Cantigny, using rifles, grenades, and flamethrowers wielded by French soldiers to kill or coerce from hiding the several hundred enemy hidden in the cellars and ruins of every bombed building. French tanks also put the fear in the defenders and provided cover for the advancing doughboys.

"They went over into the fighting singing, laughing, joking, absolutely unafraid, uncaring," Company E's 1st Lt. Irving Wood wrote. "They couldn't move forward fast enough, and some who were wounded struggled to their feet with smiles on their faces and kept going."

The 2nd Battalion and Companies B and D of the 1st Battalion then moved east as planned, leaving small details to wipe up the remaining resistance in the village, while Company A swung from the Cantigny Woods to the south to block the road to Montdidier.

Once out on the plain and exposed to German machine guns in the wheat, and to the artillery lurking in the dense Framicourt Woods to the center and the Laval Woods on their left, both battalions suffered severely as they attempted to connect shell holes into a forward line of resistance. Some companies endured casualties of 30 percent in just minutes as bullets and shells ripped into their forlorn positions.

"Digging a trench under these conditions is not the pleasantest occupation I know," Company B's 2nd Lt. Neilson "Net" Poe—a distant cousin of the late poet Edgar Allen and one of six Poe brothers who had starred in football at Princeton between 1882 and 1902—would write.

"Most of our losses occurred at this spot and our company was as badly cut up as any," Poe, forty-one, of Baltimore, would add. "In about an hour we had a trench dug deep enough to get some protection from the machine gun bullets, and it was then just a case of digging deeper and joining the trenches with the company on our right and left."

"There was a queer sense of unreality about the whole thing," Irving Wood recalled, "for though many of our men were wounded, dead or dying, and though the Huns were lying around in heaps, still it seemed more like a dream, a movie show or one of our many practice battles."

The presence of a French signal corps photographer on the battlefield only added to the sense of "unreality"; as the company dug in, 2nd Lt. Wilmer Bodenstab, a twenty-four-year-old former bond seller at the Guaranty Trust Company of New York, posed for some shots.

"He was laughing at the photographer who was taking the picture of his men digging in in front of him," 2nd Lt. Hugh Flanagan of Company H recalled. "Just then a shell came over and he was instantly killed"—as was the photographer.

Because of the previous day's raid and the quick death of Bodenstab,

Company E had just three officers on the line that morning—Wood, 2nd Lt. John Curry, and Capt. Edward Johnston.

The three survivors "walked around there either smoking cigars or cigarettes, superintending the digging of the new trenches, under full view of several German machine guns that were just raking our position with fire . . . There was so much to command our personal attention that we forgot our personal danger," Wood added. "It was natural to ignore the bullets."

(Wood would be reminded of his peril when he took a bullet in the hip and Johnston sent him to the rear. Another sniper's bullet "struck its mark" later in the day and killed John Curry "instantly," Wood would write.)

Axel Rasmussen's replacement as commander of the regiment's 2nd Battalion was also mortally wounded early that morning. The only battalion commander to step into the fight, Lt. Col. Robert J. Maxey at one point stopped a massacre-in-the-making among a group of doughboys who, their blood up, were about to kill a dozen Germans in cold blood.

Not long after, the forty-five-year-old Mississippian himself was hit by a machine-gun bullet; "although fatally wounded he gave detailed directions to his second in command as to just what to do and caused himself to be carried to the Post of Command . . . to give information to his Regimental Commander that he considered very important," his posthumous citation says. That second in command, Company G's Capt. Clarence Huebner, would assume command of the battalion.

On the left, the 3rd Battalion advanced with Company L on the left, Company K in the center, and Company M to the right, flanked on its right by Company F of the 2nd Battalion. The gap between Company L and the nearest French unit to the north was filled by German machine gunners, who ploughed severe enfilade fire into Company L's men in particular as they moved across the open ground north of Cantigny.*

---

* Years later, upon reading Laurence Stallings' 1963 book *The Doughboys,* Newhall would write that the author's map of the battle "puts my company in the wrong place in the line," and instead had Company K on the northern flank of the advance and Company L in the center. Battalion commander Jesse Cullison in his after-action report would write that the

The punishing fire caused some of Company L's men to flinch and drift south to mingle with Capt. Henry Mosher's Company K, which also suffered from the machine guns on the left as it advanced, and caused a few men to return to the safety of the jump-off trench or go to ground in shell holes that pocked the ground.

Others continued on. "We had not advanced very far before Germans began jumping out of shell holes and beating it for the rear," 2nd Lt. Samuel I. Parker, a twenty-six-year-old native of Monroe, North Carolina, would write. "The boys couldn't stand it. They let out a terrible 'rabbit-hunting' yell and began cutting them down with their rifles."

As they rushed the first-line trench, "one big burly cuss, with whiskers, thought he would stay us off. He threw a grenade right between my sergeant and me, but it did not explode until we had rushed past. The big brute saw that his grenade did not phase our bunch, that we were coming after him; so he jumped out of the trench with his hands up yelling 'Camerad.' Sergeant said, 'Yes, a Hell of a Camerad,' and shot his bayonet clear through him."

Company K's 2nd Lt. John G. Mays, who had discussed the "new death" with George Redwood just thirty-six hours before, led his platoon on the right flank of the second wave in "mop up" duty.

"When our second wave sighted the Boche running out of their trenches they closed up into the front wave, so as to get a better shot at the enemy," Mays wrote. "I had to drive our men back at the point of my pistol, so they would begin digging our trench before the enemy counter attacked. This shows their magnificent valor—they wouldn't stay in any rear wave once the enemy was sighted.

"We did mop up those trenches," he would add. "I myself killed two Boches and took three prisoners—perhaps I should have killed them, too, but when they came toward me with their hands up crying 'Kamerad, Kamerad,' I just couldn't do it."

His platoon killed "approximately 25 of the enemy" while "capturing

---

battalions advanced in the order "M, K, and L, respectively, and numbered C1, C2, and C3, extending north from the Junction with the 2nd battalion." Van Natter would also note that Company L "was assigned to the left of the 3rd Battalion" in the assault.

in excess of 20. We passed on to the line of resistance . . . and commenced digging in. We made good progress at digging in but suffered severely from machine gun fire on the left."

"Advance was swift and unchecked," Company K's 2nd Lt. Lafayette Irwin Morris would report. "Very few casualties during the advance, and these were due mostly to machine gun fire coming from the left front."

Reaching the German first line, "considerable numbers were shot down in places," Morris wrote. "Two squads of automatic riflemen ran up and down the parapet pouring their fire into the trench and at least 50 of the dead were left there."

Company M, on Morris's right, had similar success in routing the German defenders. "The French tanks were right along with us, but were not needed very much as the German machine gunners either ran or threw up their hands," 2nd Lt. Gerald Tyler wrote.

"Just before we reached their front lines they swarmed out and soon began trying to put as much distance between themselves and us as possible. Run! They simply faded away. Our rifles got many of them.

"Most of the Boches however came out of their trenches running toward us waving hands frantically over their heads and yelling, 'Kamerad!' These were taken prisoners."

Upon reaching the line on which the 3rd Battalion was to dig in, German machine-gun fire quickly took a toll. In just minutes, twelve of Morris's men were killed and four wounded. Retribution was swift: Morris and four of his men pinpointed one of the machine guns raking his company from a hidden position in the wheat and captured it.

"There were about 15 of the enemy in the post and we killed all but four of them and we returned them as prisoners," he wrote. "The gun was then slewed around and we commenced firing at the enemy who could be seen on the reverse slope of the hill, just in the edge" of the Laval Woods. They then carried the weapon back to their lines.

Newhall's "crony," Company K's Henry Mosher, advanced not with his prized bolo, as he had said he would, but with a cane hooked over his left arm and a pistol in his right hand.

"He dealt death to five Germans, shooting them down with his automatic as nonchalantly as at target practice," John Mays would remember.

Mosher, anticipating a German counterattack, sent out patrols to establish a line of surveillance far in advance of the company's position. Cpl. Jesse D. Gillespie, of Aiken, South Carolina, was one of those chosen for the perilous duty.

Mosher "sent me out with a detail of five men," he would remember. "We went forward about seventy-five yards, established ourselves in two adjoining shell holes that afforded a measure of protection, and began filling bags with dirt to shield us somewhat from the enemy fire."

Within an hour, two of Gillespie's men had been "picked off," while a third, "badly wounded, left the outpost to take chances on crawling back to the American lines."

Before long, "a high explosive shell struck near the outpost, throwing its metal fragments in all directions," Gillespie would remember. "I pulled myself together to find one of my comrades who had already received machine gun wounds, with additional injuries, the other unharmed, and myself in a bad way.

"A good sized piece of the metal had gone through my right leg breaking it about six inches above the knee, the left leg was slightly injured, and the right hand and wrist were shattered by another fragment of shell that had ploughed its way through."

Gillespie made a tourniquet for his leg from his shoelaces while his uninjured private bound his wrist. "In a few minutes my helper was killed by rifle fire, leaving us two wounded fellows alone."

He, like Richard Newhall, would spend the rest of that day and two more "listening to the music of warfare as it spent itself in the air above No Man's Land."

While digging in, meanwhile, two of Company K's young officers were quickly killed. The first was 2nd Lt. Paul Waples Derrickson, a twenty-six-year-old from Norfolk, Virginia. Just days before, in anticipation of the assault, the 1915 graduate of Washington and Lee University had written his will and addressed it to his brother-in-law, with instructions to pass it on to his mother in the event of his death.

In it, he bequeathed his $10,000 in war-risk insurance and several hundred dollars in bonds to his widowed mother, Mary, and his sister, Helen.

"You won't get this letter if all goes well," he wrote, "and of course that being the case I sincerely hope that you won't get it . . . Mother, I want you to give Helen a college education . . . and especially to see a good time yourself with the insurance which with what you already have ought to keep you fairly well off."

Reaching the consolidation point on the morning of May 28, Derrickson paused and was reaching out a congratulatory hand to Lafayette Morris "when a machine gun bullet struck Derrickson in the forehead over the right eye," Morris would later say.

Stunned, Derrickson reeled and dropped to the ground. "He said to me, 'Morris, come over here and fix me up,'" Morris remembered. "When I got to him he had passed away."

Falling soon after was 2nd Lt. Clarence Drumm, the twenty-eight-year-old son of a Bigelow, Kansas, farmer and a former semipro baseball player in the Nebraska state leagues. Drumm had just returned from visiting the outposts and was directing the consolidation when he was hit and killed instantly by a bullet, Morris remembered.

Lt. Gerald Tyler was wounded soon after Company M halted and began to dig in. Told that there was a gap between his platoon and the one on his left, he went through increasing machine-gun and sniper fire to talk to the other platoon commander.

"When I went over to see the Lieutenant something hit me in the right thigh and knocked me down," he would write. "It was the sniper's bullet. I crawled to the hole a couple of men were digging and not a moment too soon for the Huns played a machine gun right over the top of it nearly all day. I spent the day in that hole."

Adding to their peril, at about 9:00 A.M. the first of what would be seven German counterattacks rolled tentatively from the Framicourt Woods to the right front of the 3rd Battalion, but was scattered by the division's artillery.

Consolidation of the ground won by the doughboys continued under heavy machine-gun and shell fire. Despite the dangers, Henry Mosher maintained his nonchalance, "checking up on the casualties walking from one place to another cheering his men," Sgt. Marshall Sanderford recalled.

At about 10:00 A.M., "he asked me with some other men how we were getting along," Sanderford would say. An instant later, Mosher fell. "I was about 10 feet from Captain Mosher when he was killed, being hit with a large piece of shrapnel at the junction of neck and shoulder."

"One of his last actions was to drag a wounded private, under heavy fire, back to a place of safety," Mays would write. "I was by the side of our captain when a shrapnel struck him and was able to catch him. Death must have been instantaneous and I am glad I was there to have my old friend and captain die in my arms."

Meanwhile, the 3rd Battalion's Company I remained in reserve, some of its men carrying munitions and other supplies to the front—among them Samuel Ervin, reinstated as a private the day before the assault with the help of George Redwood.

Leading a carrying party, Ervin encountered a wounded German soldier as he waded through a field of high grass. Kneeling to tend to his foe's broken arm, Ervin was shot through his left foot by a machine gunner.

Wir sind verdammte Schweine ("We are damned swine"), the wounded German told Ervin, who managed to hobble back to the company's position at the village cemetery.

With no way to know that Newhall lay stunned and bleeding, George Haydock led Company L's 1st Platoon east toward the German first line.

A long way from Fresh Ponds, where the Harvard Regiment had played at war in the spring of 1916, Haydock was at last meeting his stiffest test, that which he had hoped would be transformative—should he survive.

As he had tried to in his many letters home, he put on a stiff upper lip and showed no fear as he directed his men to subdue a German machine-gun post just east of the road leading into Cantigny, then paused to reorganize before leading the assault on the German first-line trench.

"We came to a halt," Pvt. John D. A. Rader would tell Louisa Haydock. "The Lieutenant walked from one end of the platoon to the other cautioning repeatedly, 'Men keep lower for your own sakes.' They replied, 'Lieutenant, you keep low, they will get you.'

"The last words he spoke were, 'They can't kill me.' "

Pvt. Douglas Woodworth would remember that the company entered a German trench labeled "Trieste" on 1st Division maps and began bombing its length with hand grenades. He and another private rousted two Germans from a "sleeping hole" dug into the trench wall.

Suddenly, a machine-gun crew partially hidden by a large beet pile fifty yards to the platoon's left opened fire, and Haydock, ignoring his men's suggestion that he keep his head down, boldly directed the fire of his men toward the gunners. Within moments, "he was hit by a machine gun bullet and died instantly," Rader would write.

Thus did the great adventure of the "fatalist" George Guest Haydock come to an end. "I suppose when the time comes I will go to the front just as I went to camp, getting a new experience and wondering if I could make good, and then if I get plugged that will be the next step," he had written all those long months ago.

He had certainly made good, then taken that "next step" of getting "plugged," as he would put it, plugged by a machine-gun bullet from the back of a lousy pile of beets; and one can't help but imagine that had he somehow been but wounded and lived, George Haydock would have made light of such a scene, squeezing every last ounce of self-deprecating humor from the ingloriousness of it all.

He had done all that the army had required and expected of him, and more; despite all of his self-doubts and fumbling, he had learned to lead men, and those same men had willingly followed him into the trenches and lastly into battle, where their safety, not his own, had been paramount, and where his courage had not faltered.

"They can't kill me," he had said, and one gets the sense that by that morning his men believed it. His posthumous citation would celebrate George for displaying "qualities of coolness and gallantry which inspired his entire platoon." Without him, his 1st Platoon, rudderless, went little farther that morning and would instead gather their line around his lifeless body; many would break and run later in the day, with no George Haydock to rally them.

His great adventure over, George Haydock would lie lifeless out on the field all that day and be buried that night "close to where he fell," Rader would say.

It would occur to Richard Newhall only years later that he might have known that something had happened to Haydock. After all, had he known that his friend lay stranded on the field of battle, "I would have risked anything to get to him."

But George never came. No one came.

Instead, Newhall lay helpless and broken, unaware of his best friend's death and "longing for unconsciousness" just a few hundred yards from Haydock's body.

Richard Newhall would remain there through the morning, as consolidation of a front line went on amid machine-gun fire and shelling, which only intensified in midmorning when the French pulled out their artillery to race south and meet yet another German offensive launched the day before, leaving the survivors of the 28th Regiment to dig furiously into the chalky earth on an arc running 1,500 yards from north to south.

Above them, German aviators soared almost at will, directing fire onto their pitiful and shallow holes, and the German 271st and 272nd regiments of the 82nd Reserve Division massed in the woods for counterattack after counterattack.

"Along in the afternoon the enemy began to shell us pretty heavily," Newhall would write. "There was nothing for me to do but lie still with my helmet over my face."

He could hear "explosions of a salvo well off to the left. Then, after a minute or two, another one considerably closer, then a third right on top of our location, then a fourth off to the right. This was repeated, perhaps three times, and then the German sights would be lifted and the shells would fall beyond us towards our former position."

One shell made a direct hit on the small trench near him, blowing off the lower jaw and fracturing both forearms of twenty-year-old Cpl. Ruffus A. Shelton, of Honey Grove, Texas. In one of Shelton's pockets was a letter to his widowed mother, Ruth Ann, scribbled while he waited to go over that morning.

"We are about to enter the first drive that the United States has made in the war," Shelton wrote. "There are some of us that will not live through it, but mamma . . . if I had lived to come back one aim in life for me was to come back and show the world that I could be somebody, and most of all to show mother how much I love her. God keep and bless you till we meet again."

As his corporal's life ebbed, Newhall "was repeatedly showered with loose dirt. A stone thrown out by one shell hit me in the left shoulder and . . . broke the collar bone. I recall thinking, 'This is the time when you're supposed to pray,' and realizing that I had no inclination to do so. I did hope very sincerely that if I was hit again I would be killed and not just wounded again."

Toward 4:00 P.M., the German fire intensified. "The enemy had moved up some machine guns on the immediate left and they were firing at us continuously," Company K's Lt. Morris would report. "The shelling continued and became very severe about 6 o'clock."

Morris noted that many of Company L's men retreated to the safety of their original jump-off trenches, taking some of Company K's men with them.

"The order was passed down from the right that the company was to retire to the support trench," John Mays recalled. "I had a non commissioned officer confirm this order and he said that it had been passed down from the right of the sector.

"He could not tell from whom the order came. No American troops remained on my left as they were continuously withdrawing. The enemy barrage had cut us off and there were only 12 men left."

His left flank "in the air" because of Company L's retreat, Mays gave the order to retire to the jump-off trenches several hundred yards to the rear, where he found one officer, three machine guns, and eight to ten enlisted men. He sent word of his position to Lt. Col. Jesse Cullison, who ordered Mays to consolidate a strongpoint where he was.

Lt. Samuel Parker would remember that at about 6:00 P.M., "word was passed down the trench that Lieut. WARD (or some such name) ordered us to evacuate at once. Not knowing who Lieut. Ward was or with what authority he gave such an order, I ordered my men to stand fast, and stand guard for the approach of the enemy." (John Mays would later blame "a German spy in American uniform" for the mysterious order to retire.)

Moving to his right, Parker sought out Lafayette Morris. "I consulted with him and we decided to remain in position until something more serious happened or we had the proper authority to withdraw."

Parker returned to his platoon sector to find that "someone" had led his men back to the company's original jump-off lines. He then went forward through heavy fire to the company's outposts, where Pvt. Jesse Gillespie lay in agony, and found the survivors "discharging their duties faithfully, with some dead and some wounded in the posts. The positions were in full view of the enemy and it seemed an impossibility to evacuate the wounded in daylight.

"I explained to the post that the company had retired but that I was going to find it and bring it back into the original position, and ordered them to hold out until the wounded were evacuated . . . I went back to the front line, then down through 'L' Co's sector but could find no one."

Company L's commander, Francis Van Natter, would write that the unit had had to halt its consolidation by 11:00 A.M. because of heavy artillery and machine-gun fire.

"By afternoon the company's left center had sustained heavy losses," he added. "Certain of the old and covered positions were reoccupied. A number of small detachments remained on the assigned objective."

Newhall, meanwhile, lay helpless halfway between the jump-off trenches and the forward line. He would remember that as the bulk of Company L's men retired to their original position, his faithful sergeant, John J. Stetz, "crawled up to me on his belly.

" 'Lieutenant, the company has fallen back to the old line and the Germans are forming for a counter-attack.' That meant that these little outposts were isolated.

" 'If the company has fallen back,' I said, 'you'd better get back as quickly as you can.'

"It was impossible to take me. I couldn't move without pain and couldn't possibly crawl. Earlier in the day one of my men had tried to pick me up but I had fainted with pain. It was impossible to get a stretcher. I was too far forward for the Medical Corps man attached to the platoon to reach me."

Sergeant Stetz "bade me quite an affectionate farewell, kissed my hand twice, and assured me he would come out for me that night," Newhall wrote. "I recall being first surprised at his action and then very much content because it made me believe that I had functioned effectively and apparently won the affectionate respect of the men." (He would learn that Stetz was subsequently wounded and thus was unable to rescue him.)

Alone and isolated, Newhall "now expected to be taken prisoner (it never occurred to me that since a battle was going on I was much more likely to be bayoneted where I lay). But the German counter-attack never got to me. The preparatory bombardment had been its worst feature and the infantry attack was easily broken up. There wasn't much fight in that German outfit."

The German attack by the 1st and 2nd battalions of the 272nd Reserve Division was launched from the Laval Woods in front of the 28th's 3rd Battalion. Automatic-rifle fire and a defensive barrage from the remaining artillery quickly dispersed the Germans, whose survivors fled into the Framicourt Woods to the south.

Company M's Lt. Rudolph Koubsky remembered that at dusk on May 28 "a number of Germans could be seen advancing across no-man's land." A wave of Germans edged out of the Laval Woods on the far left of the field, only to be "beaten off with heavy losses, by our rifle and auto rifle fire which lasted until dark."

Amid the chaos, 3rd Battalion scout George Buchanan Redwood flitted about, mapping German strongpoints and machine-gun posts and racing to and fro from the front line to battalion headquarters in the St. Eloi Woods.

He was, it seems, in his glory, all of his life pointing to this morning.

Prior to the regiment's advance, Redwood was hit by a machine-gun bullet in his right shoulder while scouting the front. The wound was "dressed by Private Washburne and Lt. Redwood went on and refused to go to the dressing station," Company I's Pvt. Robert Flagg would remember.

Heading back to the front, Redwood was again wounded, this time in the jaw, and he went to the aid station behind the lines. "He told them at the dressing station that he was going to die with his outfit and he made his third start," Flagg would write.

Sam Ervin remembered encountering Redwood just prior to jump-off. "I remarked to him that he was somewhat recklessly exposing himself to machine-gun fire," Ervin would write. "He merely smiled in his quiet, cool way and said he had already been 'slightly wounded.'

"About two hours later," Ervin added, "I returned from a second trip to the rear with materials, and some one came to the strong point with news that Lieut. Redwood had been wounded severely a second time."

With permission from his platoon commander, 1st Lt. Charles McKnolly, Ervin "searched innumerable shell holes" for Redwood and in one found "the overseas cap he wore. I could find no trace of him, save this."

It wasn't until Ervin himself was in the hospital that he found out the fate of his former billet mate. "I learned that he had gone to the aid station and his wounds had been dressed," Ervin wrote. "He was tagged for the hospital. Heavy firing began—probably a counter attack by the Germans—and he went back toward the front lines. Thus he met his death, manifesting a most unusual and courageous devotion to duty."

Company M's Lt. Gerald Tyler recalled Redwood crawling to his shell hole and asking "how things were going. I gave him what information I could and advised him to get under cover because the area was being subjected to heavy machine gun fire. I noticed that he was holding his right hand up to his chest at this time.

"He replied that he had already been wounded and intended to proceed at once to Bn. Headquarters to make his report. A few minutes after this, word was passed to me that he had been killed by shell fire."

A postbattle citation would claim that Redwood "volunteered to obtain information of the enemy's line which was reported to be under consolidation within our own barrage area" and that he was killed while "making a sketch of the enemy's positions and, although wounded by their fire, continued to complete the sketch."

Company M's Sgt. Max Rosenbaum offered a very different—and eyewitness—version of his death.

Redwood, he would write Mom-Mom, had found the severely wounded Rosenbaum and "administered first aid to me, and regardless of his own safety, he carried me thru intense machine gun and intense artillery fire to the back area.

"While assisting me he was severely wounded, and instead of receiving first aid treatment as I asked him to, he attempted to reach the lines again, in order to lead a retreating company (Comp. K) up to their line of resistance. While doing so a high explosive shell burst near him killing him instantly.

"I am the only living man who was an eye witness to your brave son's heroic death. You can imagine my sorrow to see the man killed, who a few moments before had saved my life."

Redwood, he would add, "is always referred to by the Officers and men as 'The Hero of Heroes' of the First Division."

Redwood's body was "picked up by soldiers of his command," Private Flagg would write. "There was a hole above his right temple and a piece of shrapnel through his heart."

Flagg and several others carried Redwood's body to a quarry several hundred yards west of Cantigny, where "Pvt. Wishburne was killed while burying him, and Corp. Crawford was wounded."

Flagg finished the job, using a propeller from a downed German plane as a cross. He later returned to place two French 75 mm shells on the grave, "and some little stones to read, 'Gone but not forgotten.'"

The sentiment that Redwood's legacy would be remembered long after the war had ended was shared by Company K's John Mays, who months later would write: "More than once I have seen him in my dreams . . . The thought brought out so strongly in Miss Kirkland's 'New Death'—that the spirits of our comrades and loved ones who have passed on to the far better life do exert a powerful influence upon us—is, to my mind, a most logical one."

Gone but not forgotten: The loss of Redwood's "powerful influence" would extend even to America's Allies. "A French officer who has been Liaison Officer with this Division in all its fighting and knew George, said the other day: 'I would rather have the man Redwood alive than to have taken Cantigny,'" Maj. Redmond Stewart would write.

Still immobile in his small hole, Richard Newhall remained unaware of all of the drama, heroism, and suffering going on around him. He hoped only for rescue from his own pitiful plight, and by nightfall on May 28, "everything was quiet except an occasional burst from a machine-gun fired into the dark at random," Newhall wrote. "I lay still, afraid to move for fear the stretchers would miss me. Nobody ever came."

He was alone, save for the body of Cpl. Ruffus Shelton, and unaware of the perilous position to which the 3rd Battalion clung through the night. (Newhall was later brought to the brink of tears when he learned that Pvt. Roy Hall had wanted to crawl out at night and rescue him "but had not been permitted to do so." Hall was later killed at Soissons.)

Only Company M, on the right, had remained in position, with no troops on its left flank. Company G of the 18th Regiment and the 28th Regiment's Company I were ordered to the forward line established that morning by Companies K and L to fill the gap.

Gerald Tyler, wounded that morning, performed the escape from the front line that Newhall could only dream about. He set his sites on a communication trench three hundred yards away that would lead him to the back lines.

The route, however, was overland, through intense shelling and random machine-gun fire. "I had been wounded for many hours, my wound needed dressing badly and I was weak from loss of blood and lack of water," he wrote. "I concluded I'd be a fool to try it, but I got right up and beat it through that hell.

"I shall never know how I made it but I remember running from one shell hole to another as best I could with my lame leg, hearing shell fragments, shrapnel and bullets whiz about my ears. I passed horribly mangled Germans and Americans, some not altogether dead. I finally reached the aid station, and since then have let other people worry over me."

While Tyler reveled in a bath and clean sheets, his surviving brother officers licked their wounds and counted heads. Some pleaded for relief—among them Van Natter, who on that first night would send a plaintive series of messages to 28th Regiment commander Maj. Hanson Ely.

(Years later, Newhall would note with delight that Van Natter had made it sound like Company L had been "completely annihilated" in his "somewhat hysterical" report. Van Natter was relieved of command of Company L on May 29; 1st Lt. Howard Hawkinson, Haydock's former coleader of the 1st Platoon, would see the survivors through the next two days.).

"My company is practically wiped out," Van Natter wrote. "I have lost Lieut. Haydock killed, and Lieut. Newhall and Lieut. Hook wounded. M.G. fire has raised havoc . . . Practically all of my noncommissioned officers are wounded."

Shortly thereafter, he wrote an addendum pleading for help: "I have thought this over very carefully for the past hour—I feel I should not ask it, but I believe I owe it to the men. My men have fought hard hand to hand all day long with the enemy, they have suffered heavy losses, no rest or sleep and little time to eat. What I should like is to have them relieved . . .

"Hawkinson's platoon held out until all their ammunition was gone and then took German rifles and ammunition to fight with. If you can effect this relief it will be appreciated."

Hanson Ely also sought a relief for his entire battered regiment, but he found no sympathy with 1st Division commander Gen. Robert Bullard, who remained concerned about the German offensive to the south and was hesitant to commit the division's reserves to the battle.

As well, the taking of Cantigny had during the day become something more than what Gen. John Pershing had originally thought of as a "simple affair."

Pershing had observed the attack but left the scene in midmorning. "I think he must, after leaving me, have encountered some of our Allies and heard them express doubt of our ability to hold what we had won,"

Bullard would write. "He meant to show them that we could and would."

There would be no relief—and no retreat, on Pershing's orders. "Inform Ely as follows," Bullard would write in a message to the 28th Regiment. "The position must be held. The C of C expects it."

For Richard Newhall, relief was not an option. He remained awake and in agony as night descended. At daylight on May 29, "I managed slowly to edge myself over to the little trench and slip into it.

"I couldn't lie flat because of the dead corporal in the other end. (That was fortunate because I never could have got to my feet from a prone position). So I sat in one corner all day slowly thinking about how I would get myself back that night."

The day brought more shelling, and more counterattacks by the now-desperate Germans. Even as Newhall was managing to squirm into the small trench that held his dead corporal, the Germans blanketed the American positions with shells, followed by an attack from the Framicourt Woods.

"As the smoke cleared away three waves could be seen advancing on our front and left front, attempting to envelope our left flank," Company M's 1st Lt. Rudolph Koubsky would report. "They were beaten off with heavy losses again."

That night, Capt. Jock Manning would take command of the company, which had been reduced from some 225 men to 1 officer and 80 men. By then, though, they had taken their own toll on the Germans: Company M, 3rd Battalion commander Jesse Cullison would write, "is the company on whose front the enemy dead lie thickest."

Yet another counterattack was mounted on the 28th Regiment's lines in late afternoon, but this one, too, was repelled. As night fell a second time, Newhall decided to make a try for Company L's lines several hundred yards to the rear.

"By midnight it was dark enough to move," he wrote. "I removed all my equipment and abandoned it, except my gas-mask and helmet. The latter got lost on the way. From the strap by which I carried the Very pistol pouch I made a sort of sling for my left arm.

"Then I got to my feet. The effort caused me to faint but I fortunately fell against the parapet and so remained upright. The cold night wind quickly revived me. Somehow I managed to get out of the trench. Perhaps I fainted again; I'm not sure.

"The only way I could move was upright which was dangerous because of the random machine gun fire, but that couldn't be helped. Movement was slow and I had to crouch frequently for rest when I got dizzy."

Moving painfully, he now worried that his own men might shoot him, thinking he was a German.

"When I began to make my way through our wire, fortunately not very thick, I was challenged from our trench," he wrote. "They were suspicious of me for fear it was some German ruse."

An American voice yelled, "Who goes there?"

"Friend, a wounded American," Newhall replied.

"Advance and be recognized. Who are you?"

"Lieutenant Newhall, L Co."

At that point "men jumped out and helped me into the trench."

His first question was whether the regiment had taken Cantigny.

"Yes," he was told.

"What about Haydock?"

"He was killed."

The three simple words sent Newhall reeling.

"I went to pieces, and cried out, probably somewhat hysterically," he would write. "I remember a voice saying, 'Captain Mosher was killed too.' "

Another doughboy's voice, "very angry and stern," immediately followed: "Don't tell him!"

The admonishing tone amounted to a "psychological slap" for Newhall: "The tone of this latter . . . helped me, I think, to pull myself together and regain control."

Stretcher bearers soon arrived, and Newhall, now suffering from heartbreak as well as his physical wounds, was taken to the aid station, "a small cave-like place," where he would learn some of the circumstances of George Guest Haydock's death in battle.

"It was a gallant end without sorrow or pain to him," Newhall would write consolingly to Louisa Haydock while in the hospital in July, "and there have been times in the last six weeks when I have thought of it a little enviously.

"George was very dear to me. His companionship made tolerable this military life which is very hateful to me. I shrink from the idea of returning to that life alone."

Dawn brought yet another German assault on the 28th Regiment's lines, but this, too, was repulsed. Throughout May 30, desultory shelling back and forth ruled the day, but it became clear that the Germans had given up hope of taking back Cantigny.

The Americans had held their lines and prevailed, though the battle had bought little military value; instead, it had served notice to the Allies—and, more ominously, to the Germans—that America was willing to spill its blood as freely as any of the combatants. As well, the set-piece attack relieved some of the pressure brought to bear on Pershing to split his army and dish it out piecemeal to the Allies.

On the night of May 30–31, the 28th Regiment's able-bodied survivors—soon to be known as "the Lions of Cantigny"—were finally relieved by the 16th Regiment and emerged sleepless and "hollow-eyed" from their trenches, Ely would say.

Thirteen officers were dead—among them Wilmer Bodenstab, Thomas H. Watson, and John Curry. In the early morning hours of June 1, Jim Quinn laid all three in a common grave. Nearby, he and several men buried "as nearly as I can remember, about fifty" enlisted men—just a small portion of the 185 enlisted men killed in action at Cantigny.

Thirty-two officers had also been wounded or were missing in action—almost every one a graduate of the first officer training camps—as were 837 men.

Some of those missing lay alive but severely wounded when the regiment was relieved. Among them was Company K's Cpl. Jesse Gillespie, whom Henry Mosher had sent forward early on the morning of May 28.

Gillespie lay next to his buddy, Pvt. William Dreger, all through the battle, until on the morning of May 30, bleeding and in desperate need of water, he decided to try to try to reach Company K's original consolidation line.

"I'll send back for you if I reach our men," he told Dreger.

"There's no need now," Dreger told him. "It's too late." (His body would, indeed, be found by searchers days later.)

Gillespie painfully pushed on his back, using his elbows for propulsion, until he reached the former front line. "Here he began his search for water, and, strange to say, the first he found was on the dead body of Capt. Mosher, who had sent him out," a newspaper account would say.

"The bodies of Lieut. Clarence Drumm and other men of Company K were recognized, silent testimony to the cost of the Cantigny victory."

19

So Much Easier Just to Die

She had pretty much always received whatever she wanted. Once, in her later years, fumbling with a zipper on the back of a gown after returning from a society party, she called the Palm Beach Police Department and asked if someone couldn't be sent over to help her unzip, and "the nicest young man you ever saw came to my assistance."

On another occasion, when inquiring about swimming conditions off the bath and tennis club, she was told by the manager that the ocean was swarming with Portuguese men-of-war. Without hesitation, she told him, "Tell the visiting Portuguese men-of-war officers that they are invited to my house this afternoon for tea."

It was an invitation that even a marine organism ignored at its peril.

What Marion Wallace Rappleye McKinlock wanted now was not help with a dress, or guests for tea. She wanted to know what had become of her only child, Lt. George Alexander McKinlock. "He is not dead," she said that July. "He is missing and they shall find him."

McKinlock had had his first taste of real action at Cantigny and endured three days of constant bombardment "in fine style," his friend Bill Morgan would somewhat bitterly note.

In understated style, McKinlock would write his mother on June 3 to say: "Well, I am safe and sound, and experienced. If you have the papers and look at the maps, you can at least know what we were doing the last week.

"I was with a barrage group of machine guns in a wood, and it was our job to fire into the Boche, well behind his lines and break up his reserves. We did not go over the top, but even so we had our share of attention from the Hun, who played continually upon our support lines with artillery.

"Barrage machine guns have a hard time, even if they are not right up on the line. The enemy takes pain to locate them, because they do great damage, and then goes right after them with artillery."

He had been hoping for such "line experience," his work on Chester Davis's staff to that point consisting mainly in "reading reports, arranging maps and dealing with conditions in the abstract." On the morning of May 28, as Davis's right-hand man, McKinlock's schooling in the realities of modern war began in earnest.

The action, he would write, was as a rule "hot and heavy. I was in a trench directly behind a couple of our guns when a shell fell out so close that the gun crews even tumbled back into the trench, one man wounded in the thigh and another in the shoulder, neither of them seriously. It was only a miracle that we all got out, of course, we lost a few but the Boche artillery was a little off in range.

"It is wearing, because even if the greater part of the shells are wide of one's position, everything is constantly jarred so that one cannot get any rest. I spent most of my time in a small trench about six feet long, two feet wide, and four feet deep, which was good protection against fragments but of course nothing against a direct hit."

As much as McKinlock downplayed his first action, his commander, Maj. Chester Davis, wrote that for those three days at Cantigny his battalion was "subjected to the most hellish fire that man can endure . . .

"It was our first experience in seeing men killed within a few feet of us. We had absolutely no shelter and after the second day, we were out of food and water."

On the night of May 29, Davis received orders to scout for better positions for the guns, which had been well sited by the Germans. "Alexander and I reconnoitered together and we got in an enemy barrage," Davis wrote. "Shells burst so near that we could feel the heat of the explosion. At one time during that barrage several shell fragments hit me in the hand and wrist.

"Alexander was probably twelve feet from me. I told him I had been hit, and supposing that it was a serious wound, [he] came over to assist me, despite the fact that shells were at that time hitting within a few yards of us. This is but an instance of his unselfish loyalty and disregard for personal safety."

By mid-June, such loyalty had led McKinlock to be appointed as an intelligence officer to the staff of 2nd Brigade commander Gen. Beaumont Buck, who would claim he took McKinlock away from Davis's staff—and over Davis's objections—"on account of his splendid qualities and abilities."

Not as impressed with himself, McKinlock likened his army career to working for his father at the Central Electric Company in Chicago, "visiting different departments and working a bit in each one."

His nonchalant attitude no doubt would have infuriated those self-promoting and ambitious peers of his who vainly sought to climb the army's chain of command—but Alexander would allow that the army "has no fascination for me; I am willing to work and do the job, but there's nothing inspiring.

"At least one doesn't feel that there's a future to be worked up to." He simply wanted to "get it over with and then clear out."

He expected to be assigned to an infantry company once the 1st Division was relieved from the lines around Cantigny, and he was pleased with the prospect. "I don't mind staff work," he wrote, "but I don't mind going with the troops.

"The only unpleasant part of staff work is the contact with the rest of its members," he would add. "About half a dozen live, eat and sleep together and stay in dug outs doing office work without exercise, so that it's easy to get scrappy when we are under a strain for a couple of days. With troops one has a certain amount of exercise and being in the open naturally is not so tiring."

He would get his wish to be with the troops, for action, for something more than stultifying staff work, sooner than he could know.

William Otho Potwin Morgan had come though Cantigny not in "fine style" but as a broken man. The three days of pounding had shaken him to the core and turned upside down his grand ideas about the war, about mankind and the better world to come, mocking his pride in having become inured to the small horrors he had previously encountered.

All had evaporated in the intense shell fire and desperate violence of those three days, to be replaced by a new and vivid sense of how precious life—his life—was to him, along with a new revulsion at the war and his part in it.

"I sort of wander around all day doing nothing," he would write Christiana Councilman on June 3. "Somehow I can't tell you all that has happened to me this last week, it is all too vivid. I can't seem to get over the shock of the terrible reality."

He and his machine gunners advanced behind the 28th Regiment on the morning of May 28 and set up strongpoints to the rear of the consolidation line, digging in to afford themselves as much cover as possible. The outposts soon became—as advertised—veritable magnets for German artillery and planes that scoured the battlefield. The singing and hilarity ended in a deluge of German shells and machine-gun bullets.

"The next three days and nights had no laughs in them," Morgan would write. "When the Germans let fly, a corporal was wounded, the man next to him killed, and two others wounded at other guns about 15 yards ahead of me. We had practically no protection, only a little digging at night."

For the first time, Morgan encountered the effects of German fire at close range. He was horrified and forever unnerved when one of his men collapsed, wounded, on top of him.

"A corporal came jumping into my little knee-deep trench, and a second later fell over on top of me, with a shell fragment through his helmet and in his head," he wrote. "I didn't know that he was hit, until I realized he was limp, so I took off his hat, and seeing the wound realized he had to be gotten to First Aid.

"There was so much lead flying around that I couldn't seem to order a man to leave his little hole and go back after a stretcher, so I made a break for it. When I got back a few minutes later, this corporal was standing so dazed he couldn't realize anything, and had consequently been hit three more times in the head. They got him back, and I think that he will live."

While the infantry of the 28th Regiment manned their thin holes and fought off counterattack after counterattack, Morgan remained with his guns until the third day.

With Maj. Chester Davis, McKinlock, and Capt. Charles Yuill, he "just lay in one spot for hours wondering where the next shell would fall," he wrote.

"It literally nearly drives you mad. You feel like tearing things to pieces and yelling. The shells throw dirt all over you, and one of our men was killed by concussion alone. I can't say enough for the infantry. They held that line hour after hour. It is unbelievable what they stood, and their spirit was beyond all words."

His love for the new science of war was replaced by horror at its flesh-and-blood realities. "One man with an arm torn off wanted to go back to the line, and the First Aid men finally had to call for volunteers to go up to the front line to dress the wounded who refused to go to the rear . . .

"I know of one case and there are probably more where a man drank his own urine. That is unbelievable, but so is it all. This whole damn business is unbelievable."

Welcome P. Waltz, in charge of a platoon from Company C of the battalion, would remember his position to the rear of the 28th's 2nd Battalion being blanketed by "large 10 inch ashcans or mortar shells" that descended through the day on May 28.

"They came over so low that one, in looking up at them in an endeavor to gauge their line of drift, had too much time for reflection and this condition made their presence very undesirable.

"One of these bombs dropped exceedingly close to my hole and the concussion seemed to create a vacuum in the hole. It also pulled all the air out of my lungs and I had to stand up, lean over and gasp for my breath. My heart ached for sometime after that. The terrific concussion had almost finished me."

On the second afternoon, the German artillery became so intense that Waltz worried "that our position was going to be pulverized and all of us churned up with it . . . The dust created by the bursting shells around our position was so great that it looked like the heaviest London fog.

"French artillery observers, afterwards, stated that it was the heaviest artillery fire they had seen delivered on a small sector in years of war."

Two long-range German guns added to the misery of the second day, pounding Waltz's strongpoint.

"These were guns so far back that we never could hear the report of the gun but our first warning of the approaching shells was a great roar in the air as the giants would twist over and then a succession of roars and when it sounded like a mountain was on the point of smashing us, we could look up and see two huge logs bearing down on us, both together.

"The earth seemed to buckle and shimmy around in a crazy manner. This type of stuff is what makes men go insane [with] shell shock."

The shells, of course, also brought death, one direct hit taking the life of Company G's "brave and courageous" 2nd Lt. Thomas H. Watson, who commanded a squad of riflemen at Waltz's position.

The twenty-three-year-old former bank teller from Roxobel, North Carolina, "was at all times very active and in his hopped up battle condition, thought it was his duty to be running constantly over to his men," Waltz wrote. "I tried to keep him down but it was no use. He was even taking his pistol and shooting at our runners, from the front line, that were coming back near the strongpoint."

During one of the many bombardments pulverizing Waltz's position that day, Watson "ran forward to see something or somebody and one of the big [shells] ranged along side of him and that was the end of a very brave officer."

"I, with several other men in the Company, got to him immediately after this explosion," Richard Newhall's former billet mate, Lt. Jim Quinn, recalled. "He was killed simply from concussion. There were no marks on his body, that we found, except the skin directly under each eye was broken, and the blood was gushing from each one of these wounds as if it were being forced out with pressure."

The continual pounding of the German artillery caused Captain Yuill to be evacuated during the second day with "shell shock." Morgan lasted until the evening of May 30 until he, too, gave in.

"I went a little to pieces, and the major sent me back to arrange for a relief for all of them," an exhausted Morgan would write on May 31. "I can't write any more, I couldn't bear to just now . . .

"All that I have ever read or imagined can't picture the hell of our attack, and it was far worse for the boche. It's an awful nightmare, and I only hope that I can get hold of myself before long."

He would add, furiously: "Alec McKinlock came through our three days in fine style, and wondered why Captain Yuill and myself gave out, when he hadn't been at the front twelve hours together in these last three months." Nevertheless, McKinlock would be awarded the Croix de Guerre for his actions at Cantigny—further rankling Morgan.

In fact, Morgan, too, would be cited by the 2nd Brigade for displaying "conspicuous leadership and meritorious conduct in skillfully having his battery repeatedly perform its barrage mission for 72 hours while under repeated heavy bombardments."

Those heavy bombardments, and the death and maiming that ranged all around him, continued to echo through Morgan's rattled brain. "It makes you think, I'll say that much, seeing these wonderful boys crumple up like so much dough, and human flesh mean nothing," he would write.

The lasting visions, and the newfound fear of shelling, left him unable to function as the 1st Division through early June improved and consolidated further the hard-won lines east of Cantigny.

"It's an awful nightmare," he wrote. "I guess I'll be able to go back now. I tried it two nights ago, but two shells in front of me made me feel so like flying to pieces that I came back. I decided I had to get up the line again, to get over my nervousness. I feel so ashamed being this way, but last night the Captain refused to send me just yet.

"When I hear a shell I get the most terrible sensation. I become perfectly tense and rigid, and I was affected the same way a little while ago when some one started an automobile engine. I don't seem to get over it as fast as the rest somehow."

Prior to Cantigny, he would add, "I laughed at the close calls that Captain Yuill and I had had, and I said there wasn't a shell in Germany with my name on it. The Major sort of smiled and said that Major Rasmussen was the only man he had heard say that. I told him I would take it all back and I certainly have."

Worse was the apprehension during the second week of June that the Germans would make a push to regain those lines—"a pleasant prospect as I had to go way beyond the line on which we intended to hold them, and all in front of this line were sacrifice troops," Morgan wrote.

"We were notified in the middle of dinner one night that the attack would start in 45 minutes. I did some hectic scrambling, but the attack didn't come until next day after all and then it missed our right flank by a few thousand yards."

He would add: "I long so to get off by myself, to crawl into some woods where I can forget the war for a minute or so. You can't look anywhere or think, or hear anything which isn't associated with war, or isn't a part of it. I am afraid I got a little too much of a dose of it at once.

"Honestly, I wasn't afraid of shells before. It is only that which gives me confidence that I will get over this. Thank heavens I can tell anyone now that I am afraid of them, for they know I used to laugh at shells.

"You should have seen the officers come out of this show. They lost awfully in weight, and looked about ten years older. I certainly don't feel the same. I used to be all enthusiasm and right on my toes, it all seemed like such good fun.

"But now it's all simple and pure determination with me. You have got to make yourself go ahead hour by hour, with no assurance that you are going to see the next day."

It was a task he was finding more and more difficult to perform.

On July 8, the 1st Division finally left the lines at Cantigny and trucked to the area around Dommartin, thirty miles northwest of Paris. Rumors abounded, one having it that its next destination was the States, to train recruits; another had the division heading for Italy, and yet another Russia. Alexander McKinlock wished only for a leave, so he could pick up a new uniform he'd ordered in Paris.

Though by no means a trench rat, McKinlock lived something like the infantry, traveling light and ready to move out at a moment's notice. "I now have the bedding roll, all my clothes are carried in it, my toilet articles in two musette bags," he would write on July 10.

"I have a bottle of spot remover which is invaluable, otherwise my uniform would look like a dish rag for I have lived in it practically all the time since the middle of December."

He would add, in what would be his last letter to Marion McKinlock: "I certainly would like to be home with you at present, I need your good influence, this life is too primitive we have nothing of the finer things at hand and unless one has ideals constantly in the foreground, why, it's easy to act like an animal."

Any hopes for a rest and a taste of the "finer things" dissipated quickly amid the continuing crisis on the Western Front, where the Germans continued the series of offensives they had unleashed on March 21. Pushing ever south toward Paris, the latest assault between Noyon and Reims gobbled the city of Soissons and continued to the north bank of the Marne, creating a pocket thirty miles deep.

The deep bulge was quickly seen as an opportunity by Pershing and the French. Plans were quickly devised for a counteroffensive that would strike east on the left shoulder of the German bulge just below Soissons and cut the Germans' ability to supply troops, munitions, and other materiel for a continuing push on Paris from the Marne.

The smaller aim of the operation was to force a German retreat from the Marne. The larger aim, if the assault could be made quickly enough, was to entrap the German forces. In an attempt to draw even more Germans into the pocket, artillery on the south side of the Marne was pulled back, as were frontline infantry positions, in expectation of an attack.

The German drive was launched early on July 15, but when the German preparation artillery began, the shells fell into unmanned trenches, and assault troops crossing the Marne were cut to shreds or left isolated by quick-arriving Allied troops—including those from three American divisions—that were rushed to the front.

On July 17, Gen. Erich Ludendorff halted the offensive, but by then, thousands of Americans and French colonial troops were marching and trucking east to jump-off trenches just south and west of Soissons.

After marching through a fierce thunderstorm on the night of July 17–18, the troops took position for the knife thrust, the 1st Division on the north flank, the 1st Moroccan Division to its right, and the American 2nd Division on the southern flank of the assault.

At 4:35 A.M. a thin, creeping barrage signaled the attack, and more than 30,000 men stepped into the thick wheat of the countryside below Soissons and began wading through tall grass toward the hidden German lines, dug in among the deep, gashing ravines, gullies, caves, and stone buildings that pocked the countryside.

The advance was swift, and costly. Almost as soon as the men left the trenches, George Redwood's former billet mate 2nd Lt. John S. Morrison was mortally wounded and died in agony.

"It was sort of a horrible death," Sam Ervin recalled. "He had a bunch of signal rockets in his knapsack on his back and some shell or something exploded behind him and ignited them and they spewed in every direction."

Jim Quinn made his fame early in the advance at a place called the Raperie, a large stone farmhouse surrounded by six-foot walls, within which lurked one hundred Germans, five machine guns, and a mortar. Several hours after jumping off, and already having been shot through the right wrist, Quinn approached the strongpoint with the sixteen survivors of his platoon.

Crouching and crawling over open ground toward the Raperie, Quinn lost thirteen more men, and took more bullets to his right arm and shoulder, before he and his three remaining men covered the 150 yards to the outer wall of the farmhouse.

There, they found that the defenders had stored mortar rounds on the outside walls, so that "the whole place wouldn't be blown up" if an American shell landed within.

Quinn and his men unscrewed the detonation caps of the three-inch rounds and pitched them into the farmyard and house, in which each exploded seven seconds later. "Then we went over the wall," he would say. "My men cleaned up with grenades and we went on."

His citation for his Distinguished Service Cross would say that Quinn and his men "captured" one hundred prisoners at the Raperie.

"That was the nicer way of writing it," he would laugh.

From north to south, the 1st and 2nd brigades pushed east, traveling four miles by 11:00 A.M., when stiff opposition on the eastern edge of Missy Ravine—a mile-wide pastoral refuge dotted with farms and small villages—held up the advance.

On July 19, another push was made through the early-morning mist and fog, but while the 1st Brigade was able to advance several hundred yards, severe machine-gun fire from a strongpoint on the left stymied the 2nd Brigade.

It was there that Company L's towering Lt. Charles Mord Stromberg, his pipe in one hand and his tobacco in another, became an easy target for German snipers and was shot dead; so, too, was company M's 2nd Lt. Robert Obadiah Purdy, the stain of his failings as an officer erased by a machine-gun bullet through his heart.

Purdy's company commander, Capt. John Speed "Jock" Manning, who had lived "a man alone and shaken" since his best pal Axel Rasmussen's death in May, was severely wounded that same morning—shot "twice in one arm, once in the stomach, and once in the leg," Sgt. Vinton Pawel would remember. Just thirty-eight, but with a twenty-year military career that included the awarding of the Victoria Cross already behind him, he died of his wounds on July 25, and so began his journey as a "willing sacrifice" to join Rasmussen at Valhalla, as Company E's Edward Johnston would write.

Fresh troops were brought up on the afternoon of July 19 and in a costly and bloody advance pushed the lines another mile, deep into Ploisy Ravine, beyond which lay the village of Berzy-le-Sec, teetering on the western edge of the Crise River Valley, through which ran a vital road and railroad, both of which supplied the German pocket on the Marne.

(Newhall's foil, Francis Marion Van Natter, having been relieved of Company L and sent in some disgrace to the regiment's supply company, joined the push and was wounded in the jaw by splinters from a German shell.)

Berzy-le-Sec had originally been the objective of the French colonial regiments on the left of the 28th Regiment, but they faced stiff opposition and had had trouble keeping up with the Americans.

The responsibility for taking Berzy—the key to the entire Soissons offensive—was instead handed to the 1st Division—and in a broad-daylight attack on the afternoon of July 20, the 2nd Brigade tried, and failed, to pry the village from the grip of the Germans.

The 1st Division's commander, Gen. Charles Summerall, who had replaced Robert Bullard just prior to Soissons, would remember arriving at the 2nd Brigade's headquarters in the village of Missy-aux-Bois, at the southern head of the ravine, after the failed assault and encountering Alexander McKinlock, whom he knew as a friend of a young aide who had also attended Harvard.

"I turned to him spontaneously as though no one else could have enlightened me as he could," Summerall would say. "He told me with poise and certainty, and even solemnity, the situation as he had just seen it on visiting the line.

"I think it was the only time I ever saw him when he did not smile, but the tragedy and the fatigue were such that no one could have thought of anything but the serious business at hand."

Summerall would add with high praise: "There was something almost spiritual about the man that made victory seem almost within our grasp, although the brigade had not moved from where it was before the assault was ordered."

Summerall ordered that another attempt be made on Berzy the next morning—and further ordered Beaumont Buck to personally lead what remained of his brigade in the attack or face cashiering.

Buck, with McKinlock at his side, visited the front lines between 2:00 A.M. and 4:30 A.M. the next morning and with flashlight and maps explained the plan of action to the several hundred sleepless, exhausted survivors of the 28th Regiment.

There were few alterations of the previous, and vain, plan: They were to form in full view of the Germans at 8:30 A.M. and attack the village while the 26th Regiment on their right advanced through the ravines and atop the hills just south of Berzy.

Jumping off behind a light artillery barrage, the men of the 28th Regiment ascended the long slope before the village and then moved steadily across the kilometer of flat ground guarding its approach. Though suffering terrible casualties, they took the village, chasing the remnants of the defenders down the twisting, narrow streets to the valley below.

Advance elements cut the railroad and road, signaling the doom of the Marne pocket, where the Germans had already begun to withdraw, their high-water mark of the war left on the southern bank of the Marne, just fifty miles from Paris.

(In the coming days, the 1st Division would tally its dead and wounded and find that it had suffered casualties of about 50 percent: 1,714 men were killed in action or died from wounds, and another 5,492 were wounded.)

While the battle for Berzy-le-Sec raged, McKinlock had manned the 26th Regiment's forward telephone station "in a little gully by the side of an unused road," Buck would write. "This was a very dangerous position."

At 1:00 P.M., having telephoned his report of the situation to 1st Division headquarters, Buck learned that Summerall wanted "a sketch showing definitely just where our advanced line was holding and the units occupying various positions, their strength, etc."

Buck ordered McKinlock to scout the front lines.

"In sending him . . . I had no idea he was to be in any danger," Buck would write, "as I and another staff officer had just come from the immediate vicinity only an hour or two previously."

Alexander set off east through Ploisy Ravine, heading for the base of the bluff on which Berzy stood, less than a mile away.

"He never returned," Buck would write.

Bill Morgan continued to fret over his feeling that Cantigny had unhinged something at the bottom of his soul, unleashing a profound fear of death or at the least the fear that he was "flying apart," something that would never do in his present circumstance, where he was expected to man his guns and do his duty, no matter what.

He struggled to convince himself that he was not a coward, but at the same time the thought of returning to the front line left him almost paralyzed with terror.

"I am not sorry for the way I wrote you these last weeks," he would tell his fiancée on June 25, "for my letters have been just the way I felt, and I couldn't write you in any other way.

"I am so disappointed in myself for being so selfish and dissatisfied. I lost sight of the big side of this war and saw only my little horizon. I thought that my flesh was more valuable than anyone else's. I lost my pep, and I wanted to get out of it."

He would finally return to the front lines in mid-June but would write Christiana Councilman, "I suppose I went back too soon . . . The mental agony I went through I can never forget. If you knew how I hated to go around the front line every night to my guns.

"I had the most terrible feeling, yet it had to be done, and I managed to pass it off lightly with the men, but it was mental hell, I can tell you—timing the intervals so I could get over certain paths between shelling, and then coming back and lying for 21 hours in the dugout which shook every time a shell came along, and twice filled with smoke from shells bursting outside the entrance."

Adding to his sense of dread and mortality was the rumored loss of his friend George Haydock. "I haven't been near Haydock's company ever since our attack, and I can't locate it or find out about him, though I have asked everywhere and rode horseback all over, and went to the hospital which he would have been in," he would write on June 18.

"I can't believe it and won't until I know first hand. Dear old George. Each of us were the only one the other knew when we were split into the different branches of the service, and went to these schools. Before our show we bet each other that the one who received a wound out of it would give the other ten dollars, just to rub it in, for a good dinner in New York. If only I knew about him."

By June 25, and "a bit all in with the usual dugout cough," he had confirmed Haydock's death, the account of which came in somewhat embellished form—perhaps the result of Haydock's June 15 1st Division citation, which claimed that George "was killed while attempting almost single-handed to take a machine-gun."

"George Haydock was killed," Morgan would write. "I heard it yesterday from a man who was near him at the time. George rushed out ahead of his men, and alone ran straight for a machine gun trying to kill the crew with his pistol, and he fell riddled with bullets.

"Thank God he probably didn't know it. George dead. It can't be. Everything through all this has struck him just the way it did me. It was all so damnably repulsive, so unnatural. It was all so appalling to us, so contrary to everything we had somehow always believed.

"The madness struck us so vividly . . . I can't help but think that his spirit and clean character were too good for Boche lead."

He would add derisively: "Some times, damn it all, I don't see the use of living. Why not rush in and go down with fellows like him? Have you ever imagined feeling that you craved to rush out and get it over with once and for all? You can imagine what a state a man gets into when his mind goes back on him that way. It's plain hell."

More hell awaited Morgan on the morning of July 18, when, still unnerved by his experience at Cantigny and Haydock's death, he jumped off into the wheat fields below Soissons.

"I scarcely know where to begin or how," Morgan would write five days later. "An all night ride in trucks; a day and night's rest; an all night ride back again; all day in a forest; march that night until two A.M.; march the next night (July 17) from nine at night until four in the morning; . . . rain; one sandwich and a piece of steak in the previous 48 hours; and then over the top without even a chance to sit down all night, for the roads were so choked that we arrived less than an hour before zero hour."

He would describe the jump-off below Soissons as "the most wonderful sight that I ever saw. As far as you could see, streams of khaki going forward through the wheat, shells bursting around, then gas. (Five of my six men went down during the first kilometer.)

"Ahead were the tanks, on the hills behind flashes from our guns looked like hundreds of fireflies against the dark green, the roads for miles choked with artillery, camions, cavalry, light armored motor cars, all waiting until we had advanced and taken the Boche artillery, then moving forward to the new line."

There was a new spirit and optimism to his voice that July 23, replacing the fearful and cynical tone of his post-Cantigny writing. For good reason: Morgan's part in the vast assault was cut short after he suffered an injury to his right foot.

Struggling to get his machine-gun company to the front at about 2:00 A.M. on July 18, "I was trying to get our four horse combat wagon through the mud, around holes and trenches when it ran over my foot," he would write. His foot apparently crushed, he limped on, but at some point that morning, the regimental surgeon happened along. The hobbled Morgan "asked him for some adhesive tape, for I knew my shoe would have to come off before long. He looked at my foot, and ordered me to go back, as I couldn't keep up with my men."

It was no doubt with a great sense of relief that Morgan, still "jittery" from his experience at Cantigny, turned west and began retracing his steps through the detritus of the jump-off. Each gimpy step brought him farther from the fates of many of the 3rd Machine-Gun Battalion's men who followed the infantry into those murderous ravines and wheat fields.

"Further of the battle I know not, except that the Huns ran or surrendered, excepting the machine gunners who did well," he would write.

The horrors of war followed him even to the back lines.

Encountering a soldier who had been gassed, Morgan told the man to follow him. "We had gotten a few steps when all I remember is a blinding flash and crash, and then a few seconds later a horrible cry behind me," he wrote. "The man had landed just at my heels, with his leg torn off just below the knee."

He bandaged the man, then headed to the rear to find a stretcher. Returning, "everywhere men would cry to me," he wrote. "One poor man, agonized, held out his arms to me, and said no one would stop to bandage him. That field, never shall I forget it. From a selfish point of view it would be so much easier to die than to see all that suffering. Somehow it hits me hard.

"Imagine a man looking the other way when he passes a dead man out here where life is so cheap. But to me it seems less cheap than ever, when I see it lying there like that."

He wound up in a hospital in Vichy and then got leave to Paris, where in August he would learn the fates of his men.

"I saw another man of my platoon, who was wounded on [July] 21st, and he said that when he left, there was only one man in my platoon who was not a casualty, and he was last seen digging-in with his mess plate under very heavy shell fire," he wrote.

"He told me that one shell landed in the middle of my entire platoon the second day while they were resting along a road, and it knocked out almost every man . . . practically the entire division was annihilated."

He went before the disability board on August 14, where a major "jokingly asked me if I was anxious to get back to the front," he would write.

"I am asking everlasting forgiveness for the lie I told him."

Marion McKinlock would learn that her only child had been killed in action when a War Department telegram reached her at the Red Cross canteen in Chicago that August.

She refused to believe the report.

"She set the message aside, drew the picture of the handsome young officer to the center of her desk, and continued her work of caring for other mothers' sons with an added attention to details and a concentration that alone told her associates of the shock she concealed in her heart," the *Chicago Tribune* would report.

"In mid-summer there was a battle at Aisne-Marne," she would herself say many years later. "In August a report came—but it wasn't possible! No one from Lake Forest had died. The report said Alexander was *dead*, but it wasn't even complete!"

She sought the place of his supposed death on the map of France hanging in the study of Brown Gables. "We couldn't find it, not even a pinpoint on the map! How could any pinpoint consume him? How could he disappear into that alien map of France?"

Word quickly spread throughout Lake Forest that her son was "the first man from Lake Forest to be killed," she would say. "Only I said no. I decided—where there was hope, there was life. He was alive."

She plunged into her work at the Red Cross, working "longer and longer hours. Under the shadow of Alexander's likely death, so long as French authorities could not find him, I was compelled by . . . pleading hope. In part, I worked because the war—between my grief and disbelief—would not permit me sleep."

She would push with all of the power of her connections in politics and business to learn what had become of Alexander, as the ensuing months brought various reports and reconstructions of his route and an intimation as to his fate.

What became known was that as Alexander picked his way through Ploisy Ravine, he encountered two French officers from the 1st Moroccan Division on a similar mission and walked and chatted with them in French.

As they approached Berzy, "several shots were fired at us but the rifle fire did not seem to me to be very accurate," Capt. George Ego would say. "Suddenly the American officer dropped on the road without uttering a word. He had been killed right away."

The other French officer, a Lieutenant Fabrer, would report that he and McKinlock talked for five minutes before Fabrer left "to proceed with my reconnaissance." When he returned, "I saw the American comrade lying dead on the road."

Fabrer and Ego both reported McKinlock's death to the chaplain of the 28th Regiment, Father Coleman O'Flaherty, who was in charge of burying the regiment's dead. O'Flaherty "went back as quickly as possible to the spot described but could find no trace of the body except a helmet which was not marked," a friend of Alexander's, Capt. Worden W. Parris, would tell Marion McKinlock.

"Upon making inquiries he was told by enlisted men nearby that the body had been removed by an ambulance, and if this is true your son was not dead as our ambulances are not allowed to carry dead bodies." Parris would add that he had personally visited "all Aid Stations, both Battalion and regimental, and have made inquiries" but could obtain no "accurate information."

Beaumont Buck, too, would report that he had "several officers search the aid stations, hospitals, etc. hoping to find your boy, and to learn he was only wounded, but no trace has been found of him."

Buck did reveal some tantalizing information to the distressed Mrs. McKinlock, however, though he hesitated to give her false hope.

"In the search made for your son a soldier was found who claimed to know that one of my staff officers was taken prisoner just as he entered Berzy-le-sec on the morning in question," Buck wrote. "As we could not find him or his body, I have been hoping to learn he is a prisoner."

Marion McKinlock held out the same hope, but more definite—and dreaded—news arrived "in the form of a letter written by a young woman Y.M.C.A. canteen worker in Paris," the *Chicago Tribune* would report.

The letter had been sent to a friend in New York, and then read aloud at a well-heeled dinner party that included Constance McCormick, the wife of McCormick heir Hamilton McCormick and a mainstay of Chicago high society.

Marion McKinlock shortly thereafter received a copy of the letter, which read in part: "It is hard not to let one's eyes fill up, but I haven't yet except once, when I heard of the death of one of the sweetest young boy lieutenants, who belonged to our battalion mess and who talked to me so often of his adored mother—Alexander McKinlock of Lake Forest."

The paper would note that the demise of her Alexander was "unverified." Marion McKinlock, the *Tribune* added, said "she would not accept the information as true until she had made a thorough investigation."

20

As if He Were Still Alive

They had maintained his room exactly as he himself had left it one year before, and it was following many entreaties and invitations that Richard Newhall found himself there, in George's room in the Haydocks' tidy and comfortable home in Milton, Massachusetts, on his first Christmas back from the war.

They'd picked him up in "the Dodge" at the train station in Boston, carried his bags up to George's room, and shown him how the latchstring worked so he could come and go as he pleased.

For just a few days Robert Roger and Annie Haydock took some comfort in the fact that if they couldn't have their George back, at least they had the next best thing with the presence of Richard Newhall, whom they gently prodded to provide his memories of their son, of what he had gone through, the things he had said and the men he had known and, in the end, just exactly how, if not why, they had lost him on that faraway battlefield in Picardy.

"I cannot tell you what it meant to us to have your son with us over the Christmas holidays," Robert Roger Haydock would write Harry Newhall, to whom he had reached out following George's death, "for he was here long enough and entered so into our family life, we making no attempt to treat him as 'company,' that we now feel that we really know him, and he too we hope knows that our home is always open to him whenever he cares to come."

Newhall himself at first had had "a feeling of delicacy about putting myself at all forward in the direction of the Haydocks. They can associate me only with a very tragic event in their family life."

That Christmas, though, unable to return to Minneapolis because of ongoing treatment for his wounds, he had patiently read through and annotated George's wartime letters and diary, marking the places George had been, and penciling in the names of some of the men George had liked and disliked, in preparation for a pamphlet the family planned to publish in George's memory.

As he did, Newhall's own memory raced back, back to his first encounters with George, thoughts of reading *Macbeth* in the Cave, lying in the spring sun talking to George, that Sunday dinner in Beauvais, and of course the battle, and his own ordeal, and that night when he had learned of George's death and received the sharp "psychological slap" in those three words—"Don't tell him!"—which shook him from his sudden despair and set him back in the realm of the quick, able to leave the dead to their own.

He had been evacuated that early morning of May 30 from the aid station to a field hospital, where doctors operated on him, and then sent to a backline hospital, where "every clear night German aviators bombed the place which was not conducive to sleep," he would write.

There, too, he once again encountered Elizabeth Bliss, with whom he and Haydock had enjoyed Sunday dinner on April 21, and whom he had last seen standing on the curb in front of the Grand Hotel de France et Angleterre in Beauvais as he and Haydock raced off to make it back to Company L.

His main concern at that point was his parents' reaction when they received the telegram saying he had been seriously wounded. He was too weak to write, so Elizabeth Bliss instead handled the duty of notifying Harry and Elizabeth Newhall their son would be okay.

("I will be eternally grateful to Miss Bliss for helping me back towards a normal state," Newhall would write that summer. "She was a wonder.")

"This is to bring you the *good* news that your son though wounded is doing beautifully and there is no cause for any anxiety," Bliss wrote to Elizabeth Newhall on June 4. "His left arm is badly broken and there is a slight flesh wound on his shoulder but his condition is not at all serious and in a few weeks he will be quite well again.

"Of course he is very much shaken from the experience and it will take time for him to get back to a normal condition, but he is not dangerously wounded and you must not worry. That seems to be all that worries him."

The Newhalls had indeed been shaken when the dreaded telegram arrived in Minneapolis that June. No further word or explanation of his fate had come until they received the letter from Elizabeth Bliss—a full three weeks after she penned it.

"My Dear Miss Bliss: Your letter of June 4th telling me the condition of my dear son Richard is just received and has brought such unspeakable joy to this household, and has lifted a load of anxiety from our hearts," Elizabeth Newhall wrote on June 26.

"The suspense we have been under since receiving the dispatch announcing the bare fact that he had been 'seriously wounded' has been exceedingly trying, and we have been watching and hoping for further news . . . It is a comfort to know that for a while at least he will not be on the firing line—but getting a good rest. I will not worry any more about him—at least not at present."

With the knowledge that their son was out of physical danger, their concerns turned to his psychological welfare. Newhall's mother, in particular, carefully probed for details of his experience, with the thought, it appears, that she might better understand what, if any, changes she should be prepared to see in him upon his return to the United States.

"There must be harrowing pictures that you would like to wipe out of your memory altogether, if only you could—and that you do not care to dwell upon—and, of course, we at this end have imaginations that have run riot, when left entirely to themselves," Newhall's mother wrote to him on July 9.

They had noted George Haydock's name in the casualty lists and "feared it might be your friend . . . We had thought we might get something from him in regard to you, after you were wounded." The silence from Haydock had confirmed their worst fears about him.

She would add, "I know you will feel the loss of your friend keenly, and I feel for you—and especially do I feel for his mother—when you are able I hope you will write to her, I think it would be a comfort to her to hear from one who had been in close friendship with her son up to the last.

"But don't get despondent thinking of it. He is out of the horrors of it all—and where he can view it with a larger vision, and see the spiritual benefits."

The Haydocks, too, had sought information concerning George's death, hoping to fill the void in their hearts with, at the least, some lasting image of his death in battle. On July 10, Louisa Haydock, ministering to some of those wounded at Cantigny, wrote to Newhall from her Red Cross station in Paris to "ask if you could tell me a little about the circumstances under which he was killed. He so often spoke of you in his letters as 'my PhD friend' and I know you meant a great deal to him.

"I have seen a good many of the men from your Company at this hospital here but they were all wounded before George was killed and some-one of them said you were near him at the time . . . If you could drop me a line and tell me as much about the attack as you can I would appreciate it very much.

"Have been nursing at this hospital ever since the attack and it has been a wonderful comfort—but well now it's hard to realize the kid is gone. Hope you are getting on and I am glad you came through as well as you did and I'm very glad you knew my brother. He was a peach wasn't he and I am very proud of him but with all that it makes your heart sick to lose him."

Newhall would tell her all he had learned about his good friend's death—of the last few moments before the advance, when they huddled in the jump-off trench; of last seeing George at the head of his platoon; of his final moments directing fire against a machine gun hidden behind a beet pile.

He would add: "I am glad I did not see him after he was killed, for now I shall never think of him as dead." They would begin a regular correspondence, but time would not quickly heal Louisa's heartbreak.

"It seems to be harder to believe and harder to bear as time goes on," she would write six weeks later. "I don't think I will ever have the courage to go home without him—and there is nothing to do but try and live up to him and what he stood for."

She would ultimately find some solace in returning to the site of George's death, the last time "with a rough sketch map which I made for her showing where George's platoon had been and where I thought he was buried," Newhall wrote.

As Louisa sought some small measure of comfort, Newhall that summer characteristically looked forward, preferring not to dwell on either George's death or his own near-demise.

"Those two days out in No Man's Land were not pleasant but they are over now and are gradually fading into the realm of reminiscence," he would write consolingly to his still-worried mother, who was certain that his mind had been "affected" by the war.

"Often you have asked me if there were memories which haunted me, which I wanted to blot out of my mind," Newhall would write in reply. "Truly there are none. Always I have been rather objective in my point of view, able to stand off and observe myself and my surroundings in rather an impersonal fashion.

"Fortunately I was spared any hideous sights. It took an effort to go and look at my first casualty, but the actual sight was not nearly as bad as I had imagined, and I can conjure up the picture now without any hesitation or shrinking."

He would add: "I have always been particularly glad that I did not see George's body. That, I think, would be an unpleasant memory."

He was plagued by more immediate troubles, including an abscess in his right armpit and a shattered left arm that remained immobilized in a sling and gave promise of becoming a permanent, and disabling, reminder of Cantigny. Just how disabling, no one would say.

"The secretiveness with which all information about my case is carefully kept from me, and even, to a large extent, from the nurse, really angers me," he would write Harry Newhall on August 14. "I resent being treated like a child.

"I am beginning to suspect that part of my arm bone near the shoulder was knocked off. What and how much I don't know, nor what permanent effects it will have . . . Still I continue to improve. Every day I am noticeably stronger. My tendency to complain is a healthy sign."

He delighted in confounding his nurses. "The nurse in charge is fine. She is capable and energetic without being at all 'strong minded,'" he wrote to his mother that August. "The assistant nurse is a plump, red-haired little person, very frank and naïve, who never knows quite how to take some of my whimsical remarks.

"Indeed, I spend many of my idle hours thinking of things to say which will make her look surprised. When I told her that I didn't desire to return to the front she said I wasn't very patriotic and got me a book to read entitled 'The Victorious Attitude' to strengthen my courage. I was much amused."

Not so amusing were some of the other patients stuck in the hospital ward with him—particularly one, a marine, wounded at Belleau Wood. His name was Laurence Stallings, the future coauthor of the antiwar novel *Plumes,* and in 1963 of the book *The Doughboys.*

"There is one man here who has acted like a spoiled child ever since he came in a month ago," Newhall wrote. "He is rather painfully wounded but he has made himself the laughing-stock even of the nurses. He has tyrannized over the ward until my patience is nearly exhausted."

Stallings had lost a leg, "but he made a most unfortunate impression on the ward because he had also lost his nerve," Newhall wrote. "So he was a most demanding and complaining patient, who claimed, with some justification, to be the most badly wounded person in the ward. The attitude of most of us, I suspect, was rather callous. Everyone was somewhat battered and no other patient was at all troublesome or demanding."

Finally a severely wounded pilot was placed in the bed next to Stallings and died the next day. "This had a temporarily subduing influence" on Stallings, Newhall wrote.

The mutual admiration between Miss Bliss and Newhall continued to grow that summer as she spent hours at his bedside, consoling him over the loss of Haydock, ministering to his wounds, and talking about books. Their blossoming relationship—it would shortly turn to love—was confirmation, perhaps, of Newhall's core belief that some good comes out of all experiences, even the most evil.

"I am writing now to give you some news about your son which has come to me from men in his company," Elizabeth Bliss wrote to Newhall's mother on July 28. "In the hospital where I am working, I have had a number of men who were in his company and it would do your heart good to hear the way they talk about him.

"Three different ones told me he was the best officer they had ever had and only today one told me they had never expected to be under an officer whom the men so universally liked. He also told me that when Lieutenant Newhall was wounded he tried three times to lead his men on before he had to give up. I am telling you this for I know you will be proud to hear it and I also know that your son would probably never tell you all of this himself."

(Newhall would be cited by the 1st Division for his short-lived actions at Cantigny—"although wounded four times," his citation reads, he "still led his platoon in an attack on an enemy strongpoint" and "retained command until he lost consciousness." Once again, the official reports had gotten things only half-right.)

Another of Newhall's admirers in Company L, Sgt. John J. Stetz, visited him on August 17. "Yesterday my Polish sergeant turned up here, much to my surprise," Newhall wrote. "I had no news of him since he kissed my hand and said farewell on the battle field, except a rumor that he had been wounded."

Stetz was able to fill in some of the blanks about the events of May 28. "When he was carried to the Battalion Aid Station he had tried to get them to send a party after me but they had their hands too full to go out after men in No Man's Land," Newhall wrote.

"I was quite touched to think that he had exerted himself so much on my behalf. And I certainly was glad to see him, truly glad. There is a simplicity and genuineness about him which appeals to me very decidedly."

By August 18, Newhall's doctor was recommending a "sea voyage," and Newhall wrote: "For the moment I am the envy of the whole ward and the prospect of once more seeing America soon and possibly you is quite enough to occupy my mind."

He sailed for home that September, even as the 1st Division once again went into battle in midmonth, taking few casualties as it drove through the St. Mihiel salient, launching its attack from the same lines at Seicheprey that Newhall had manned the previous March.

Newhall reached New York in late September, as his old division was about to jump off yet again, this time in the Meuse-Argonne, where twelve days of severe fighting in the hilly, wooded terrain would leave 35 officers and 816 enlisted men—almost all replacements for those lost at Cantigny and Soissons—dead and another 7,703 men wounded, gassed, or missing.

Early October found Newhall at Army General Hospital Number One in Williamsbridge, New York; later the same month, he transferred to Walter Reed General Hospital in Washington, D.C., and went to work for the Bureau of Public Information. On the day Newhall left New York, October 17, Robert Roger Haydock came into the city expressly to meet him. They lunched at the Belmont Hotel, where Newhall told him his reminiscences of the past year.

As they parted, Robert Haydock invited Newhall to spend Christmas in Milton. Newhall, not physically able to face the long train journey to Minneapolis, accepted, setting aside his worries that he represented a "very tragic event" in their lives.

On November 11, the Armistice went into effect, and those 1st Division officers who had survived the war looked back at the past six months in wonder. "I feel that I am quite lucky to be able to go back at all. There are many fine fellows who will not go back," Company M's Lt. Gerald Tyler would write of his fellow 28th Regiment officers who had not made it through.

"Whenever I think of some of the men I've known who went through what they did, and then so willingly give up their lives, I feel a little bit like a slacker. The spirit of some of these men was the kind that would have developed them into the big men that our country could have used to more advantage in the future."

Newhall by then also felt lucky to have been wounded, and put out of the war, as early as he was. "Probably I would have been hit later, and perhaps worse," he would write his father. "The policy of headquarters seems to have been to keep sending a division to the attack day after day until it was used up and then putting in another."

It was a strategy with which he, interestingly, had few qualms. "In the long run it was the most economical policy as the results show."

He had continued to correspond with Miss Bliss, and on December 20, she at last returned from France, having tended the 1st Division's wounded during its final big drive in the Argonne.

"Well—here I am—and very unreal it seems!" she wrote. "And now—I want to see you! Isn't it absurd—but already I ache for those who've been 'Over There'—those who understand. As you do. And I want a *real* visit with you now you're well."

She would add: "I'm sorry you couldn't get to Minneapolis for Christmas, especially as I know how disappointed your family must be—but after all the Haydocks need you most just now and you will help them through a hard moment so I'm glad you can be there."

Even as Elizabeth Bliss and thousands of doughboys sailed west for home, a lone figure sailed east on a special, and singular-minded, mission. The instructions Daniel Woodhead had received were simple, if daunting: Find the missing 2nd Lt. George Alexander McKinlock and bring him home—dead or alive.

In the months since Alexander's disappearance, Marion McKinlock had fretted and worried but still not accepted that he was dead and might instead be eking by as a prisoner of the Germans.

With war's end, and with traffic increasing at her Red Cross canteen in Chicago, through which more and more doughboys passed on their way home to points west and south, Marion hatched a plan to determine Alexander's fate once and for all—with or without the help of the U.S. Army.

Woodhead, Alexander's football coach at St. Mark's and a sales representative at the McKinlocks' Central Electric Company since 1909, sailed for France in December 1918 and once there headed for Berzy-le-Sec, where Alexander was last seen.

By then, even John Pershing had taken personal notice of McKinlock's disappearance, having "cabled his sister-in-law that Lt. McKinlock was killed in action July 21st," one report says. Beaumont Buck, however, "thinks this is a mistake," the report added. There was still strong suspicion McKinlock had, in fact, been the officer seen being taken prisoner that day.

"Jesse Spaulding, a Captain, U.S.A. and a Chicago man, now stationed in Tours, in charge of German prisoners there, and who is in constant communication with prison camps in Germany . . . feels sure that Lt. McKinlock is still alive and a prisoner," the same report would say. Spaulding had found two American lieutenants in German camps who had also been listed as missing for many months, "so the father and mother of Lt. McKinlock still have hopes of Alexander's being found."

However, by the time Woodhead arrived at Berzy, some more definite, and disturbing, information had been gained. Capt. Adelbert Stewart of the 3rd Machine-Gun Battalion had reported that Alexander's body had indeed been found five hundred yards in front of Berzy-le-Sec by the 28th Regiment's chaplain, Coleman O'Flaherty, who with a "Captain (Doctor) Gage" of the regiment had carried his body "into the town and buried him in a small garden in the town.

"Have been unable to get in touch with Dr. Gage," Stewart added in a Graves Registration report. O'Flaherty, in the meantime, had been killed in the Argonne in early October. A flurry of orders circulated within the army, Graves Registration Service, and Red Cross in early 1919, as the McKinlocks pulled strings and brought the pressure of their connections to bear on the case. "Have all means exhausted to locate grave," one memo written on January 8, 1919, says.

Woodhead, meanwhile, sought to have the bodies of four "unknown officers" in the area around Berzy-le-Sec disinterred, so that "he might identify his friend from one or other of these bodies." He would write the Red Cross that as he had known McKinlock for a decade, "I feel that there is every possibility that should he be in one of those four graves, his identification would be a simple matter." At the least, he sought to examine two of the unmarked graves.

On March 30 one of the graves in Berzy-le-Sec was opened, with

Woodhead present. "Grave believed to be that of Capt. McKinlock," the Graves Registration Service headquarters was notified in a telegram, was "that of unknown enemy soldier. Period."

While her envoy continued to search for her son's grave, Marion McKinlock continued to bury herself—and her fears—in her Red Cross work.

"Every boy was her Alexander," the *Chicago Tribune* would say.

"We had so many dear boys to care for!" she herself would remember. "Thousands of young soldiers hailing from Antigo, Beardstown, Grundy, Pocahontas—American towns I'd never heard of, just pinpoints on the map. We changed bandages and poured coffee for truckloads, trainloads of feverish, homesick young men . . . and each one named his hometown with love. They came from so many places, they seemed to spring from the pores of the map—until, gradually, the world expanded—paper and ink seemed to yield flesh and blood—*until I knew.*"

Finally, in the spring of 1919, Marion McKinlock was asked to go to France and help coordinate Red Cross activities. She accepted "eagerly," the *Tribune* reported. "It was a chance to trace her boy."

She sailed on April 16 and upon landing was met by an excited Woodhead, who thought he had finally located McKinlock's grave in the garden of a home in Berzy-le-Sec. On May 14, Marion McKinlock "went almost direct to his grave, which the army authorities in France, after a ten-month search, had been unable to locate," the *Tribune* would report.

"There, hanging on a little cross, was his helmet, with his name inside. On the cross it was written, 'McKinlow,' which had up to then been sufficient to conceal the grave from the keen scrutiny of those hunting for it."

Woodhead would cable George Alexander McKinlock Sr. with both sad and happy news. "We have found Alexander's body," he wrote, "and have identified it. Mrs. McKinlock is here, bearing up with the splendid spirit that has marked her service throughout."

Choosing not to notify the army or Graves Registration Service of the find, Marion McKinlock had Alexander's body removed from the plot, and with Woodhead's assistance, she had him reburied in a small cemetery.

Later, she had the body cremated and the ashes sent home to Lake Forest, where they were placed in a tomb. "After we brought his body home I seldom glanced at the map of France," she would say. "Just once in a while, I'd hold it up to the light. Where the pin used to be stuck through Aisne a la Marne, there's just a hole."

There was a hole, as well, in the army's paperwork regarding the young officer. He would be carried as missing until November 1921, when in a routine follow-up Alexander's former commander Maj. Chester Arthur Davis let it slip that he was aware that Alexander's remains had been found and sent to the United States.

Davis subsequently found himself in some hot water, apparently, being "requested" to report to the chief of the Army Cemeterial Division in Washington, D.C., and explain "upon what facts or circumstances" he knew that Alexander's remains "are now in the United States when the records of this office do not show that his body was ever recovered."

Davis appeared and explained; by November 29, 1921, the strange case of George Alexander McKinlock Jr. was closed, "identification having been made by mother on the ground," Capt. Charles J. Wynne would write.

Left bereft, and now childless, the very wealthy McKinlocks poured some of their vast fortune into memorials for Alexander—more than half a million dollars each for a freshman dormitory at Harvard and a downtown Northwestern University campus in Chicago; another donation for construction of a terrace at the Chicago Art Institute; all to be named after a second lieutenant who spent most of his short army career at a desk in brigade headquarters, and who had performed no greater heroic deed than simply surviving Cantigny and being shot down while scouting the extent of positions much farther forward than he had ever trod in battle.

Exactly how much, or how little, Alexander had done in the war didn't matter to his parents, or to their sympathizers in society. As the *Chicago Tribune* would write, "Perhaps he was no braver, no more heroic than millions of other young men who have since 1914 laid down their lives on life's very threshold, but he typifies them all."

That might have been the limit to his legacy, had not another very,

very wealthy scion of the city's industrial elite stepped into Marion McKinlock's life: Muriel McCormick, granddaughter not only of Cyrus McCormick, "the Harvester King," but of John D. Rockefeller, the founder of the Standard Oil Company.

At some point in the early 1920s, her mother, Edith Rockefeller McCormick, indulged her idle hours in a then-fashionable interest in "psychical research." She had even startled a dinner party by announcing that she had been the first wife of King Tutankh-Amen, whose lavish tomb had recently been discovered and even then was being excavated from the desert sands of Egypt.

Raised amid wealth and emotionally scarred when her father, Harold, left her mother for the "temperamental" Ganna Walska, Muriel in her early twenties left her divorced mother's mansion on Rush Street and took an apartment overlooking its gardens. She started working on her career, which was to be in grand opera, and leading "a free and independent life," the *Tribune* would report.

"But it was a lonely life for a young woman to lead, and perhaps Muriel McCormick began to feel the need of some deeper interest in her affairs . . . Muriel, while not in sympathy with many of her mother's psychic friendships, may have felt that something in that line would serve to round out her life to a certain extent."

So it was that Muriel McCormick herself attended a "spiritual" gathering. "She is reported to have been called by name by one shade on her very first visit," the *Tribune* would report, "and during later visits, the spirit was identified by friends."

The voice was that of the "dashing"—and quite late—Lt. George Alexander McKinlock Jr. Muriel's friends told her that he was "one of the handsomest and most interesting of all the younger Chicago set in which he had moved prior to his death.

"A curious sort of spirit wooing followed" between Muriel, who had never met the young lieutenant, and the spirit said to be Alexander's. "Private séances were arranged in which only the medium was present to interpret the words of the shade of young McKinlock. The spirit's love-making was said to have become increasingly passionate, and Miss McCormick became increasingly interested in her gallant spectre."

One night, "the wooer" asked Muriel to go to Marion McKinlock and comfort her. "So she went to Mrs. McKinlock and told her the strange story. Her news and her patent belief in its truth was healing to the heart of the mother who had been desolated since her son's death."

Marion McKinlock attended further séances with her young and now constant companion. Marion, the *Tribune* reported, also presented Muriel "with a miniature of her dead son that Muriel is said to wear constantly about her neck."

Muriel and the mother of her dead boyfriend became "inseparable," to the point where McCormick moved into the McKinlocks' estate of Brown Gables. They visited the site of Alexander's death in France, and Marion McKinlock "was never seen without the Rockefeller heiress at the Saddle-Cycle Club, the Opera Club, or any of the smart places where Chicago society congregates," the papers would report.

Muriel McCormick also had a wedding ring fashioned of platinum, appropriately inlaid in black—"and warns all men with ambitions that she considers herself bound to the fallen war hero as firmly as if he were alive and waiting for her at home."

She announced as well that she considered the McKinlocks to be her "adopted" parents—solace, certainly, to the heartbroken and childless Marion McKinlock, who would say that her constant companion "had made my dead son an ideal. I believe that all her latent love of country is being poured out upon my boy who died so gloriously."

That Alexander McKinlock had somehow died "gloriously" was to become a mantra through the 1920s. Even former 1st Division commander Gen. Charles Summerall would say as much at the dedication of the new freshman dormitory, McKinlock Hall, at Harvard on June 7, 1927.

"He need not have been killed," Summerall said. "He could have stopped as he approached this fire-swept zone, and his courage would never have been questioned . . . Nothing could stop or swerve him from the responsibility. His life was on the altar of his country, and he was above such reasoning as life and death."

Muriel McCormick would eventually tire of her strange affair with Alexander's spirit and in 1931 she wed Elisha Dyer Hubbard, a wealthy gentleman farmer from Middletown, Connecticut, at the summer home of the McKinlocks in Deep Cove, Maine.

Her actual marriage dissipated the public fascination and interest in her spirit lover, George Alexander McKinlock Jr., who had become more famous in death than in life. His strange legacy would further be reduced as the Great Depression took hold and wiped out much of the McKinlocks' fortune (enough was left, however, to provide for Marion McKinlock to reign as the doyenne of Palm Beach society and live in some splendor in her villa, Casa Alejandro, until her 1964 death).

Shortly before his December 1936 death the elder McKinlock asked Northwestern University to cancel his contract to finance the twenty-one-acre Chicago campus because he "could not meet his pledges." The university agreed and returned $778,000 in five annual installments to Marion McKinlock.

There was a small catch, however.

In June 1937, workers chiseled a word from a sign on the $25,000 wrought-iron gate at what had been known as the McKinlock Campus. The word "campus" was removed and replaced with the word "gates."

"Then it read Alexander McKinlock Memorial Gates," *Time* magazine would report. The university's "famed" McKinlock Campus, it added, would in the future be known as the "Chicago Campus."

"It seems as though everyone were in Paris," Bill Morgan would write on August 20, 1918. "I was at the Hotel Crillon yesterday, which is the rendezvous for all Americans at the bar every afternoon, when in came Tom Brookes, on leave from Brest. He looked at me, and his eyes nearly popped out of his head, and his jaw dropped, and making one big jump for me he said, 'My God, I thought you were dead!' "

Another friend had reported that Morgan had "gotten it" at Soissons, "because they had seen me go over, and because I went to a French hospital instead of an American one, they lost track of me."

He took the premature news of his passing in stride. "After all," he would write, "I don't know why I am alive after all this time. It is a big gamble, but it is really only a question of time."

Morgan remained conflicted, his nerves "live wires," even while on leave in Paris that late summer. He spent long afternoons that turned into evenings in the bars and cafés, but he told himself he'd be all right eventually. In the meantime, "if any soft job comes along I have made up my mind to take it for a while and get quieted down a bit, for I can always go back to the line," he would tell Christiana Councilman.

In fact, he had little real intention of returning to the war. In Paris, he learned the fates of numerous others he had known—Carleton Burr; Oliver Ames Jr.; McKinlock; Eddie Hines, whom Morgan knew from the OTC camp at Fort Sheridan and who "cracked under the strain the other day. He came back to the hospital and broke down, then caught pneumonia and died."

There was also "Spike" Shell. "I saw him before the last show," Morgan wrote. "He was a wreck, and had great deep lines in his face. He got a bad wound and didn't have strength enough to pull through."

Of course, there was George Haydock—"Old George and I had been together from the day we landed until he was killed," he would write, "and I think that I have felt his death more than anyone else's.

"I have made hundreds of friends," he would add, "and I never remember picking up a casualty list without seeing at least one name that I know."

Wherever he turned that fall, Morgan saw the faces of dead friends, the dead from his platoon, his corporal toppling onto him at Cantigny.

"I feel that since Cantigny I have lacked visions, and without them I felt that I was lost," he wrote on September 8. "I couldn't grasp the things in life which I once held as ideals. I gave in and wasn't able to face the reality of war.

"Those men, *real* men in every sense of the word just going down as if human life and flesh were worth nothing . . . I don't know what really happened to me yet. I was just sort of swamped. Life was turned upside down, and all my foundations in life seemed to be swept out under me."

Others, perhaps, took the war's horrors in stride, took the loss of friends philosophically, thought little of the violent acts they had witnessed or committed themselves, found ways to rationalize and move beyond; Morgan's mind remained haunted by what he'd seen and encountered on the battlefields at Cantigny and Soissons.

"The shocks I couldn't get over afterwards were such as seeing a Boche fall bayoneted, quite dead, and then see the bayonet rammed though him two or three times more," he would write.

Such an image created "a living picture" made of "a thousand horrible memories which I wish I could forget. Those sights have been so near to me in their realism, so vivid because I was too sensitive to them. My vision is more like a ghostly mirage, a transparent picture, through which I can plainly see the endless little incidents which we don't talk about.

"It does get to you to see the men with whom you are living so intimately 'go away' one after the other, or to be joking and laughing with a bunch, and a second later see half of them ripped to pieces. It hits you between the eyes, and it takes an awful lot of reasoning to be able to think it all out.

"I have seen such horrible things that I hate to read a newspaper, for I know every sound, and every single thing that each word of the 'communiques' mean. I am trying to get away from it all for a while but I can't forget. Only today at the hospital I heard the most awful yells from some poor fellow."

He would add: "I may be able to laugh, and everyone may think that I am fifteen years old, but underneath I feel a hundred."

When, finally, he was given the opportunity to become an instructor at Gondrecourt, he grabbed it. "It is about time that I pulled a wire or two," he would write. "I shall proceed there after going to Chaumont, to try to get sent home."

While at Gondrecourt, his own name would turn up in the casualty lists—a "wild tale of my being shellshocked. Unless it is qualified and explained, it is no fun to be kidded about, because it is what everyone [says] in order to get back from the trenches, when they get cold feet in the middle of things," he would write with some embarrassment.

The casualties among his friends continued to climb. On leave in Paris in late October, "I heard of four others, one of whom was Nat Simpkins. The other three nearly finished me. I went up to my room and prayed that it couldn't be. Ever since, I have felt like a yellow quitter . . . If only I could have lasted out and kept enjoying it the way I did the first three or four months. If only it would all end."

When it did end on November 11, Morgan did not know "whether to lie down and go into hysterics, or stride forth breaking things into small bits. I can laugh with the best of them, but underneath there is a Hell which can't be forgotten."

After the Armistice, he found himself more adrift than ever, trying vainly to sort out the meaning of his "Great Adventure." On November 24, he would write Christiana Councilman's father, William, and say: "I feel that I have learned a great deal, and the only explanation I can give myself is that life is very, very simple, just as simple as human nature is. My life of idealism had led me to believe that life was complex, deep, something for great minds to meditate over for years.

"The full significance of your toast, 'Babes in the Woods' is beginning to dawn on me. There I was thinking that I knew what life consisted of, and I had only seen life from the second story window of the AD club. I thought I could judge men . . . I thought I was democratic, and had seen the extremes of life.

"All this you knew, Pa, and didn't tell me. I'm glad you didn't now."

The war over, his "day to day existence" past, he looked to the future—and saw nothing. "My dreams are at an end," he would write.

Desperate at that point to return home, and with no intention of joining the 1st Division in its march to and occupation of the Coblenz area on the Rhine, Morgan pulled enough wires to land a plum job as a courier to the American Commission to Negotiate Peace.

After a hectic four months traveling Switzerland, Austria, and France, he returned to the United States in April 1919 "with his faculties less than intact and with a bitter contempt for high ideals," Claire Douglas would write, as the failures of the Paris conference, and subsequent Versailles Treaty, only further clouded his original vision of the very purpose for which he had gone to war.

His fiancée had also changed during his absence. Christiana had found a new sense of esteem, and a purpose, in working as a Red Cross nurse, experiencing some of the horrors of the age as she tended to Boston's victims of the Spanish influenza in the fall of 1918. She was no longer "the young postdebutante Boston girl he had left behind," Douglas wrote. "She now knew that she could do something, and do it well."

Nor was Bill Morgan, Douglas adds, "the plucky Harvard lad who she had sent off to war . . . He had lost forever the high ideals with which he had catapulted himself into the battlefield. Bill returned with much of his strength, health, and vigor gone; these lay trampled and wounded in fields where his friends had fallen, and he emerged far less whole than Christiana."

After almost two years of carrying on through letters, they married on May 9, 1919, and embarked on a "complicated" life as man and wife, together representing "two poles of the mood in America just after the war: Bill's the bitterness of the sad young men who had watched much of themselves die with their comrades in the trenches; Christiana's the elation in a new world made possible by a war that had swept away the old," Douglas wrote.*

---

* From Douglas's *Translate This Darkness: The Life of Christiana Morgan, the Veiled Woman in Jung's Circle*. Princeton, N.J.: Princeton University Press, 1993.

21

There Was a War

Nothing had been quite right, been the same, since he died; no more letters from France addressed "Dear Sir" and signed "Your affectionate brother," and sometimes illustrated with cannons and locomotives and soldiers of various nations, all meant to entertain and inspire the imagination of the young Francis Tazewell Redwood.

He had lost his father when he was just one year old and that father's surrogate, George, when just thirteen. As much as Francis struggled to come to terms with the loss of his older and revered brother, there's a sense as well that he labored under the shadow of George's postdeath lionization and elevation to near-sainthood.

After George Redwood's death, his old rivals at the *Baltimore Sun* would editorialize: "At thirty he has passed away with a record which few men twice his age can equal. And the record is peculiarly beautiful, inspiring, and touching, even to this day when heroism has become a commonplace of daily life.

"It appeals to us especially not merely because he died in battle, not merely because he showed a courage that never flinched, but because there was behind and in it all the rare spirit of knighthood at its best, of a loving and lofty self-sacrifice that made this war to him almost a sacrament, and made peril in a great cause almost a religious rite."

In late 1918, the city council would vote to rename Baltimore's German Street "Redwood Street" in his memory; on "Armistice Sunday"—November 9, 1919—a tablet was laid in the Cathedral of the Incarnation in Baltimore. A CRUSADER BLAMELESS AND WITHOUT FEAR, the inscription read.

Letters of condolence poured in to Mom-Mom; her son, one said, was "like Sir Galahad, a 'stainless knight' so brave and pure"; he died "bravely, unselfishly trying to help others," read another; "so good, clean and pure," read yet another; "he died gloriously, with his face to the enemy," another read. As well, several would claim, he had become a "martyr" in the cause of "righteousness."

Of course, America needed heroes that summer of 1918, and even more as the new year turned and some began to question what, exactly, had been accomplished Over There.

Still, one can't help but feel that Redwood the man, and not the myth, would have scoffed at all the purple prose thrown toward his memory and laughed off the idea that he was somehow "blameless," somehow the embodiment of the Crusades, somehow the martyr, rather than just a man wrapped in the hilarity of his job, the good sport of putting one over on the enemy—and the hard work of providing for and caring for his men.

Three who served under Redwood—Pvt. Anthony Tack and Cpls. Newell "Paddy" Davis and Ben B. Allen—would give him that due. Certainly their words would have pleased him most, speaking as they did plainly, and directly, to his legacy.

"His was the highest type of service and he was the finest type of soldier, never thinking of himself, but always of his men, looking to their comfort and welfare, and we all loved him and would have died for him," they would write Mom-Mom. "His wonderful coolness and courage under fire always inspired us to do our duty to the utmost."

Nevertheless, the newspapers did their best to canonize him. Mom-Mom, of course, allowed all the testimonials to wash over her and assuage her grief as if they were drops of holy water, while the truth was more complex, and Redwood the man too enigmatic to conveniently label one way or another.

Call him a hero, call him a "knight"—in the end it's easy to sense that

George Redwood was one of those that indeed died smiling at Cantigny, and perhaps for no greater cause than his own simple enjoyment of the battle, the "hilarity of heroism" he found in the excitement, in the way his wounded flesh simmered with adrenaline and in the way his spirit soared with a sense of purpose.

He may, simply, have taken Donald Hankey's admonitions to heart. "As for personal danger, he must not think of it," Hankey had written in *A Student in Arms*. "Every man who goes to war must, if he is to be happy, give his body, a living sacrifice, to God and his country. It is no longer his. He need not worry about it."

Don't worry. Redwood by all accounts seemed not to fear death but to embrace it that day. Carefree and reckless, he seemed to feel it was expected of him to die in battle. Or perhaps, in the end, he simply expected it of *himself,* sensing that by going on ahead he might set the bar for those he led, and those who would follow. So had Jesus Christ died; so, too, did the Christian soldier George Buchanan Redwood so willingly sacrifice his life—not so much as a martyr but as an example.

As for young Francis? One wonders if the elevation of George to near-sainthood left him with too much to prove, too much to live up to, as the younger brother of Baltimore's most famous war hero.

Mom-Mom, the *Baltimore Sun* would say, found "hope and consolation in the lad whom calamity had left her. Bright and talented, he promised to bring light into her darkness."

Where George was confident and outgoing, though, Francis "was an introspective person, a very quiet boy, never making himself conspicuous in any way," his cousin Jack Redwood would remember.

"Having lost his father at a very early age and then an older brother, the war hero, must have weighed heavily on what appears to have been a very sensitive nature," family historian John Redwood III would add.

He was a brilliant student and a gifted writer and poet—although "there is a good deal of a plaintive, sad note in some of those poems," Jack Redwood would write, adding: "I won't dwell on that any more."

He attended the same prep school as George had, and then the Hill School in Pottstown, Pennsylvania—where he was ranked at the top of his class and was known for his "remarkable literary ability."

He was making plans to attend Harvard, and in early April of 1923, Francis, then eighteen, came home to Baltimore for spring break. On the morning of April 5, just an hour and a half before his 11:00 A.M. train was to leave to carry him back to school, he went to the home of a friend, Jere Wheelwright, ostensibly to say good-bye to Mrs. Annie O'Connor, the Wheelwrights' housekeeper.

Francis was let in by the butler, but "the boy did not look for Mrs. O'Connor at all," the *Baltimore Sun* would report. "He went directly to the middle room on the third floor—young Jere Wheelwright's room. He knew the room almost as well as his own at home. He knew that in the drawer of the desk lay a blue steel Colt pistol and cartridges."

Within seconds, a single shot rang out. Mrs. O'Connor was the first to find Francis's body. "The bullet hole was in his temple and the bullet was in the ceiling," the *Sun* reported. "He had used only one cartridge—had put only one in the pistol."

Francis lay dead on the floor; there would be no more "hope and consolation" for Mary Redwood, now left bereft and grieving a third time. "If there be tears in Heaven," the *Sun* would write on April 6, "angels themselves might weep for her . . . Her house and her heart are left desolate. The pathos of it paralyzes the tongue and pen.

"If there is a God of mercy, as we believe there is, may He give her strength and courage to bear this last and most cruel cross of all."

Mom-Mom carried that cross until death unburdened her in 1940. No "hint" of a motive could ever be found for young Francis Redwood's suicide, the police would say.

"I can hardly wait to get into the trenches," he had written. "I sometimes feel so impatient to be where I can really see these Huns and possibly take a shot at them. You could scarcely believe me when I should tell you how much I should like to stick one of the Boches with my bayonet."

Those lines from October 1917 would haunt Bill Morgan, echoing an increasingly dim image of the person he had once been, and the ardor and naïveté with which he had gallantly gone to war.

He had changed; war had changed him. He had survived, but the passionate and patriotic Harvard schoolboy was dead, gone to dust in those same trenches for which he had so longed as an innocent.

"I did not desire anything which war meant once I realized that war was a cruel delusion and untruths had been believed by me because I was innocent of men," he would write in the early 1920s. "Then it took strength and in my blinders of wrath over any illiteracy I was unscrupulous.

"I said things which were cowardly. I told the truth to some men as I saw it—it was shameless—and I wanted to get away and let others take my place to be made fools of."

He racked his mind to convince himself, and perhaps Christiana, that he had tried valiantly to overcome his weakness for life and its inherent flip side—the fear of death. "I have called on every bit of strength in me to give me courage and to over come fear in the war," he would write.

Yet he remained shaken and haunted by the mental images he carried back—the German soldier, way past dead, being run through over and over by a doughboy; the bits of brains and flesh that attached themselves to the wall of the backline kitchen at Seicheprey; recollections of the unending pounding of the earth, visions of men without legs, men without arms, at Cantigny.

Such was the glory of war.

"At first wounded men didn't affect me," Morgan had written in September 1918. "Then the magnitude of it gradually dawned on me. A dead man being blown to pieces didn't bother me at the time, but afterwards I couldn't shake it out of my mind."

His gradual appreciation of the fragility of human life, of *his* life, in the end had turned him against the war, and he became determined not to be another of its faceless victims.

"I did not want to go helplessly along—ordered and used as if I was the same as the other ignorant men who were with me—or the less enlightened ones clamoring at home," he would write bitterly.

Such lines were a far cry from those he had written aboard ship while heading to France, heading to war, in September 1917. "I realize that this great effort which lies ahead of me—this test which is taking every bit of my will to face—will be a great thing for me," he had written.

"For after I have been thru it I shall have the confidence to undertake anything. Obstacles which come in my way will be small indeed, and I shall be able, as I should never be otherwise, to meet and to conquer them."

Even then he had sensed that if he survived, "life can never be the same—there will be a shadow in the background."

As the war receded, that shadow loomed larger than he could ever have imagined. His view of life—and death—had hardened. Summoned home to "suffocating" Highland Park, Illinois, in late 1919, where his mother, Clara, lay slowly dying from cancer, he would write: "It is too pathetic. It is so pathetic that you pity—and with such pity I must express myself in a more solemn way—I must have sympathy—for as you look at her lying there, struggling so hard against a life, a world, which is ruthless, ungiving, hard, resisting you sorrow over her—helpless and trusting that some one's strength will take care of her and protect her.

"Poor little thing—born to die—born into a life which frightened her, fluttering through it."

Of those gathered around, he expressed contempt for not understanding what he now knew. "It depressed me so that I couldn't say a word—I could have opened their eyes but somehow it stunned me to find them so completely taken up with the little petty things from aches to furnace."

Though embarrassed to be classified as such, Morgan seems to have become a victim of "shell shock," which today falls under the psychiatric umbrella of post-traumatic stress disorder. Certainly he shared the symptoms of post-traumatic stress as laid out by one expert.

"Three assumptions are shattered," Peter W. Howorth wrote, "the belief in personal invulnerablility, the perception of the world as meaningful and comprehensible and the view of oneself in a positive light. Victims are continually afraid of a recurrence, see themselves as weak and vulnerable, and question whether there is any meaning to the world."

"Courage is will-power, whereof no man has an unlimited stock; and when in war it is used up, he is finished," Charles Wilson, a.k.a. Lord

Moran, Winston Churchill's physician and a veteran of the Great War, would write in his study of the nature of courage.

"A man's courage is his capital and he is always spending. The call on the bank may only be the daily drain of the front line or it may be a sudden draft which threatens to close the account. His will is perhaps almost destroyed by intensive shelling, by heavy bombing, or by a bloody battle, or it is gradually used up by monotony, by exposure, by the loss of support of stauncher spirits on whom he has come to depend, by physical exhaustion, by a wrong attitude to danger, to casualties, to war, to death itself."

Morgan's account was certainly in arrears, gone not in one single rush on the bank but in a dollop here and there until finally the three days at Cantigny bankrupted him. He had long complained of having to man the lines for weeks on end while the infantry rotated in and out; he had sought vainly as time went on to harden himself, and his mind, sought to "kill" his imagination and not think about whether the next shell, or the one after that, might be the one to leave him dead or, perhaps worse, maimed beyond recognition.

Yet in the end he had given out—not physically but mentally, and not once but twice. Worse, he saw his name in the papers next to the term "shell shock," which by then was associated with cowardice, with "malingering." It was a term the British Army had first invented and then banned, ordering that such cases be labeled "not yet diagnosed, nervous," which by all appearances fit the condition of Bill Morgan by May 31, 1918.

Where the standard treatment of such cases was to allow a rest with plenty of food and "encouraging" words before a quick return to the lines, Morgan, it seems, had been left to his own devices, left to inhabit a fog of angst, of dread, and to wrestle alone with the notion that he was weak and, as he would write of himself, "a yellow quitter."

At the same time, he had seen little reason to continue on. He had come to believe that the war was a farce, and that his friends were dying around him for no good reason.

It was for obvious reasons, perhaps, that the "not yet diagnosed, nervous" Bill Morgan happily opted out of it all on the morning of July 18,

1918, and packed off for the back lines even as other walking wounded were performing the heroic deeds that eluded him—among them the Medal of Honor winner 2nd Lt. Samuel I. Parker of the 28th Regiment's Company K, who, although "painfully wounded in the foot," helped lead the regiment through the German lines to Ploisy on July 19, where he consolidated the new lines while being "compelled to crawl on his hands and knees on account of his painful wound."

There were more heroes, some who had lived, and some who had died, while fighting on despite severe or even mortal wounds. By that July 18, though, Morgan seemed outwardly happy to let them have their glory; he would keep his life.

At the same time, he would never get over feeling that he had failed the "test" of war and betrayed the heroic ideal he and Christiana Councilman had held so high; and it would be Christiana, and not Bill Morgan, who would set the pace of their postwar lives, while he spun his wheels and sought vainly to keep up.

Against her wishes, Christiana became pregnant, and a son, Peter, was born on September 6, 1920. The young family moved to New York, where Bill worked as a banker and then a trader, taking long absences from Christiana and work to visit his dying mother in Highland Park.

His work bored him, and it disappointed Christiana, who preferred he become a "political journalist." In fact, Morgan did pen a piece that ran in the October 1, 1919, issue of the *New Republic*. It expressed his disillusion with the hijacking of the Versailles Treaty by politicians, imperialists, and capitalists; his disgust with Woodrow Wilson for allowing his famous Fourteen Points to be compromised, and his grand idea of a League of Nations to be dashed; and his own optimism that the principles for which he fought—a coming "internationalism"—would one day come to fruition.

"Mr. Wilson has sold us," Morgan wrote. "The politicians of the world have sold their peoples. The diplomats of the Allies have had the opportunity to bring about a new era. Any policies that may follow which bring us into another war will not be the fault of the peoples who will then be called upon to fight that war. The great mass of workers by hand and by brain recognize their power. Without their support there can be no wars."

He would claim to be willing to devote the rest of his life "to the bringing about of principles which we have seen trampled upon by Five Men working secretly." Speaking for his fellow doughboys, whom he felt had also been sold out at Versailles and by anti-Wilson forces at home, he would conclude:

"We know what war is. We saw the trenches in 1917 as soon as our President allowed us, and we will continue that work, begun there, until the last vestige of this dishonorable treaty has disappeared."

In fact, Morgan would devote the rest of his short life not to fighting for the principles for which he went bomb-silly in the trenches but to trying to find some calling that would focus his restless and scattered mind. As well, he would devote much of his energy to trying to keep up with Christiana, who was disappointed in Morgan's "weakness and lack of vigor," Claire Douglas would write.*

Christiana would eventually begin having affairs—the first with the heroic RAF bomber Cecil Dunmore Murray, the second with the Zionist Chaim Weizmann, who would become the first president of Israel. An interest in "depth psychology," meanwhile, would lead her to a young Boston doctor, Henry A. Murray, with whom she had a forty-year affair.

Bill and Christiana would remain married but lead very different lives. Christiana's path led her to be psychoanalyzed by Carl Jung, and she and Murray became part of a group that initiated the Harvard Psychiatric Clinic.

Bill Morgan would pursue a graduate degree in England, first in biochemistry and then in anthropology. Continuing to experience the "hyperarousal and fragmentation of chronic post-traumatic stress," Douglas wrote, he was "too jittery to settle down to his studies and found them as barren as journalism, the bank, and business."

He had horrid nightmares: of asphyxiating on his own breath, of a brown-skinned figure, its pupils clear and its skin brown—"the warning of coming DEATH in heavy large letters," he would write.

---

* See Douglas, Claire. *Translate This Darkness: The Life of Christiana Morgan, the Veiled Woman in Jung's Circle.* Princeton, N.J.: Princeton University Press, 1993.

Upon his return to the States, his health indeed began to deteriorate, and he was diagnosed with asthma; doctors recommended Morgan spend time away in the dry air of the Southwest. It was there, beginning in 1929, that Morgan began anthropological field studies of the Navajo, ultimately producing two monographs—one on Navajo dreams and the other on Navajo treatment of illness.

It was only in the final years of Morgan's "brief and tragic life," Douglas would write, that he "found a profession that engaged him" and succeeded in describing "a disintegrating world and vanishing way of life that in many ways echoed his own."

Morgan's asthma was in fact tuberculosis, perhaps contracted in the trenches, or in those crowded billets at Toutencourt or Gondrecourt. He went home to Cambridge, Massachusetts, in 1933; he died there in May 1934, at the age of just thirty-nine.

While Morgan may, as Douglas wrote, have been one of the "last casualties" of the Great War, all that can be said with certainty is that the war deadened him, its stark displays of human butchery and brutality, and the ponderous and probing steps of the German artillery at Cantigny, sucking the life out of him.

In the end, it may be that he asphyxiated not on his own poisoned breath but on the visions of who he had once been, and the cancerous emptiness that had replaced his once-vibrant spirit.

"This is Cantigny Day," Robert Roger Haydock would write Richard Newhall on May 28, 1922, "and as I raised the flag at 6:45 I saluted George and his comrades who have gone, and you and your comrades who have suffered, as well as those who fought and came through unscathed.

"It was a fateful day, and one that will stand out more and more as the perspective clears and history is written."

Richard Newhall's own perspective on the signal experience of his life—and on the nature of his most profound friendship—would evolve over the years. Unlike Bill Morgan, however, whatever lingering effects he suffered in the war were mostly physical, as his strong bedrock personality and beliefs went untouched by the snipers' bullets that left him incapacitated at Cantigny.

"What have I brought home from the war?" he would write in answer to a question posed by Miss Bliss on the first day of 1919. "I have not grown from an 'average kid' into a 'thinking man' because I had reached the latter stage before I went to war, and in a measure it was a disadvantage because it kept me in a questioning state of mind, not about the big things of the war, I settled them long ago, but about the matters of daily performance."

Instead, he wrote, "I learned how to do things that I despised and how to see, in silence, things done which angered me and revolted my sense of justice. Was that educating? Demoralizing, I claim. That is my great indictment of the army.

"As for men, I came to see as I had not seen how the men whom I loved and admired stood out from the majority, according to my standards, not according to the rewards of the army. They were the salt of the earth and I had not known it. That is a great discovery. And as to the common run of men who made up the rank and file, my respect for them is increased, and with it my hopes for democracy."

Of course, he also brought home the fresh memory of George Haydock, and his memory of George remained with him even as he pushed his other, less pleasant memories of the military aside and eased into civilian life that year, accepting a teaching position at Harvard and marrying Elizabeth Bliss on June 21. The newlyweds afterward spent some time with the Haydocks. "It was a great pleasure to have you really settle down as part of our family," Robert Roger would write Newhall after one visit.

The Newhalls once again were put up in George's room. "It is our intention," Robert Roger Haydock told Newhall, "to leave George's room just as it is, and we hope you will use it often again in memory of what you went through together . . . Come when you will and stay as long as it may suit you . . . The latch-string is out, so that all you have to do is to pull it and enter without further formality."

Later that year, Newhall took a teaching job at Yale, and in 1924 he published his first book, which had grown out of his doctoral thesis—*The English Conquest of Normandy, 1416–1424: A Study in Fifteenth-Century Warfare*—and dedicated it to George Guest Haydock, with whom he had spent so many hours visiting cathedrals and Roman ruins in the back lines. The same year, Newhall accepted a job at Williams College in Williamstown, Massachusetts—where he would spend the rest of his days.

Each May 28, Newhall sent roses in memory of George to Robert Roger and Annie Haydock, the gesture ending only with their deaths in 1928 and 1948, respectively; George's sister Louisa, who had married the airman William H. Hackett in Paris on October 1, 1918, would receive a bouquet each subsequent year until Newhall's own death.

Like Morgan, Newhall was disappointed that the war had not, in the end, brought about lasting peace; he alone of those five Harvard men watched as the world slipped into another world war. Still, he remained stoutly proud of and satisfied with his small part in the effort, and his own sacrifice.

Ever the iconoclast, however, he refused to join the American Legion—begun by former doughboys to promote the "Americanism" he detested—and he also disagreed when veterans pushed for a federal war bonus in the 1930s, considering their "selfish" motives "contemptible and disgraceful."

His left arm remained crippled. "It was impossible not to be aware that he carried his left arm, obviously useless, in a sling," wrote Russell Bostert, who first met Newhall in 1948. "His left hand, encased in a grey glove, dangled as he adjusted it from time to time with a firm right hand."

Thus he needed no flag-raising to remind him of Cantigny Day through his long life, even as the world rushed on to another world war and his sacrifice, and the sacrifices of the 28th Regiment, dimmed.

He soon found, to his irritation, that the American memory could be short; at a dinner party in the 1920s, when one "bold soul" asked Newhall what had happened to his arm, Newhall replied icily and to the point, "There was a war, you know."

Teaching history, heading the Williams History Department, a houseful of children, and an eventual temporary stint as president of

Williams College filled his days until 1956, when he retired and was named the college's Brown Professor of History, Emeritus.

It was with a slackening of his pace that he turned more toward his own history, his own experiences in a war and what those experiences had left him—and especially to the subject of George Guest Haydock, and how their brief friendship had shadowed his life.

His grief over the loss of George had of course ebbed over the years, but thoughts of their friendship remained "very persistently near the forefront of my mind," and there's little doubt that with each step Newhall took in life—marriage, children, professional advancement, grandchildren—the memory of George Haydock, and a conscious appreciation of all that had escaped George, walked with him.

He cherished the short time he had had with George—lolling in the sun, reading *Macbeth* in the Cave, quiet conversations and griping about the army way on warm spring days in their cottage at Maisoncelle, shopping and visiting cathedrals while on the slog to Picardy.

In sum, their friendship, he would write in 1966, was "something idyllic, a relationship of mutual sympathy and companionship in circumstances which gave it a natural simplicity and a quality of depth unique in my experience. If it be urged that I have built up over the years a sentimentally exaggerated image I can only say that I don't think so."

Considering that their friendship had blossomed amid the carnage of a world war, Newhall would add that his chief concern during that long-ago spring had been "how my dear friend in my company, with whom I billeted, would remember me" had he, and not Haydock, been killed.

"Certainly if he had remembered me the way I have remembered him . . . I could indeed feel happy."

However, half a century's "long pondering" led Newhall to realize that it was Haydock's premature death in battle that had frozen in his mind the fond memories of their friendship. George's death, he came to understand, may have altered the natural course of their relationship—and prevented the eventual spoiling of Newhall's treasured lifelong memories of a "most perfect" friendship.

On Cantigny Day, 1972—at the age of eighty-three and just a little more than a year before his own death—Newhall attempted to sort out the issue of his friendship with Haydock for the last time, at least on paper.

"What I find demands thoughtful consideration," he wrote, "is what I have lost by the fact that our friendship was part of my half-century of living only as a memory. Maybe it has enjoyed a sentimental vitality, with many happy features, because it has not been subjected to any of the usual, unavoidable strains and stresses characteristic of human relations."

He had come, by then, to appreciate the likelihood that had he and Haydock both lived to return home, "each would have been fitted again into the patterns of social-professional living from which we had emerged in 1917. These could not help [but] emphasize the differences in our ways of life and, very probably, lead each of us off in a different direction. (This was practically a certainty with respect to my friend Stromberg).

"The possible erosion of friendship brought on by becoming aware of such differences is an experience sure to be disappointing. That I have been spared it could be looked upon as an item of good luck, even if I can believe that it might not have happened like that."

He also recognized that their differences in personalities and backgrounds might have become more conspicuous once removed from the exigencies of wartime.

"George was part of a social pattern into which I could fit, after a fashion, but with somewhat limited success," Newhall wrote. "The possibility that, away from the Army situation, certain of my temperamental peculiarities might become more obvious and that this might prove unattractive to him, is, in my opinion, a real one. It never got tested."

His revisionism extended even to George's family. Although the Haydocks "could not have been kinder or more friendly," Newhall would write:

"It seemed clear to me, as time advanced, that the members of the family, perhaps unconsciously, thought of me as 'not quite their sort,' and they were probably correct. Since, for me, this didn't involve George himself it was insignificant. But I can be pleased that he was not involved."

Newhall in the end was content to trade all of the might-have-beens for the enduring memories of his brief, but intense, friendship with George Haydock.

"Perhaps what this all adds up to is that, faced with an imaginary choice in my own mind between the actual treasured memory of an unusual, and for me unique, friendship of short duration under extraordinary circumstances of living, and the possible experience of a long period of intermittent friendly contact in the ordinary circumstances of living, it seems to me that the memory, which is real, seems probably preferable to what the event of May 28, 1918 prevented," he would write.

"If this looks like philosophical acquiescence in Fate both for George and for me, I am not troubled by that appearance.

"Certainly," he would conclude, "repining is a futile activity."

On June 18, 1973, life released him six days after his eighty-fifth birthday. Fifty-five years and twenty-one days following the jump-off at Cantigny, Richard Ager Newhall passed on, taking with him that last image of his great friend George Guest Haydock, the perpetually youthful first lieutenant ever advancing with a secure and firm step as he led the 1st Platoon of Company L into terrible battle.

August 7, 1967
Williamstown, Massachusetts

Last night I dreamed of George Haydock. This has never happened before. With his picture before me for many years my memories of him are always clear and my mind treasures these as the expression and realization of a perfect friendship, which is best described by the second movement of Beethoven's piano solo (Pathetique).

Yet in all of 49 years, I have not dreamt of George, nor is there anything recent to suggest an explanation. My memory of the dream is somewhat vague, but we seemed to be going somewhere together until we came to a place where I turned aside and he went on, and I kissed him on the cheek.

Notes

In the entries below, the abbreviation *WWR* stands for U.S. Army, *World War Records, First Division, A.E.F. Regular.* 25 vols. Washington: USGPO, 1928–30.

The abbreviation ROQC stands for Records of the Office of the Quartermaster General, Cemeterial Division, 1915–1939. U.S. National Archives, College Park, Maryland. Record Group 92.

Armstrong, Edward. Account of March 29, 1918, patrol found in the George Redwood Folder, Harvard University Archives (see Redwood entry below) and in the George B. Redwood Papers, MS 3023, Maryland Historical Society.

Avery, Charles. Account of his wounding at Cantigny from Johnston, *Americans vs. Germans* (see bibliography) and letter to sister of Lt. John Curry in *Wilkes-Barre* (Pennsylvania) *Evening News,* May 28, 1919.

Birmingham, Daniel J. Letters describing the front at Seicheprey from his file in the Robert R. McCormick Research Center, First Division Museum, Wheaton, Illinois.

Bliss, Elizabeth Howe. Her account of refugees from *New York Times,* May 5, 1918. Information on the Smith College Relief Unit from *New York Times,* July 22, 1917, and *Independent*, August 11, 1917. Letters to Richard and Elizabeth Newhall found in the Richard A. Newhall Papers (see Newhall entry below).

Brown, Jerome. Letter regarding assignments to the 28th Infantry Regiment found in the George Redwood Folder, Harvard University Archives (see Redwood entry below).

Buck, Beaumont. Letters regarding Alexander McKinlock from the George A. McKinlock Jr. file in the Harvard University Archives (see McKinlock entry below). See also Buck's *Memories of Peace and War* in the bibliography.

Burr, Francis H. Biographical material from *Norwich University, 1819–1911: Her History, Her Graduates, Her Roll of Honor,* by Grenville M. Dodge and William Arba Ellis (Montpelier, VT: Capital City Press, 1911). Anecdote about being "dugout king" from handwritten annotations made by former Company M soldier Floyd Weeks in a copy of *The Story of the Twenty-Eighth Infantry in the Great War,* provided by the Robert R. McCormick Research Center, First Division Museum, Wheaton, Illinois.

Carter, Paul Dillard. Letter describing backlines and trenches from November 25, 1917, letter in *Phi Gamma Delta* 21, no. 6 (April 1918).

Curry, John. Account of rescuing Charles Avery from Avery letter in *Wilkes-Barre* (Pennsylvania) *Evening News,* May 28, 1919. Account of death from Wood letter in same. Clipping graciously provided by Jim Nolan, Curry's great-nephew.

Dacus, Herman. Dacus's 1984 reminiscences about the battles of Cantigny and Soissons come from letters Dacus wrote to Ed Burke, president of the Society of the First Division, copies of which were provided to the author by Col. Stephen L. Bowman. Further Dacus material comes from the World War I Veterans Survey Collection, U.S. Army Heritage and Education Center, Carlisle, Pennsylvania.

Davis, Chester Arthur. Biographical information from his obituary in *Washington Post,* January 26, 1965. Letters to Marion McKinlock regarding Alexander McKinlock found in McKinlock's file in the Harvard University Archives (see McKinlock Jr. entry below).

Davis, Newell B. Account of March 30, 1918, patrol and other material from the George Redwood File in the Harvard University Archives (see Redwood entry below).

Dearing, Vinton A. Dearing's comments on Axel Rasmussen from Dearing, *My Galahad of the Trenches* (see bibliography).

Derrickson, Paul Waples. His letter of May 15, 1918, and biographical material from the Mary George Derrickson Papers, Library of Virginia Archives, Accession No. 38655, Richmond, Virginia. Account of death from his burial file, ROQC.

Drumm, Clarence Milton. Account of Drumm's death from his burial file, ROQC.

Edwards, Maurice M. His "Fragments from France" from *St. Lawrence University in the World War, 1917–1918: a memorial* (see bibliography).

Ervin, Sam J. His account of being relieved of command from Ervin, *Preserving the Constitution* (see bibliography). Account of Redwood's death and his character from May 2, 1920, letter to Mary Redwood in The George B. Redwood Papers (duplicate found in Ervin's file at the Robert R. McCormick Research Center, Wheaton, Illinois). His account of the Battle of Cantigny from Clancy, *Just a Country Lawyer* (see bibliography).

Flagg, Robert. Account of George Redwood's actions and death at Cantigny from the George B. Redwood Papers, Maryland Historical Society.

Flanagan, Hugh. Account of Wilmer Bodenstab's death from Bodenstab's burial file, ROQC.

Gillespie, Jesse. His account of the Battle of Cantigny from the *Aiken* (South Carolina) *Journal and Review,* August 29, 1928.

Graham, John B. Account of wounding and death from Summerall, *The Story of the Twenty-Eighth Infantry in the Great War* (see bibliography). Biographical information from Irving Wood letter in *Wilkes-Barre* (Pennsylvania) *Evening News,* May 28, 1919.

Hadsell, George Arthur. His account of landing in France from Yale University *Daily News,* February 2, 1918. Biographical material from *Hartford* (Connecticut) *Courant,* February 19, 1918.

Hartney, James Leo. Description of Axel Rasmussen's funeral comes from Hartney's May 5, 1918, letter to his fiancée. Graciously provided to the author by his grandson Dr. Thomas Harney.

Haydock, George Guest. Haydock's letters and diary were graciously provided to the author by Robert Gould Shaw, Haydock's great-nephew. Biographical material also found in Howe, *Memoirs of the Harvard Dead in the War Against Germany,* vol. 2 (see bibliography). His citation from *WWR,* vol. 23. Account of death from his burial file, ROQC.

Huebner, Clarence Ralph. See Blumenston and Stokesbury, *Masters of the Art of Command* (in bibliography).

Johnston, Edward Scott. His portrait of Axel Rasmussen and the early days of the 28th Regiment from the chapter "Portrait of a Soldier" in Johnston, *Americans vs. Germans* (see bibliography). His account of the German raid on Company E from "The Day Before Cantigny" in the same book, and his monograph of the same name (see monographs section in bibliography).

Joslin, Ruth. See "With the Doughboy in France," *Independent,* August 11, 1917.

Maxey, Robert Jayne. Account of death from his burial file, ROQC. His posthumous citation from *WWR*, vol. 23.

Mays, John Glascock. Account of the Battle of Cantigny from the Atlanta *Constitution,* July 7, 1918; *WWR,* vol. 13, *Operations Reports, 28th Infantry Regiment*; and Records Group 117, Entry 31 (see U.S. National Archives in bibliography). His discussion of the "New Death" from letter to Mary Coale Redwood in George B. Redwood file, Harvard University Archives (see Redwood entry below).

McCormick, Muriel. Account of wedding to Elisha Dyer Hubbard from *Time,* September 21, 1931. For citations regarding their relationship and her "spiritual wedding" to Alexander McKinlock, see Marion McKinlock entry below.

McKinlock, George Alexander. Biographical information from Currey, *Chicago: Its History and Its Builders* (see bibliography) and the Lake Forest, Illinois, *Lake Forester,* December 24, 1936. Erosion of fortune and change of name of McKinlock Campus from *Time,* November 29, 1937.

McKinlock, George Alexander, Jr. McKinlock's letters from France, accounts of his military career, and letters regarding his disappearance found in the George A. McKinlock Jr. Folder, Call #UAV874.269, Box 74, *Records of the Harvard War Records Office (World War 1), 1916–1927,* Harvard University Archives, Cambridge, Massachusetts. Their use comes courtesy of the Harvard University Archives. Charles Summerall's reminiscences of McKinlock from *Field Artillery Journal* 18, no. 6 (November–December 1928). Additional information from Howe, *Memoirs of the Harvard Dead in the War*, vol. 2 (see bibliography) and Benson, *Saint Mark's School in the War Against Germany* (see bibliography.) His return of an interception for a touchdown from *Harvard Crimson*, October 11, 1915. Correspondence on search for his body from his burial file, ROQC.

McKinlock, John. Biographical information from Currey, *Chicago: Its History and Its Builders* (see bibliography).

McKinlock, Marion Wallace Rappleye. Account of her wedding to George A. McKinlock from *Chicago Daily Tribune*, December 3, 1890. Account of Lake Forest's estates from *Chicago Daily Tribune*, August 11, 1907. Her being "peeved" from *Chicago Daily Tribune*, August 25, 1916. Accounts of learning of son's death from *Chicago Daily Tribune*, September 4, 1918. Accounts of finding son's grave from *Chicago Daily Tribune*, July 27, 1919; April 9, 1919; and May 15, 1919. Accounts of friendship with Muriel McCormick from *Waterloo* (Iowa) *Evening Courier*, June 23, 1923. Portugese men-of-war anecdote from *Life*, January 21, 1952. Anecdote about police helping with gown from the *Ft. Lauderdale Sun Sentinel*, November 14, 1992. Information on using a map of France to trace Alexander McKinlock across France from 1964 memorial tribute provided by the Lake Forest–Lake Bluff Historical Society.

Morgan, Christiana. Biographical material and diary entries from Douglas, *Translate This Darkness* (see bibliography).

Morgan, Otho Herron. Biographical information from *Manufacturing and Wholesale Industries of Chicago* and Dunn, *Indiana and Indianans* (see bibliography.) Further information on Morgan's artillery battery in the Civil War from *Indiana at Chickamauga: Report of Indiana Commissioners, Chickamauga National Military Park* (Indianapolis: Wm. B. Burford, 1901).

Morgan, William Otho Potwin. Morgan's wartime and postwar letters to Christiana Councilman, and his diary from September 1917 to December 1917, can be found in The Christiana Morgan Papers, 1881–1930, in the Schlesinger Library, Radcliffe Institute, Harvard University. Used with permission of his granddaughters Hilary and Christiana Morgan and the Schlesinger Library. Biographical material from Douglas, *Translate This Darkness* (see bibliography).

Morgan, William Potwin. Biographical information from *Memorials of Deceased Companions of the Commandery of the State of Illinois, Military Order of the Loyal Legion of the United States* (Chicago, 1901). Also Douglas, *Translate This Darkness* (see bibliography).

Morris, Lafayette I. Morris's account of night patrol from the *Lexington* (Missouri) *News,* May 2, 1918. His account of the Battle of Cantigny from *WWR, vol. 13, Operations Reports, 28th Infantry Regiment.*

Morrison, John S. Account of Morrison's death at Soissons from Clancy, *Just a Country Lawyer* (see bibliography). Additional biographical material provided to the author by Morrison's grandson, Don Keller.

Mosher, Henry Ephraim. John Mays's account of Mosher's death from letter in the *Atlanta Constitution,* July 7, 1918. Mosher's April 17 and 20, 1918, letters to his sister, Gertrude, provided to the author by Mosher descendant Paul Densmore. Biographical information on Henry Mosher from Downs, *History of Chautauqua County, New York, and Its People* (see bibliography), and the *Jamestown* (New York) *Morning Post,* June 8, 1918.

Newhall, Richard Ager. Biographical material from Bostert, *Selected Papers of a History Teacher at a New England College 1917–1973* (see bibliography). His letters and reminiscences were found in The Richard A. Newhall Papers, Williams College Archives and Special Collections. Material was used from the following: Elizabeth Bliss letter to Elizabeth Newhall, June 4, 1918: Box 5, Folder 21; correspondence between Elizabeth Newhall and Elizabeth Bliss, June and July 1918: Box 5, Folder 22; Newhall's reminiscences about the Battle of Cantigny: Box 5, Folder 23; correspondence between Richard Newhall and Elizabeth Bliss, October 1918–January 1, 1919: Box 5, Folder 24; Richard Newhall's letters to Elizabeth Newhall, January–February 1918: Box 5, Folder 27; Richard Newhall's letters to Elizabeth Newhall December 1917 to May 1918: Box 5, Folder 28; correspondence between Elizabeth and Richard Newhall, July and August 1918: Box 5, Folder 29; Richard Newhall's letters to parents, October 1918–April 1919: Box 5, Folder 30; Richard Newhall's letters to Elizabeth Newhall, March–April 1918: Box 6, Folder 2; Richard Newhall's letters to his parents while in a hospital in France, August 1918; Box 6, Folder 3; reminiscences about George Haydock: Box 7, Folder 13; Richard Newhall's reminiscences about his youth: Box 7, Folder 14; Harry Newhall letter to Richard Newhall, April 5, 1917: Box 7, Folder 15; Newhall's reminiscences about Capts. Henry Mosher and Francis Van Natter and Lt. Col. Jesse Cullison: Box 7, Folder 16; correspondence between Robert Roger Haydock and Richard and Harry Newhall, correspondence between Richard Newhall and Louisa Haydock, Newhall's 1972 reminiscences of George Haydock, and Newhall's August 7, 1967 account of his Haydock dream: Box 8, Folder 9; Richard Newhall's letters to parents, May–August 1917, and his reminiscences about Plattsburg training: Box 10, Folder 22; Richard Newhall letters to Elizabeth Newhall, April–August 1918: Box 12, Folder 5; Richard Newhall letters to Elizabeth Newhall, September–April 1917, and reminiscences about George Haydock: Box 12, Folder 6. Used with permission. Some descriptions of life at the front, the First Division, and the lead-up to the Battle of Cantigny were found in his postwar article "With the First Division," (see bibliography). His citation from *WWR*, vol. 23.

Parker, Samuel I. Parker's account of the Battle of Cantigny is from the *Monroe* (North Carolina) *Enquirer Journal*, July 15, 1918; also *WWR*, vol. 13, *Operations Reports, 28th Infantry Regiment*. Account of his part in Soissons battle from his Medal of Honor citation found in his response to the World War I Veterans Survey Collection, U.S. Army Heritage and Education Center, Carlisle, Pennsylvania.

Poe, Neilson. His account of the Battle of Cantigny is from the *Baltimore Sun*, July 21, 1918. Biographical material from the *Princeton Weekly Bulletin*, October 3, 2003, "Memories of the Poe Brothers."

Purdy, Robert Obadiah, Jr. Biographical material from *The History of South Carolina*, vol. 1, by Yates Snowden and Henry Gardner Cutler, (Chicago and New York: Lewis, 1920). Memo from Willis J. Tack and subsequent findings from the investigation of Robert Purdy from family records provided to the author by Robert O. Purdy IV.

Quinn, Jim. Quinn's reasons for enlisting from the *St. Louis Star-Times*, February 5, 1934; his account of Soissons from the same paper, February 6, 1934. Both accounts provided to the author by his son, William M. Quinn, as was the November 1, 1957, letter from Clarence Huebner describing Quinn as an officer.

Rappleye, Cythera. Biographical information from *John Seeley Wallace vs. Cythera M. Rappleye et al.*, found in *Reports of Cases at Law and in Chancery Argued and Determined in the Supreme Court of Illinois*, vol. 103, 1882.

Rappyle, Nicholas B. Information on court cases and financial affairs from *Chicago Daily Tribune*, January 3, 1879; February 11, 1879; and February 25, 1881.

Rasmussen, Axel Severin. Rasmussen's Canadian service records from Library and Archives Canada, Accession 1992-93/166, Box 8102-5. J. W. Pegler's accounts of "the Lost Legion" from the *Clearfield* (Pennsylvania) *Progress*, July 6, 1918; *Marshall* (Michigan) *Evening Chronicle*, July 2, 1918; and *Lebanon* (Pennsylvania) *Daily News*, June 29, 1918. Cobb's portrait of Rasmussen's life and death from the November 23, 1918, *Saturday Evening Post*. Rasmussen letter about being gassed from the *Portland* (Oregon) *Journal*, May 8, 1918. Edward Johnston's account of Rasmussen's impact on the 28th Regiment from *Americans vs. Germans* (see bibliography).

Redwood, George Buchanan. Mary Coale Redwood's memories of her son George B. Redwood's pre-1917 letters, and accounts of his military career and death, from the George B. Redwood Papers, Maryland Historical Society. Redwood's letters from France, and further reminiscences about and testimonies to his life and military activities, from the George Redwood Folder, Call #UAV.874.269, Box 94—*Records of the Harvard War Record Office (World War I), 1916–1927*, Harvard University Archives, Cambridge, Massachusetts. Their use comes courtesy of the Harvard University Archives. Jack Redwood's *Memoirs* graciously provided to the author by his son James Redwood. John Redwood III's unpublished family history *The Redwoods of Virginia and Maryland* also graciously provided by John Redwood. Account of Redwood patrols also from "Redwood Took Huns and 'Eats'" in *Washington Post*, August 25, 1918. Published accounts of March 29, 1918, patrol from *Stars and Stripes*, April 5, 1918; *Baltimore Sun*, March 30, 1918; and *Warren* (Pennsylvania) *Evening Times*, March 30, 1918. His posthumous citation from *WWR*, vol. 23.

Redwood, Mary Coale. Editorial regarding the loss of her husband and sons from *Baltimore Sun*, April 6, 1923.

Redwood, Francis T. Obituary for George Redwood's father ran in *Baltimore Sun*, November 30, 1906.

Redwood, Francis Tazewell. Account of suicide from *Baltimore Sun,* April 6, 1923.

Redmond, Stewart C. Account of his investigation into the demotion of Sam Ervin and comments on Redwood's legacy from the George Redwood File in the Harvard University Archives (see Redwood entry above).

Seeger, Alan. Account of his life and death from Howe, *Memoirs of the Harvard Dead in the War Against Germany,* vol. 1 (see bibliography).

Senay, Charles T. Senay's unpublished memoir, *From Shavetail to Captain,* was graciously provided to the author by Charles Senay's son, David, and grandson, Tim Senay.

Shelton, Ruffus A. His last letter from *Galveston* (Texas) *Daily News,* February 25, 1919. Details of his death from his burial file, ROQC.

Stone, Edward Mandell. Account of his life and death from Howe, *Memoirs of the Harvard Dead in the War Against Germany,* vol. 1 (see bibliography).

Stromberg, Charles Mord. Account of Stromberg's death is from his burial file, ROQC. Biographical material on Charles Stromberg and John Alexander Stromberg and Charles's letters to his sister Elizabeth provided by Stromberg descendant Don W. Lowe of Grand Prairie, Alberta, Canada. Used with permission.

Tyler, Gerald Rudolph. Tyler's account of the Battle of Cantigny is from the *Aiken* (South Carolina) *Journal and Review,* July 10, 1918, and Record Group 117, Entry 31, Box 184 (see U.S. National Archives section in bibliography). Postwar letter from *Journal and Review,* April 30, 1919.

Van Natter, Francis Marion. His request for relief at Cantigny from *WWR,* vol. 13, *Operations Reports, 28th Infantry Regiment.* His account of the position of Company L from Record Group 117, Entry 31, Box 184 (see U.S. National Archives section of bibliography). Account of wounding at Soissons from memo titled "Incidents of July 19th, South of Soissons," found in the Francis M. Van Natter Collection at the Robert R. McCormick Research Center, Wheaton, Illinois, which is also the source for Van Natter's memoir "Organizing the Indiana Mexican Border Veterans." Used with permission.

Waltz, Welcome P. See his *Operations of Company C . . .* (in monographs section of bibliography).

Watson, Thomas H. Account of death from Welcome Waltz's *Operations of Company C . . .* (see monographs section of bibliography). Jim Quinn's description of body from Watson's burial file, ROQC.

Wood, Irving W. Account of May 27, 1918, raid on Company E from Johnston, *Americans vs. Germans* (see bibliography) and the *Wilkes-Barre* (Pennsylvania) *Evening News,* May 28, 1919, from which is also drawn his account of the Battle of Cantigny.

Woodhead, Daniel. Information on the search for Alexander McKinlock's body from McKinlock's burial file, ROQC, and *Chicago Daily Tribune,* May 15, 1919.

Bibliography

BOOKS

Adams, Myron E., and Fred Girton. *The History and Achievements of the Fort Sheridan Officers' Training Camps*. Fort Sheridan, IL: The Association, 1920.

American Battle Monuments Commission. *American Armies and Battlefields in Europe*. Washington: USGPO, 1938.

———. *1st Division, Summary of Operations in the World War*. Washington: USGPO, 1944.

Bacon, Margaret Hope. *The Quiet Rebels: The Story of the Quakers in America*. Baltimore: New Society Publishers, 1985.

Berry, Henry. *Make the Kaiser Dance: The American Experience in World War I*. New York: Doubleday, 1978.

Benson, Albert Emerson, ed. *Saint Mark's School in the War Against Germany*. Privately printed, 1920.

Blumenson, Martin, and James L Stokesbury. *Masters of the Art of Command*. Boston: Houghton Mifflin, 1975.

Bostert, Russell H. *Selected Papers of a History Teacher at a New England College, 1917–1973*. New York: Peter Lang, Publishing, 1989.

Browne, G. Waldo, and Rosecrans W. Pillsbury. *The American Army in the World War: A Divisional Record of the American Expeditionary Forces in Europe*. Manchester, NH: Overseas Book Company, 1921.

Buck, Beaumont B. *Memories of Peace and War.* San Antonio, TX: Naylor, 1935.

Bullard, Robert Lee. *Personalities and Reminiscences of the War.* Garden City, NY: Doubleday, Page, 1925.

Bunker, Mary Powell, comp. *Long Island Genealogies.* Albany, NY: Joel Munsell's Sons, 1895.

Clancy, Paul R. *Just a Country Lawyer: A Biography of Senator Sam Ervin.* Bloomington: Indiana University Press, 1974.

Clifford, John Garry. *The Citizen Soldiers: The Plattsburg Training Camp Movement, 1913–1920.* Lexington: University Press of Kentucky, 1972.

Coffman, Edward M. *The Old Army: A Portrait of the American Army in Peacetime, 1784–1898.* New York: Oxford University Press, 1986.

———. *The Regulars: The American Army, 1898–1941.* Cambridge, MA: Belknap Press of Harvard University Press, 2004.

———. *The War to End All Wars: The American Military Experience in World War I.* New York: Oxford University Press, 1968.

Currey, J. Seymour. *Chicago: Its History and Its Builders: A Century of Marvelous Growth.* Chicago: S. J. Clarke, 1912.

———. *Manufacturing and Wholesale Industries of Chicago.* Chicago: Thomas B. Poole, 1918.

Dawson, Coningsby. *Carry On: Letters in Wartime.* New York, The John Lane Company, 1917.

Dearing, Vinton A. *My Galahad of the Trenches: Being a Collection of Intimate Letters of Lieut. Vinton A. Dearing.* New York, Chicago, London, Edinburgh: Fleming H. Revell, 1918.

Dedmon, Emmett. *Fabulous Chicago.* New York: Random House, 1953.

Douglas, Claire. *Translate This Darkness: The Life of Christiana Morgan, the Veiled Woman in Jung's Circle.* Princeton, NJ: Princeton University Press, 1993.

Downs, John P., ed. *History of Chautauqua County, New York, and Its People,* vol. 3. Boston, New York, and Chicago: American Historical Society, 1921.

Dunn, Jacob Piatt. *Indiana and Indianans: A History of Aboriginal and Territorial Indiana and the Century of Statehood.* Chicago and New York: American Historical Society, 1919.

Eisenhower, John S. D., and Joanne Thompson Eisenhower. *Yanks: The Epic Story of the American Army in World War I.* New York: Free Press, 2001.

Ervin, Sam J. *Preserving the Constitution: The Autobiography of Senator Sam J. Ervin, Jr.* Charlottesville, VA: Michie, 1985.

Evarts, Jeremiah M. *Cantigny: A Corner of the War.* New York: Scribner, Press 1938.

Farr, Finis. *Chicago: A Personal History of America's Most American City.* New Rochelle, NY: Arlington House, 1973.

Ferris, Richard, and Edward S. Farrow. "Machine Gun" and "Machine Gun Tactics," in *The Encyclopedia Americana: A Library of Universal Knowledge*, vol. 18. New York and Chicago: Encyclopedia Americana, 1919.

Foulds, Elfrida Vipont. *The Story of Quakerism, 1652–1952.* London: Bannisdale Press, 1954.

Ganoe, William Addleman. *The History of the United States Army.* New York and London: D. Appleton, 1924.

Garey, E. B., O. O. Ellis, and R. V. D. Magoffin. *The American Guide Book to France and Its Battlefields.* New York: Macmillan, 1920.

Gilbert, Martin. *The First World War: A Complete History.* New York: Henry Holt, 1994.

Hall, Clayton C. *Baltimore: Its History and Its People.* New York: Lewis Historical Publishing, 1912.

Hankey, Donald. *A Student in Arms (Second Series).* New York: E. P. Dutton, 1917.

Harbord, James. *The American Army in France, 1917–1919.* Boston: Little, Brown, 1936.

Harries, Meirion, and Susie Harries. *The Last Days of Innocence: America at War, 1917–1918.* New York: Vintage Books, 1997.

Hart, Abner Bushnell, ed. *America at War: A Handbook of Patriotic Education References.* New York: George H. Doran, 1918.

Hatcher, Julian S., Glenn P. Wilhelm, and Harry J. Malony. *Machine Guns.* Menasha, WI: George Banta, 1917.

Heller, Charles E., and William A. Stofft, eds. *America's First Battles, 1776–1965.* Lawrence: University Press of Kansas, 1986.

Howe, M. A. De Wolfe. *Memoirs of the Harvard Dead in the War Against Germany*, vols. 1 and 2. Cambridge: Harvard University Press, 1920, 1922.

Huelfer, Evan Andrew. *The "Casualty Issue" in American Military Practice: The Impact of World War I.* Westport, CT: Praeger, 2003.

Jacob, Caroline N. *Builders of the Quaker Road, 1652–1952*. Chicago: Henry Regnery, 1953.

Johnson, Douglas V., II, and Rolfe L. Hillman Jr. *Soissons, 1918*. College Station: Texas A&M University Press, 1999.

Johnston, Col. Edward S., et al. *Americans vs. Germans: The First AEF in Action*. New York: Penguin Books; Washington: Infantry Journal, 1942.

Keegan, John. *The Face of Battle*. London: Penguin Group, 1978.

———. *The First World War*. New York: Vintage Books, 2000.

Kennedy, David M. *Over Here: The First World War and American Society*. New York: Oxford University Press, 1982.

Manual of Voluntary Aid. Washington: National Committee on Voluntary Aid, 1916.

Mead, Gary. *The Doughboys: America and the First World War*. Woodstock, NY: Overlook Press, 2000.

Miller, Richard F. *Harvard's Civil War: A History of the Twentieth Massachusetts Volunteer Infantry*. Hanover, NH: University Press of New England, 2005.

Moran, Charles M. W. *The Anatomy of Courage*. Boston: Houghton Mifflin, 1967.

Piehler, G. Kurt. *Remembering War the American Way*. Washington: Smithsonian Books, 1995.

Pugh, Irving Edwin, and William F. Thayer. *Forgotten Fights of the A.E.F.* Boston: Roxburgh Publishing, 1921.

Renehan, Edward J., Jr. *The Lion's Pride: Theodore Roosevelt and His Family in Peace and War*. New York: Oxford University Press, 1998.

Roosevelt, Theodore, Jr. *Average Americans*. New York and London: G. P. Putnam's Sons, 1919.

Russell, Elbert. *The History of Quakerism*. New York: The Macmillan, 1942.

St. Lawrence University in the World War 1917–1918: A Memorial. Canton, NY: The University, 1931.

Society of the First Division. *History of the First Division During the World War*. Philadelphia: Winston, 1931.

Stallings, Laurence. *The Doughboys: The Story of the AEF, 1917–1918*. New York: Popular Library, 1964.

Stephen, Leslie, and Sidney Lee, eds. *Dictionary of National Biography*, vol. 25. New York: Macmillan, 1891.

Stories from the Harvard Advocate. Cambridge: Massachusetts, Harvard University, 1896.

Summerall, C. P. *The Story of the Twenty-Eighth Infantry in the Great War*. Nep.: American Expeditionary Forces, 1919.

Thomas, Shipley. *The History of the A.E.F.* New York: George H. Doran, 1920.

Thwing, Charles Franklin. *The American Colleges and Universities in the Great War, 1914–1919: A History*. New York: MacMillan, 1920.

Toland, John. *No Man's Land: 1918, the Last Year of the Great War*. Garden City, NY: Doubleday, 1980.

Tuchman, Barbara W. *The Guns of August*. New York: Ballantine Books, 1962.

U.S. Adjutant-General's Office. *Congressional Medal of Honor, the Distinguished Service Cross, and the Distinguished Service Medal Issued by the War Department Since April 6, 1917*. Washington: USGPO, 1920.

U.S. Army. *World War Records, First Division, A.E.F. Regular*. 25 vols. Washington: USGPO, 1928–30.

U.S. War Department. *Infantry Drill Regulations, United States Army, 1911*. New York: Military Publishing, 1911.

Wells, H. G. *Mr. Britling Sees It Through*. New York: Macmillan, 1916.

PERIODICALS

Amory, Cleveland. "Its Opulence May Be Dimmer Now, but Old Guard is Still 'En Guarde.'" *Life*, January 21, 1952, 90.

"College Arrogance." *Harvard Advocate*, May 17, 1889, 91–92.

Deneen, Sally. "Who Says South Florida Doesn't Have a Past? High Society—and Low Society—Give Us a Colorful History." *Ft. Lauderdale Sun-Sentinel*, November 14, 1992.

Howorth, Peter W. "The Treatment of Shell-shock: Cognitive Therapy Before Its Time." *Psychiatrist* 24 (2000): 225–27.

Ireland, Corydon. "Somber, Joyful Service Marks 75th Birthday." *Harvard Gazette*, November 15, 2007.

Jones, Edgar, et al. "Shell Shock and Mild Traumatic Brain Injury: A Historical Review." *American Journal of Psychiatry* 164 (2007): 1641–45.

Kirkland, Winifred. "The New Death." *Atlantic Monthly*, May 1918, 577–89.

Morgan, William O. P. "An American Soldier in Vienna." *New Republic,* October 1, 1919, 258–61.

Newhall, R. A. "With the First Division—Winter 1917–1918." *Historical Outlook,* October 1919, 357–62.

"Our Young Officers Trained in Newest Tactics." *New York Times,* July 15, 1917.

Schenck, Frederic. "Training for the National Defense: Harvard Men at Plattsburg." *Harvard Alumni Bulletin,* October 5, 1916, n.p.

Stillwagon, John. "The Artist on Campaign: An Examination of the Illustrations of A. C. Redwood." *General Orders,* June 2002, 2–3.

Warwick, Frances Evelyn. "The God of Mr. Britling—and of Our Fathers." *Bookman* 45 (March–August 1917): 145–47.

White, Hannah Hastings. "Rolling-Pins, Fruit Trees and Shoes: The First College Women's Unit to Work in France." *Independent*, August 11, 1917, 226–27.

MONOGRAPHS

The following are entries in the series *Monographs of the World War,* compiled by the U.S. Army Infantry School, Fort Benning, Georgia, and in the collection of the Donovan Research Library there.

Johnston, Edward S. *The Day Before Cantigny: Personal Experiences of a Company Commander.*

Parker, Paul B. *The Battle of Cantigny.*

Waltz, Welcome P. *Operations of Company C, 3d Machine Gun Battalion at Cantigny.*

Yuill, Charles W. *Operations of Co. B 3d MG Bn (First Division) in the Aisne-Marne Offensive, July 16–July 23, 1918.*

U.S. NATIONAL ARCHIVES

Record Group 94, Entry 91, Records of the Adjutant General's Office, 1780s–1917; Register of Enlistments in the U.S. Army, 1780s–1917.

Record Group 117, Entry 31, Box 184, Records of the American Battle Monuments Commission, Correspondence with Former (First) Division Officers.

Record Group 120, Entry 1241, Records of the American Expeditionary Forces, First Division Document File.

Record Group 120, Entry 1241, Records of the American Expeditionary Forces, Organizational Records First Division.

Record Group 120, Entry 1241, Records of the 28th Infantry Regiment.

Record Group 391, Entry 2133. Records of Regular Army Mobile Units, 28th Infantry Regiment.

Record Group 407-A, Records of the Adjutant General's Office, Commissions of Officers in the Regular Army, National Guard, and Officer Reserve Corps, 1917–1940.

Index